BRITISH MAIL STEAMERS TO SOUTH AMERICA, 1851–1965

Modern Economic and Social History Series

General Editor: Derek H. Aldcroft

Titles in this series include:

British Conservatism and Trade Unionism, 1945–1964
Peter Dorey

The International Order of Asia in the 1930s and 1950s
Edited by Shigeru Akita and Nicholas J. White

Personal Capitalism and Corporate Governance
British Manufacturing in the First Half of the Twentieth Century
Myrddin John Lewis, Roger Lloyd-Jones, Josephine Maltby
and Mark David Matthews

A Decent Provision
Australian Welfare Policy, 1870 to 1949
John Murphy

Commerce and Culture
Nineteenth-Century Business Elites
Edited by Robert Lee

The Eclipse of 'Elegant Economy'
The Impact of the Second World War on Attitudes to Personal Finance in Britain
Martin Cohen

The American Reaper
Harvesting Networks and Technology, 1830–1910
Gordon M. Winder

Land, Proto-Industry and Population in Catalonia, c. 1680–1829
An Alternative Transition to Capitalism?
Julie Marfany

The Making of a World Trading Power
The European Economic Community (EEC) in the GATT Kennedy Round Negotiations (1963–67)
Lucia Coppolaro

Eastern European Railways in Transition
Nineteenth to Twenty-first Centuries
Edited by Ralf Roth and Henry Jacolin

British Mail Steamers to South America, 1851–1965

A History of the Royal Mail Steam Packet Company and Royal Mail Lines

ROBERT E. FORRESTER

LONDON AND NEW YORK

First published 2014 by Ashgate Publishing

2 Park Square, Milton Park, Abingdon, Oxon OX14 4RN
711 Third Avenue, New York, NY 10017, USA

Routledge is an imprint of the Taylor & Francis Group, an informa business

First issued in paperback 2016

British Library Cataloguing in Publication Data
A catalogue record for this book is available from the British Library

The Library of Congress has cataloged the printed edition as follows:
Forrester, Robert E.
British Mail Steamers to South America, 1851–1965: A History of the Royal Mail Steam Packet Company and Royal Mail Lines / by Robert E. Forrester.
pages cm. – (Modern Economic and Social History)
Includes bibliographical references and index.
1. Royal Mail Steam Packet Company – History. 2. Postal service – Great Britain – History – 19th century. 3. Postal service – Great Britain – History – 20th century. 4. Mail steamers – Great Britain – History – 19th century. 5. Mail steamers – Great Britain – History – 20th century. I. Title.
HE6935.F67 2014
383'.142098–dc23 2013035958

ISBN 978-1-4724-1661-2 (hbk)
ISBN 978-1-138-26970-5 (pbk)

Contents

Modern Economic and Social History Series General Editor's Preface

Economic and social history has been a flourishing subject of scholarly study during recent decades. Not only has the volume of literature increased enormously but the range of interest in time, space and subject matter has broadened considerably so that today there are many sub-branches of the subject which have developed considerable status in their own right.

One of the aims of this series is to encourage the publication of scholarly monographs on any aspect of modern economic and social history. The geographical coverage is world-wide and contributions on the non-British themes will be especially welcome. While emphasis will be placed on works embodying original research, it is also intended that the series should provide the opportunity to publish studies of a more general thematic nature which offer a reappraisal or critical analysis of major issues of debate.

Derek H. Aldcroft
University of Leicester

List of Illustrations

List of Tables

Preface

After 1834, the General Steam Navigation Company of London, under contract to the Lords of the Admiralty, who were responsible for the carriage of mails, began its service to near-European ports. At the same time, liner companies such as the Peninsular Company (later P&O) and Cunard developed services, also contracted, to more distant parts, for example Southern Europe and the USA. In 1839 the Royal Mail Steam Packet Company was granted a Royal Charter 'for the conveyance of mails to and from Great Britain and the West India Islands and North and South America and other foreign parts'.

In early 1840 a contract was agreed with the Admiralty for a service from a Channel port to Barbados and a number of other destinations within the Caribbean. Extensions northwards would serve New York and Halifax, Nova Scotia. The requirements of the contract were onerous and, it transpired, unsustainable; significant adjustments were quickly made to the route network. A proposed service to South America was deferred. Annual payment was to be £240,000 for a 10-year period. It was not until 1850 that the subvention was increased by £30,000 for the additional, monthly, service to South America.

Royal Mail's steamers progressively replaced the Admiralty's expensively maintained fleet of small, slow and unreliable sailing brigs. The shipowners argued, reasonably, and government concurred, that the contract payments would support the development of vital, faster trading links, with political and commercial advantages. The financial input contributed greatly to Britain becoming the world's greatest maritime nation through the next century.

The first Royal Mail sailing for Brazilian ports, by the paddle-steamship *Teviot*, left Southampton in January 1851, terminating in Rio de Janeiro with onward transit of mails and a few passengers to Montevideo and Buenos Aires in a smaller vessel. From 1869 the main line service was extended through to Montevideo and Buenos Aires. That service ended a century later when, in early 1969, *Aragon* called at Southampton, en route to her home port of London.

Several factors govern the success, or otherwise, of shipping operations, quite apart from effective management control of the many facets of the business. First and foremost is the political and economic situation of the countries involved in the trades. Social and political unrest and war were commonplace in South America almost throughout the period of this history. Droughts, disease and depression inevitably affected profit and loss, as did trade developments and cycles in the UK and other European countries. This context is essential to an understanding of the operation of Royal Mail's services, and these considerations are explored in some detail in this book.

R.E.F., London, 2014

Chapter 1
1840: The West Indies Mail Contract

Much has been written of the early days of steam shipping, largely a British phenomenon. These works have, in the main, explored the development from the late 1830s to the 1850s of the oceanic steamship services of, among others, the Peninsular Company, later P&O, and Cunard, driven by the entrepreneurial spirits of, respectively, Brodie Willcox and Arthur Anderson, and Samuel Cunard, all three of them with prior experience of the business of steamship operation. Coastal and short-sea routes have not been ignored: a great pioneer of the steamship trade was, from 1824, the General Steam Navigation Company, which was established to serve routes from London to the east coast of Britain and to near-Continent ports. Thomas Brocklebank and William J. Hall, both shipowners, were prominent in the creation and development of this important and successful company. All these companies benefited from government subsidies for the carriage of the mails.

The early steamships were paddle-steamers, small, built of wood and powered by space-consuming, heavy and unreliable engines. A major problem for the transatlantic shipowner, especially, was ensuring that his vessel was capable of carrying a sufficient amount of coal to enable it to safely reach distant ports, although a full set of sails was always carried. The quantity of coal required occupied the greater part of the space available below deck, thereby inhibiting the carriage of cargo to usually no more than 100–200 tons in a vessel of 2,000 tons. For this reason owners ensured that accommodation was available for as many passengers as possible in order to maximise revenues.

The outstanding benefits of the steamship over the sailing ship, from the point of view of the owner, the passenger and the cargo shipper, were reliability and speed. The steamer was able to make more voyages than the sailing ship and, much less affected by wind, weather and tide, was capable of operating to a schedule, a major consideration for all.

Steam shipping was capital intensive, tonnage costing two to three times that of an equivalent-size sailing ship. Repairs and maintenance were major costs, the work usually being carried out by the ship's builder, although Royal Mail, in common with other larger companies of the period, in an effort to control standards and contain costs, established its own repair facility in Southampton. The availability of considerable financial resources was essential: changes to company law between 1865 and 1872 introduced limited liability and extended the means of raising capital.[1]

---

[1] P.L. Cottrell, 'Domestic Finance, 1860–1914'. in Roderick Floud and Paul Johnston (eds), *The Cambridge Economic History of Modern Britain, Volume II: Economic*

This was still the age of the sailing ship: in 1850 there were 7,149 sailing ships of an average of 299 tons, making a total of 2,143,234 tons, employed in Britain's foreign trades. Steamships numbered only 86 of an average of 525 tons, the majority owned by the four or five liner companies established in the early 1840s. These companies, with the benefit of mail subsidies, became major players in the development of British maritime power over the next one hundred years. The majority of steamships, 320 of an average of 169 tons, were employed in the home trades, where shorter routes ensured that assistance was closer to hand in the event of engine breakdown or accident. Much of the early experimentation with stronger iron hulls and more efficient steam engines was carried out on these smaller vessels, as was government-financed research on General Steam Navigation's *Rainbow* into the effects of iron hulls on the magnetic compass.[2]

A New Venture

The Royal Mail Steam Packet Company, hereafter Royal Mail or the Company, differed from the other steamship companies established in the 1830s and 1840s in that its leading figure was neither a steamship owner nor experienced in the shipping trades. James MacQueen was a plantation manager in the West Indies. Having returned to Britain, in 1837 he developed and presented to the government a plan for, initially, an efficient, necessarily subsidised, steamship mail service (he was critical of the existing packet service, which he rightly considered unreliable and inadequate for commercial purposes) between Britain and the West Indies. This plan was followed by a proposal for a worldwide mail service operated by steamships.

The Admiralty had already granted two mail contracts: the first was to the General Steam Navigation Company in 1834 for a service from London to Hamburg and Rotterdam with an annual subvention of £17,000. The service was terminated in 1853 when the Post Office opted for the shorter sea route from Harwich. The second was to Willcox and Anderson's Peninsular Company for a service to Spain and Gibraltar with an annual subvention of £29,600 from 1837. The contract to Cunard for a North Atlantic service was granted in 1840.

MacQueen, who was responsible for the preparation of detailed plans for the service and for negotiations with the government, was successful in obtaining, in 1840, the West Indies contract, although a proposed extension of that service

Maturity, 1860–1939 (Cambridge, 2004), pp. 261–2 and Ronald Hope, *A New History of British Shipping* (London, 1990), p. 303.

[2] John Glover, 'On the Statistics of Tonnage during the First Decade under the Navigation Law of 1849', *Journal of the Statistical Society*, Vol. XXVI, March 1863, 'Table VII, Sail, Steam and Politics'; Ewan Corlett, *The Iron Ship: The Story of Brunel's S.S. Great Britain* (London, 1990); see also Basil Greenhill, 'Steam before the Screw', in R. Gardiner (ed.), *The Advent of Steam* (London, 1993), p. 24.

to Brazil was deferred. The following year he travelled widely over the entire proposed route network, meeting colonial governors, Post Office officials, and merchants and appointing agents. He also noted and warned of the dangers of access to some of the ports on the routes. The importance of the mail services to the West Indies and other parts lay in the communication of information vital to businesses, for example the condition of crops, products available and shipments already made, ships in port and sailed, weather conditions and so on. MacQueen was strongly of the opinion that mail services were for the conveyance of the mails and of passengers. He wrote: 'The mails can never be carried either with regularity or certainty in vessels the chief object and dependence of which is to carry merchandise', although it is likely that he soon became aware of the need for additional revenues from that source.[3]

Supported by influential London merchants and bankers with interests in the West Indies, a Royal Charter was granted to the Company in September 1839 and a detailed and demanding contract with penalties for late port arrivals and departures was agreed with the Admiralty on 20 March 1840 with an annual payment of £240,000 for a period of 10 years.[4] The level of payment, which was described, predictably, by competitors as 'staggering', nevertheless offered no guarantee of profit – it barely covered ship operating costs in the early years – and required that additional revenues from passengers and freight were forthcoming. In fact, the operating costs in 1846 totalled £285,478 before allowances for repairs and maintenance. Other shipowners argued that the contracts conferred near-monopoly commercial benefits and ineffectually pressured government to open them to public bidding. The subsidies were timely: they gave British shipowners the essential financial support that enabled them to lead in the development of ship design and propulsion and of worldwide trade; it must also be borne in mind that the subsidies were greatly advantageous to the British government in terms of political and commercial prestige.[5]

At the outset Royal Mail's intention was to raise capital of £1.5m through the issue of 15,000 shares of £100, but, in the event, only £60 was called in on each share for a total of £900,000. It took until 1845 to raise the greater part of that sum, and it was 1855 before the full sum became available. Through to the end of the century the Company's nominal and issued capital remained unchanged and, arguably, inadequate. By contrast, the Peninsular & Oriental Company's nominal capital was £3.5m, of which £2.9m was paid up, and the Pacific Steam Navigation Company, which received a mail contract in 1840 for a service to the west coast of South America, had capital of £2,956,530. The modest level of Royal Mail's capital would be a problem for the directors over many years.

---

[3] T.A. Bushell, *Royal Mail. A Centenary History of the Royal Mail Line 1839–1939* (London, 1939), p. 4.

[4] Ibid., pp. 9–10.

[5] R.H. Thornton, *British Shipping* (Cambridge, 1959), p. 30.

The contract required that a fleet of 14 wooden paddle-steamers of 1,800 gross tons be built in yards around the country to maintain the transatlantic and inter-island services, and these were duly ordered at cost of approximately £67,500 each.[6] Three small sailing vessels were also built. A stipulation of the contract was that the Admiralty should exercise control over vessel construction, ports of call, frequency of service, speed on passage, time in port and so on, with penalties for delays, thus imposing time limitations on passenger embarkations and disembarkations. More importantly, this constrained the time available to load and discharge freight, a growing problem as more space became available for cargo. A naval agent was carried: he was responsible for the mails and he exercised considerable authority in all matters and could, in certain circumstances, overrule the ship's master. The schedule restrictions were adjusted as subsequent contracts were negotiated.

The Company, which operated out of offices in Moorgate, London from 1841, was required to maintain a packet service from Southampton with a complex route network throughout the Caribbean and north to New York and Halifax, Nova Scotia, providing 'good, substantial and efficient steam vessels' maintained and improved as opportunity permitted. The building materials were not specified, although the ships 'were to be of such construction and strength as to be fit and able to carry guns of the largest calibre now used on board Her Majesty's steam vessels of war'. Sailings were to be twice per month from Southampton, with calls outward and homeward at Falmouth to load and discharge mails. Quite soon some minor alterations were made to the network to accommodate the need for coaling and other facilities, and St Thomas in the Virgin Islands became the base of operations, with mail and passengers trans-shipped from the Atlantic vessels to the smaller inter-island steamers.

In the first six months of operations in 1842 it became clear that the initial plan was overly ambitious: performance was chaotic. Royal Mail had not previously owned ships, unlike others that had been awarded contracts, so that the business of planning routes, availability, or otherwise, of pilots, lighthouses, anchorage and harbour facilities, and manning and operating a substantial fleet to a schedule and over an extended, complex and navigationally difficult route network was entirely new to the directors.[7]

None was a shipping man: rather they were businessmen, men of influence in the City of London, and they relied on the energetic services of MacQueen for guidance and direction, although he, too, lacked the essential nautical background. He assumed the position of general manager, travelling widely in the Caribbean and visiting the USA.[8] However, he retired in 1842, aged 64, 'probably finding the routine duties of commercial life too strenuous', states Bushell discreetly.

[6] RMSP, Cost and Outfit of Steamships, 1839–1912.

[7] Thornton, *British Shipping*, pp. 17–19. Duncan Haws, *Triumph of a Great Tradition 1840–1990* (London, 1990), pp. 6–15.

[8] Bushell, *Royal Mail*, p. 20.

One writer asserts that MacQueen was held responsible for the Company's early failings and was dismissed, a charge he, MacQueen, vigorously repudiated. It may well be that his attitude to the carriage of cargo was at odds with the views of the directors, who must quickly have appreciated that freight income was essential for profit.

Bearing in mind the great difficulties experienced by even the experienced shipowner Samuel Cunard (his 1840 contract for a transatlantic service was revised four times in the first year of operation), there is more than a hint that MacQueen was being made a scapegoat. The first marine superintendent was a Lieutenant Kendall RN, who was assistant to MacQueen. Kendall resigned in November 1840 and was replaced by Captain Edward Chappell RN, who became marine superintendent and company secretary, in effect MacQueen's superior. Chappell's appointment was a shrewd move: he had been involved in overseeing the transition of the Post Office packet service to Admiralty control a few years previously and had experience of being in charge of a mail station, so that he was familiar with Admiralty personnel and practices.[9] He retained the position for some years.

The Company had no corps of experienced masters and deck and engineer officers, so that great responsibility was placed on men with little or no experience of steamship operations in the dangerous waters of the West Indian islands in which five of the six ships lost before 1850 were wrecked. A number of Royal Navy lieutenants were employed as ship masters – men most probably with limited prospects within the naval service. No fewer than four of the six ships lost were thus commanded.[10] Inevitably, there were problems with the vessels, mainly in the engine-rooms, and operational difficulties in the many ports, including stores and coal bunkering and facilities for the handling of mails and passengers, added to the problems.

Uncertain Prospects

The annual report for 1842 conceded that the contract was 'of too sanguine a character', one that could not profitably be maintained.[11] This was an understatement: Greenhill refers to inefficient management and a service that was 'thoroughly disorganised – calls were omitted without notice, mails left behind, vessels were unavailable'.[12] A much-modified plan was agreed by the Admiralty with no subsidy reduction. A fundamental change was the elimination of the Havana to New York and Halifax route, which contributed to an annual reduction of

[9] Captain Chappell was agent for the Post Office packets at Milford Haven from 1826 to 1828.

[10] Bushell, *Royal Mail*, p. 32.

[11] RMSP, Annual Report to Shareholders, 30 March 1843.

[12] Robert G. Greenhill, 'British Shipping and Latin America 1840–1930: The Royal Mail Steam Packet Company' (Ph.D. Thesis, University of Exeter, 1971), p. 30.

nearly 300,000 miles, almost 45 per cent of the mileage, with attendant reductions in the costs of coal, wages and provisions.

The results for the first full year of operation, 1842, were disastrous. A loss of £79,790 was incurred, despite which the directors stated that they saw 'every reason to encourage them to persevere'. Their determination resulted in a much-improved situation in 1843, with an operating surplus of £94,219. Throughout the remainder of the decade, management remained under constant pressure from the Admiralty to maintain the mail schedules efficiently, and from commercial interests unhappy with the speed and reliability of the service, although it could not fail to be more efficient than that of the Admiralty sailing brigs that preceded it.

Royal Mail's first wooden paddle-steamers had accommodation for 100 passengers, with limited space set aside for the stowage of mail and specie. The Company histories make few references to the carriage of cargo – not surprising, perhaps, when James MacQueen's words are borne in mind. However, it is clear from the published notices that some freight was carried from the outset: small-volume cargo was sought – boxes, barrels and packages that could be man-handled into the low-ceilinged spaces available below deck. Specie, frequently carried in large quantities, was charged at 2 per cent of value; spices, quicksilver and the like were carried, as well as coffee. Turtles were charged at £1 5s per hundredweight for those landed live in Southampton. On one occasion it was noted that packages were carried in the saloon, to the discomfort of passengers. Coal stowage in the 'tween decks and holds was always the priority, to the exclusion of cargo, and, as engines became smaller and more efficient, some further hold space was made available for high-value, low-volume cargo.

The Company's chosen home port of Southampton was agreed with the Admiralty only after much debate, the directors' initial preference being for Dartmouth or Falmouth. Southampton developed rapidly in the 1840–50 period with the opening of its first docks, in competition with the already substantial ports of London and Liverpool. The Liverpool Chamber of Commerce petitioned the Treasury, pressing, unsuccessfully, the advantages of the existing dock system and facilities. Bushell notes the Company's preference on the grounds that it had 'a safe and commodious anchorage, and after the opening of the London and South Western Railway, on May 11th 1841, was in direct communication with London'. Royal Mail began to use the new dock only in 1845 for the discharge of inward mails, cargo and passengers, by which time the depth of water was sufficient to accommodate the shallow-draught ships. Outward bound, the ships anchored off Netley in Southampton Water to complete coal bunkering and take on passengers, with draught appreciably increased in the process. An inner dock opened in 1859 was claimed to be able to accommodate the largest ships afloat.

A hulk moored offshore, near to the dock, was used in the early years for repair work and stores, but in 1847 land was acquired close by the dock entrance on the Itchen riverfront on which to build engineering workshops and a foundry. By the early 1850s the facility was able to handle all the Company's repair and refit requirements, with graving (or dry) docks available within the dock itself.[13]

The history of a shipping company is, inevitably, tied to the political and commercial development of the countries with which it trades. Vital to Royal Mail's success in the new South American venture, particularly when the additional £30,000 mail subsidy was removed in 1875 (to be replaced by a much lower payment by weight carried), was the erratic development of the import and export market potentials of Argentina and Brazil. (Montevideo in Uruguay was always a regular call north- and southbound, but its revenues from passengers and cargo were never greatly significant.)

This work seeks to focus on the Company's trade with those countries against the background of their turbulent political and economic situations in the latter part of the nineteenth century and into the twentieth. Equally important was the economic situation in Britain, much affected by periods of boom and depression and European wars. Without these considerations and an understanding of the highly competitive nature of business with South America, no appreciation of the development of trade and of the operations of Royal Mail is possible.

In tracing the history of the South American service of Royal Mail, some essential details have been given of the Company's early days, and further substantial background of two other vital aspects of the Company at the turn of the century are explored. The first is the establishment of the refrigerated meat trade from Argentina in the late 1800s. Regular shipments at premium rates became a vital profit source for the Company over many years. Second, and equally important, is the decline in the Company's fortunes in the late 1890s and early 1900s. This is explored at some length: the reductions in profits, dividends and share prices, and the introduction of Owen Cosby Philipps as a director and, within weeks, chairman in 1903.

Philipps's style was vastly different from that of his predecessors, yet it was very much of its time. In the early 1900s the trend among certain well-established shipping interests was to consolidate through acquisition, usually, but not always, of competitors. Philipps, in conjunction with his brother John, a City of London financier, began in 1905 a programme of purchases of controlling interests in other companies that, in time, totally transformed Royal Mail and led to it becoming, in only a few years, the largest shipping group in the world. In this process the focus of the Company's interests altered dramatically, from the West Indies to the South American routes. A number of large liners were built, the forerunners of those that would maintain the Company's prestigious passenger and cargo services through to the late 1960s, when it effectively ceased operations.

By the late 1920s the Royal Mail Steam Packet Group was vast: it owned 140 companies associated with ship operations and building. In a difficult period of intermittent worldwide trade depression, the Group's finances were severely

[13] J.F. Clark, 'Railway Ports. Southampton', *The Railway Magazine*, March 1909, pp. 238–41.

stretched and it was unable to meet demands for debt repayment. The Group collapsed, and from the subsequent legal and financial debris several shipping companies emerged, including, in 1932, Royal Mail Lines Ltd, also referred to in the text as the Company.

No history of the Royal Mail companies has, to date, covered in any detail the Company's post-Second World War recovery and the effects of the trade downturn from the mid-1950s, which resulted in a struggle to remain profitable in a dramatically changing business environment. Few, if any, shipowners anticipated the drastic increases in world tonnage in the period with heightened competition and, inevitably, uncertain freight rates. The situation was made infinitely more difficult by the determination of most countries, including Brazil and Argentina, to develop their own merchant shipping fleets to the virtual exclusion of long-established British and other European tonnage. Royal Mail's profits collapsed from 1960 and the company was taken over by Furness, Withy in 1965.

Sources

The main sources used were the Royal Mail Steam Packet Company archives in the Caird Library of the National Maritime Museum at Greenwich and in the Special Collections Library of University College, London. T.A. Bushell's centenary history of the Company, *Royal Mail 1839–1939*, was invaluable. He was assistant company secretary at the time of publication and enjoyed full access to archive material. Shortly before his death in Australia in 2008, Stuart Nicol, whose two-volume history of the Company, *MacQueen's Legacy*, was published in 2001, produced a *Scrapbook* of more than 1,800 pages. A Company employee in the publicity department until the late 1960s, at the time of the takeover of Royal Mail by Furness, Withy, Nicol was researching, for the Company, a centenary history of the South American service, which was then abandoned. Clearly he had access to and retained a substantial collection of archive material. Information in *Scrapbook* is selective and much of it is in abbreviated form, but it is an important addition to the record and a very considerable work of research. Greenhill's thesis, 'British Shipping and Latin America 1840–1930', provided further useful information.

The archive is very far from complete: the Greenwich Maritime Museum holds some material unavailable at University College, London and vice versa, with a fair amount of duplication. Vast numbers of documents, many of which would now be regarded by the historian as invaluable, were destroyed at the time of the Furness, Withy takeover. Useful further material from the post-Second World War period is held at the Merseyside Maritime Museum in Liverpool. Southampton Maritime Museum has a small collection that does not include key material, although it does have detailed staff and other records.

Important accounts documents are missing, that is, profit and loss accounts and balance sheets, so that it is, at times, difficult to be certain of profits, reserves and the like. There are incomplete sets of hand-written reports of shareholders' meetings and, sadly, the daily minutes of the board of managers, as opposed to directors' minutes, end in 1854, although *Scrapbook* offers some information beyond that date. Little or no information has been found on the backgrounds of the Company directors during the nineteenth century, or, perhaps more importantly, the personnel and responsibilities of the second-ranked board of management, which provided a measure of expertise and exercised considerable influence on the activities of the Company.

The reports to shareholders were, at least in the early years, brief and followed a standard format. They are interesting for what they do not say rather than for what they say, a point highlighted on a number of occasions by shareholders. Press reports of shareholder meetings are rather more helpful in that, on occasion, they record shareholders' reactions to the chairman's statement, which relate mostly to pressure for greater dividend payments. On infrequent occasions, usually in the latter part of the nineteenth century, they reflect strong criticism of the performance of management. *The Times* is especially helpful in this respect, most meetings right through to the 1960s being given some coverage.

Through the nineteenth century financial information made available to shareholders, and to competitors, was entirely at the discretion of the directors. A profit and loss account was considered no more than 'desirable'.[14] So far as can be established, Royal Mail's accounts were relatively straightforward through that period, although presentation altered periodically. From 1903, with the advent of Owen Philipps as chairman, the form of accounts altered significantly, sometimes year on year. A major change was the deletion of detail of income sources, passengers, freight and so on. Some items were moved from the profit and loss account to the balance sheet and vice versa, others changed their names, some simply disappeared, to the confusion, perhaps deliberate, of shareholders and competitors. The Company carried it own insurance costs from 1843, setting aside annually to an insurance fund 5 per cent or thereabouts of the value of the fleet. Throughout, the measures used as an indicator of management performance are those of interest to shareholders: dividend and share price.

Company accounts covered the full range of routes and services, so that no separation is available against which to assess the success, or otherwise, of the new South American venture. It was not until the 1890s that a measure of its potential, as opposed to its profitability, became evident when the directors began to build new liner tonnage specifically for the service. From that time meaningful insight into the financial viability of the South American routes becomes even more difficult as the nature of the accounts presentation altered and new and unidentified income sources, and dividends from shareholdings in other companies, for instance, appeared.

A list of passenger and refrigerated cargo ships involved in the South American trade is included, with rather more information than that provided by Bushell,

---

[14] Edgar Jones, *Accountancy in the British Economy 1840–1980* (London, 1981) p. 52.

certainly a reliable source. Some details of the fleet are given in each chapter, which usually covers a decade or a period of special significance – the First World War, for instance. Shipbuilding developments from the 1850s with larger ships of constantly improving design propelled by increasingly efficient engines have been noted as these significantly affected operating costs and passenger and freight revenues.

The performance of directors and senior management has been focused on, necessarily across the range of the Company's activities, in order to try to assess the effectiveness of their decision-making processes and the implementation of those decisions. The meetings of the directors are referred to as meetings of the board rather than of The Court, a term that applied when a company operated under a Royal Charter, as the Royal Mail Steam Packet Company did.

Chapter 2
1851: Across the South Atlantic

Andrew Colville, chairman of the 12-man court of directors (hereafter board of directors) in 1850, was one of six who had been with the Company since its earliest days. So far as can be established, none of the directors had business interests in Brazil or the Argentine. Indeed, shipping business experience continued in short supply, with influence and connections favoured. Thomas Baring MP and Russell Ellice were both bankers. Former Royal Navy officers and, for a time, a distinguished ex-soldier were appointed later in the decade. Colville died in 1856, his son, Eden, succeeding him as a director and Captain C.E. Mangles RN becoming chairman.

There existed at a lower level a board of management, although little information concerning its structure and functions is available, apart from one or two references that indicate that it was chaired by a director. Importantly, the marine superintendent and the engineer superintendent were members. Without doubt, it was this body, with its experience and expertise, that directed the development of the Company's services and the progressive modernisation of the fleet.

Contract for the South American Mails

In 1850, following protracted negotiations with the Admiralty, a revised 10-year mail contract commencing 1 January 1851 was agreed for the West Indies service, with an extended route network, greatly increased mileage and speeded-up services. An additional £30,000 (making a total of £270,000) payment was offered for a monthly mail service from Southampton to the east coast of South America, the only major destination from Britain still served by the Admiralty sailing packets. The service would terminate in Rio de Janeiro, with a smaller vessel making the onward transit to Montevideo and Buenos Aires.[1] London

---

[1] J.N.T. Howat, *South American Packets, 1808–1880* (York, 1984, published by the Postal History Society). Alan K. Manchester, *British Pre-eminence in Brazil. Its Rise and Decline* (Chapel Hill, 1933), p. 320. The writer, quoting Brazilian sources (*Relatorio dos Negocios Extrangieros*, 1851, notes 8–16, and 1852), states that of the Brazil mail contract two-thirds was to be paid by the British government and one-third by the Brazilian government. It is highly unlikely that the British government would be involved in such an arrangement, although inducements were certainly offered to the Company by individual trade groups within Brazil. See the later reference to payment for the Maceio service begun in 1879. Manchester also notes that Brazil's first concession to a foreign government

representatives of the countries involved had given reassurances that the privileges already granted to HM mail packets, the waiving of port and other charges and dues, would be extended to the new service, and now five steamers, larger and faster, were urgently built for the West Indies services; they made their maiden voyages in 1852–53. Older tonnage was used on the South American service.

The new contracts implied not only close and influential contacts within government and the Admiralty, but also a recognition that, despite difficulties resulting in failures to consistently meet contractual requirements, the Company had made significant commitments, financial and otherwise, to the West Indies services. On one occasion, concerned by the prospect of a second company, the General Screw Company of Liverpool, having been awarded a contract for a South American service, the company secretary visited a Mr Hamilton at the Treasury. He pleaded that it would be unfair if the government, after obtaining a contract on very low terms for conveyance of the Brazil mails by steam vessel, was now to subsidise another company to run in direct opposition. Mr Hamilton was unimpressed: he commented that he did not consider £30,000 a low sum for the Brazil mails.[2]

Business interests in the north claimed 'great inconvenience and loss' due to what they regarded as an unsatisfactory mail service, although the situation was infinitely better than it had been recently: *The Times* reported the arrival in Falmouth on 19 May of Her Majesty's packet *Penguin*, which left Rio on 23 March.[3]

The Times, anticipating the start of the new service, noted the government cost savings, unspecified, against the new £30,000 contract. The last of the six or seven small naval brigs used on the South American mail service, *Seagull*, left Falmouth on 6 December 1850 and returned on 30 April 1851. At that time the Falmouth packet establishment, 'maintained at considerable expense', was to be closed. The new contract 'will effect a considerable saving over the old plan'.[4]

Merchants and other interested parties in Liverpool were greatly exercised. A letter in *The Times* argued vigorously that a 'manifest injustice was perpetrated against the interests of Liverpool and the manufacturing towns of Lancashire and Yorkshire by the adoption of a south coast port for receiving and dispatching the mail', and demanded that the West India Company, that is, Royal Mail, 'commence the South America service urgently or surrender the contract'.[5] The

for a steamship service was to France in 1843 for a monthly service from St Nazaire using warships.

2 RMSP, Daily Minutes, Board of Managers, 6 November 1852.

3 *The Times* (London), 21 May 1850.

4 *The Times* (London), 31 December 1850. Howat, *South American Packets*, p. 87. The first combined Brazil and River Plate mail service left Falmouth on 7 September 1832 in the Post Office packet, *Lady Mary Pelham*, for Rio, the connecting vessel reaching Buenos Aires on 24 November.

5 *The Times* (London), 2 January 1850. The letter was submitted by *The Liverpool Albion*. Press reports of Company ships usually identified Royal Mail by its correct name.

case was reasonable in light of that port's already well-developed dock system and its proximity to the major manufacturing areas of much of the produce that was shipped to South America. Southampton, by contrast, boasted only one tidal dock, opened in 1842, although the depth of water was insufficient for company ships to moor alongside.

Competitors argued that the subsidy was unfair in that it gave Royal Mail a monopoly, which was undoubtedly the case. Other interested parties could hardly be expected to present a balanced assessment in the circumstances. Although the Company certainly did enjoy the benefits of being one of the first regular steamship services, any monopoly within the Brazil trade would be short-lived as other companies entered the market within a few years. Royal Mail was, without doubt, advantaged by the prestige of the mail contract but, more importantly, it offered passengers and cargo shippers a regular, fast service between South America and Europe, thereby aiding the development of trade. There was always competition for freight from the vast numbers of sailing ships that were able to offer reduced rates, and as the numbers of steamships on the route increased, freight-rate inducements were part of the commercial scene.

The naval sailing brigs that had previously operated the mail service were, predictably, slow and unreliable, subject as they were to wind and weather, and the Post Office was under great pressure from government and from trading houses for improved services. Royal Mail's much faster service resulted in an increase in the volume of mail and improved trading ties with the South American countries, so that postage rates to Argentina were lowered in 1852 and those to Brazil in 1853.[6] Even so, the sailing schedules were still subject to much criticism by business interests: the northbound vessel arrived in Southampton several days after the southbound vessel departed, so that it could still take three months to receive a reply in London to a letter sent to Buenos Aires.

Within government there was much criticism throughout the 1850s of Royal Mail's close association with the Admiralty, which was based from the outset on the availability of Company vessels for naval service, as and when required. The concept was challenged as unworkable, the vessels being unsuited for the purpose. In 1859 a Select Committee accused the Admiralty of administrative failures and was critical of the methods for allocating mail contracts.[7] The outcome of much parliamentary and commercial pressure was that from 1860 the Post Office

---

However, references to Company meetings were frequently headed 'Royal Mail Steam Company (West Indies)', or some variation, as in *The Times*, 25 April 1861. An alternative was 'The Royal West India Company'.

6 Howat, *South American Packets*, p. 116. The author notes that the Tenth Report of the Postmaster General stated that the total of letters carried in 1856 was 146,328; by 1863 the total was 242,000.

7 *PP 1860 XIX, Report of the Select Committee into Packet and Telegraph Contracts*, quoted in Robert G. Greenhill, 'British Shipping and Latin America 1840–1930: The Royal Mail Steam Packet Company', pp. 36–7.

became responsible for the negotiation and enforcement of mail contracts, with final approval from Parliament.

Preparations for the First Sailing

In August 1850 a sailing ship, *Southampton*, was chartered to carry the first shipment of coal to the new coaling stations at St Vincent in the Cape Verde Islands and in Rio de Janeiro where the Company had been granted land for the purpose, and for establishing repair facilities. Additionally, coal was available at Madeira and in Bahia and Montevideo. Stocks were regularly maintained using chartered sailing ships. Passengers on board included Mr J.W. Macauley, appointed superintendent in Rio, and Captain Evans, who took charge of the depot in St Vincent. A few months later a Captain Liot travelled out to Brazil in *Esk*, a small wooden vessel with a detachable screw, to assist with arrangements in all the ports.[8] Major considerations for the new service were that the schedules served only eight ports to which access was relatively safe and no complex network of feeder services was required, as in the West Indies. Further, only three ships were required to maintain the service, with, as needed, a fourth available on standby and the route benefited from generally fine weather conditions when compared with the less predictable North Atlantic.

At the annual general meeting in London in April 1851 (for the year 1850) the mood was buoyant. The South American service had started three months earlier: 'a large increase in freight and passage money' was reported and the 'five new ships on order were funded by 1850's profits and the reserved fund [sic] with no need to make a call on proprietors'.[9] No references have been found to shed light on the Company's anticipation of profit from the Brazil service, although Chairman Colville, commenting to shareholders on the new service, noted: 'It would be premature to hazard any conjecture at so early a period, as to what may prove the eventual advantages to be derived from this portion of the service, but it is sufficient to state that the prospects so far are of an encouraging nature.' Profit in the early years in an untried trade was, inevitably, uncertain: the commitment of three or four ships with high fixed costs to 12 voyages per year against contractual income of £30,000 was a considerable risk. Running costs were high, so that good passenger numbers and high-freight specie outward and homewards were essential, with packages of cargo contributing to revenues, although carrying capacity remained limited due to the need to carry large quantities of bunker coal.

---

8 Bushell, *Royal Mail*, p. 56.

9 Note that it is impossible to establish what, if any, profit was derived specifically from the South American service as the Company accounts covered all routes. It is likely that, at least in the early years of the service, some voyages were loss-making, a common situation in the liner shipping business, which operated through economic booms and downturns.

The deliberations of the directors in respect of the prospects for the new trade are not recorded, although it is clear that they had hoped for a larger contribution from government. They had every reason to expect that a share of existing export and import business would be attracted to the service. However, those directors who had been with the Company from the outset would recall only too well the difficulties experienced in the early days of the West Indies trade. The decision to proceed with the new service implies some measure of confidence in the prospects, although their judgement would prove to be not always sound.

Trade with Brazil, already significant, was served by large numbers of sailing ships, some operating to regular schedules. Harrisons of Liverpool had been involved irregularly in the, mainly, north Brazil trade from 1847 and a regular steamship service was begun in 1864 following a visit to the area by Thomas Harrison.[10]

A few months later, with a measure of ambition and foresight, the directors were able to advise shareholders that they had applied for, and been granted, a second Royal Charter permitting expansion of services beyond South America and the West Indies. The Charter required that the new services be 'auxiliary branches to the several lines of communication which the Company have established'. In announcing the extended opportunities, the directors commented that a service between Panama and Australia must surely soon be operating, with or without a mail contract.[11]

The Fleet

The fleet in 1850 numbered 14 vessels, totalling 21,213 tons gross, all wooden paddle-steamers except for *Esk*, with nine ships remaining of the original 1842 fleet. Of the eight ships out of service in the 1840s, five were lost in the dangerous Caribbean waters. Several of the ships were employed on the extensive services within the Caribbean. Four different builders were used in order to speed the process of constructing the five new and faster ships. All were paddle-steamers, capable of 12 knots, although contracted operating speed was appreciably less, and with capacity for 100 first-class passengers. They were equipped with simple side-lever engines of 800 hp, heavy and space-consuming. A replacement, purchased in 1847, was *Great Western*, acquired from the Great Western Railway. Brunel was involved in her building, as engineer and designer, and she opened a service from Bristol to New York in 1838.

In the first instance, 'supposing the Admiralty not to object', it was the Company's intention to build two of the new ships of iron, and three of wood.

---

10 F.E. Hyde, *Harrisons of Liverpool* (Liverpool, 1967), pp. 51–2.

11 RMSP, Half-year Report to Shareholders, 9 October 1851. The Company's service to Colon was by now well established, offering connections with Panama. The new charter was dated 30 August 1851.

However, the Admiralty, within two weeks, made clear that iron was not acceptable on the grounds that it offered 'ineffectual resistance to the striking of shot'. The building contracts were reallocated to other yards.[12] It was only in 1853 that a Treasury Committee on Postal Contracts determined that 'contracts for the conveyance of mails should be wholly free from stipulations of that nature'.

Orinoco (2,245 tons) and *Magdalena* (2,318 tons) were built at Pitcher's Northfleet yard, *Amazon* (2,256 tons, Green's Blackwall yard), *Parana* (2,943 tons, Money, Wigram, Southampton) and *Demerara* (2,318 tons, Patterson's, Bristol). Two of the five were lost very quickly, *Demerara* breaking her back when proceeding down the River Avon en route to the Clyde to be engined, and *Amazon* suffering an engine-room fire and becoming a total loss in the Bay of Biscay on the first day of her maiden voyage. Thirty-seven passengers and 68 officers and crew were lost.[13] Building specifications were altered in light of the *Amazon* catastrophe, delaying the introduction of the other three vessels.

Replacements were urgently sought: Cunard's *Arabia*, a wooden paddle-steamer, was bought when she was fitting out in Glasgow for near to £114,113 and renamed *La Plata*.[14] Five more ships were added in the 1853–54 period. *Atrato* (3,467 tons) cost £112,687. She was the largest vessel afloat and the Company's first iron ship, a paddle-wheeler. Built in Greenock by Caird & Co. and fitted with *Demerara*'s engine, she was capable of 14 knots, well in excess of contractual requirements, and was fitted to carry 224 first-class passengers. Captain Chappell, the marine superintendent, having inspected the ship, concluded that she was well suited to the Company's needs, and would give 'great speed'; he estimated that she had cargo space for about 1,000 tons.

Solent (2,230 tons), *Tamar* and *Tyne* (each 1,850 tons), wooden paddle-steamers, and *Wye* (819 tons, iron with screw propulsion), all built for inter-island service in the West Indies, entered service in 1853–54.[15] A further six ships were built or

---

[12] RMSP, Special Reports to the Court, Vol. 1, 7 June 1850 and 18 June 1850. The Admiralty was of the view that wooden hulls were preferable in ships that might be taken up for war service, the hulls absorbing, in some measure, direct hits by cannon balls. (The ships were required to be able 'to carry guns of the largest caliber now used on board Her Majesty's steam vessels of war.') Cunard built a number of small iron-screw ships in the 1850s but these were not used on the North Atlantic mail service.

[13] It was usual for ships to be towed to a specialist engine-building yard from the builder's yard close by: the Pitcher ships, for instance, were engined by Maudsley, Sons & Field, also on the Thames. *Demerara*'s planned lengthy tow from Bristol to the Clyde was unusual, as was *Parana*'s rather more successful tow from Southampton to the Clyde where the vessels were to be engined by Caird & Co. in Greenock.

[14] RMSP, Special Reports to the Court, Vol. 1, 1850. *La Plata* was at that time the Company's most expensive vessel by far. *Arabia* was Cunard's last wooden-hull vessel.

[15] Bushell, *Royal Mail*, pp. 72–6. *Wye* was Royal Mail's second screw-propelled vessel. *Esk* (232 tons) was equipped with an auxiliary screw. She was acquired on the stocks in 1849, in anticipation of the new South American contract, to maintain the Rio to Buenos Aires service. RMSP, Annual Report to Shareholders, 12 April 1855. *Tamar* cost £76,123.

bought in the period 1850–60. In 1858 the first of a trio of iron paddle-steamers was launched in anticipation of an extension of the mail contract: *Parramatta* (3,439 tons) was followed in the next two years by *Shannon* and *Seine*. In 1859, *Mersey* (1,039 tons), an iron paddle-steamer, was built for the Rio to Buenos Aires service. The other two vessels, *Oneida* (2,293 tons, 1855) and *Tasmanian* (2,956 tons, 1857), were iron, screw-propelled steamers acquired in part settlement of a debt. They were built originally for the Suez to Australia mail service and were capable of carrying 250 passengers.

It was about this time, with the introduction of iron hulls, screw propulsion and more compact engines, that Company ships became capable of carrying greater cargo loads. *Tasmanian*, with a vertical direct-acting engine with reduced coal consumption, could carry 1,100 tons of cargo. Other ships were fitted with steam super-heating apparatus, including *Avon* (1842), *Tyne* (1854) and, in 1859–60, *Shannon* (3,609 tons) and *Seine* (3,440 tons) for the same purpose.[16]

Significant demands continued to be made on the insurance fund in the 1850s. In addition to those already mentioned, two vessels were wrecked in the West Indies, *Tay* in 1856 and *Parramatta* in 1859, on her maiden voyage. *Severn* and *Great Western* were broken up in 1856 after service during the Crimean War, the cost of refitting them being considered too great for ships already 15 or more years old.[17] *Orinoco* survived only six years, being broken up in 1858 due to extensive dry rot. The directors were always at pains to reassure shareholders that the ships, their main asset, were maintained in good condition and operated efficiently. The Company's repair yard at Southampton was a valuable facility: machinery and boilers were regularly repaired and updated, the first experiments with super-heated steam being made in 1859.[18] Hull repairs and re-coppering were effected in the dry dock. In 1854 *Atrato* and *Wye*, both building at Caird's yard in Greenock, were delayed by strikes and completed at Southampton.[19]

South to Rio

The first sailing of the monthly South American service was by the nine-year-old re-engined and refurbished paddle-steamer *Teviot* (1,744 tons, 1841), on 9 January 1851. She was fitted with 'patent feathering paddle floats and her speed

16 RMSP, Annual Report to Shareholders, 25 April 1860.

17 *Great Western* was built in 1838 for the Great Western Steamship Company and was famed, along with *Sirius*, for making the first transatlantic passages, to New York, under steam. She was acquired by Royal Mail in 1847 to replace the lost *Tweed*.

18 RMSP, Report of Half-year Meeting. The directors noted that it was too soon to say what value it (super-heated steam) might have in terms of fuel cost-saving.

19 *The Times* (London), 29 April 1853. A report on the launch of *Atrato* stated that she was fitted to carry 250 first-class passengers with their servants.

has been thereby increased about two miles per hour'.[20] With 45 passengers and a small amount of cargo, she sailed from Southampton and made calls at Lisbon, Madeira, Tenerife, St Vincent (for coal bunkers), Pernambuco and Bahia. She reached Rio de Janeiro, her terminal port, on schedule, on 7 February, to the delight of the inhabitants and, no doubt, the relief of the Company.[21] The direct line from Southampton to Lisbon was an immediate advantage to passengers, both outward and homeward, as it reduced transit time between the two ports to about four days. *The Times* of 31 December 1850 noted that the service 'in consequence will be extensively resorted to by travellers between England and Portugal in preference to the indirect and slower route of the Peninsular steamers'. The Montevideo and Buenos Aires mails, passengers and specie were transferred to *Esk* (232 tons, 1849), a wooden screw steamer acquired for the extension service.[22] She collected the first mails from *Teviot* on 7 February, reaching Montevideo on the 16th and Buenos Aires on the 18th.

STEAM COMMUNICATION with the BRAZILS and RIVER PLATE.—ROYAL MAIL STEAM-PACKET COMPANY.—On the 9th January, 1851, the "Teviot," Captain Revett, and thenceforward on the 9th of each month, one or other of this Company's Steamers, will leave Southampton, with Mails, Passengers, &c., for Madeira, Teneriffe, St. Vincent (Cape de Verds), Pernambuco, Bahia, and Rio de Janeiro, and from thence by branch steamer to Monte Video and Buenos Ayres, returning by the same route to Southampton.

Particulars, as to rates of fares, freights, &c., may be had on application at the Company's Offices in London, or at Southampton, where parcels, packages, and publications will be received for the places above mentioned.

Goods taken on moderate freight outward to Rio de Janeiro, and homeward from the same place, as well as from Pernambuco, St Vincent (Cape de Verds), Teneriffe, and Madeira.

Passengers are recommended to make early application for securing proper berths.

E. CHAPPELL, Secretary, No. 55, Moorgate-street, London.

Figure 2.1 Advertisement in the press for first sailing on 9 January 1851

[20] *The Times* (London), 31 December 1850. *Teviot* was refitted at the Company's engineering factory in Southampton.

[21] RMSP, Daily Minutes, Board of Managers, Vol. 5. Passage money was £1,471, freight, £871, total £2,342; *The Hampshire Independent*, 14 June 1851. On her homeward passage *Teviot* carried 129 passengers on the Atlantic crossing, of whom 23 landed in Lisbon.

[22] Bushell, *Royal Mail*, p. 58. The River Plate estuary was, and is, wide and shallow. Even the small *Esk* was obliged to anchor 7 miles from the shore, passengers being first transferred to a small steamer and then to a whaleboat that was rowed to a small wooden jetty. It was not until the 1890s that water depth and harbour facilities improved significantly.

There were some difficulties with the early sailings: cargo was carried only for Rio because arrangements at Lisbon, Pernambuco and Bahia were not yet concluded. At Lisbon, negotiations were still in hand regarding harbour dues, which were greater than the freight rates, and there was insufficient water at Pernambuco for the ships to enter the harbour.[23] These particular problems appear to have been sorted out fairly quickly, although port facilities on the route improved only slowly, transfers of passengers and cargo usually being effected from anchorages and subject always to weather conditions. A major benefit to carriers of the mails was that they generally enjoyed special privileges and concessions when in port, as did naval ships, in terms of harbour dues and other expenses and berth/anchorage preference, important for the handling of passengers and cargo. Royal Mail received a grant of land at Rio for coal storage and repair facilities, clearly an advantage over competitors.[24]

The schedule required by the Admiralty was demanding, with penalties for failure to maintain it: the outward run to Rio was to be made in 28 days and 19 hours at an average speed of 'nine miles per hour'. Homewards to Southampton, 29 days and 23 hours was allowed. An additional seven days were permitted for the branch steamer to Buenos Aires. A few months later the directors were able to state that 'the Brazil service has been maintained with perfect regularity'. Nevertheless, despite the fact that the schedules must have been the result of many hours of consideration by all parties, the timetable was adjusted within six months to allow for more time in the ports of Brazil.[25] The normal pattern of the service was for three, on occasion four, ships to maintain the 12 sailings in the year. *Teviot*, *Tay* and *Severn*, all built in 1841, made the bulk of the voyages in the first year, *Medway* taking one sailing. In this way commanders became familiar with the route and established contacts with the Company's representatives and with agents and officials in the various ports in order to develop the commercial aspects of the trade.

Encouraging Prospects

The accounts offer no breakdown of receipts and costs as between the West Indies and South American trades, so that an accurate assessment of the impact of the new service is impossible. Comparison of the revenues and costs in 1850 and 1851, the first full year of the service, gives an imperfect indication (see Table 2.1). Total receipts increased by 24 per cent while operating costs increased by only 18 per cent. The figures tend to support the chairman's cautious optimism, although the

[23] *The Times* (London), 11 February 1851.

[24] D.C.M. Platt, *Business Imperialism 1840–1930. An Inquiry based on British Experience in Latin America* (Oxford, 1977), pp. 122–3.

[25] Stuart Nicol, *MacQueen's Legacy. A History of Royal Mail Line*, Vol. 1 (Stroud, 2001), p. 66.

essential nature of the mail contract receipts, 52 per cent of the total in 1850, must be noted. The chairman, pointing out that nearly half a million pounds had been expended on the new tonnage, recommended a prudent, 'usual', half-year dividend of £2 per share, for total in the year of £4.

Table 2.1 Income and expenditure, 1850–51

1850		**1851**	
Receipts	**£**	**Receipts**	**£**
Mail contract	240,000 (52%)	Mail contract	270,000 (48%)
Freight income	84,607 (19%)	Freight income	105,856 (19%)
Passage money	132,653 (29%)	Passage money	190,428 (33%)
Total	457,260 (100%)	Total	566,284 (100%)
Disbursements*	313,897	Disbursements*	369,299
Surplus	143,363	Surplus	196,985
Profit and loss account		**Profit and loss account**	
Dividend	59,360 (£4 = 6.6%)	Dividend	59,360 (£4 = 6.6%)
Balance sheet (selected items only)		Balance sheet (selected items only)	
Cost and outfit of ships	782,163	Costs and outfit of ships	831,516
Investments	190,000	Investments	75,000
Profit	115,670	Profit	35,610
Insur. & general res.	225,657	Insurance reserve	104,669
Capital**	890,400	Capital**	890,400
Total* **	**1,268,731**	**Total*** **	**1,084,298**

* Includes coal, wages, provisions, insurance, repairs, office costs.

** There were arrears of calls made on the £60 payment required on the £100 shares.

*** This total is the balance sheet total and it is not the sum of the selected items listed.

Shareholders were never slow to express their concerns regarding the lax accounting procedures of the time: in 1854, at the annual meeting, some advanced the view that 'they [the accounts] fail to exhibit the results in a clear and intelligible manner'. The directors conceded and agreed the desired alterations. As we shall see in future chapters, the comments of shareholders were scathing at times: they reflected little knowledge of the operation of the Company but a keen interest in dividend payments and the share price. The annual accounts consisted of a working account, a profit and loss account and a balance sheet. These were usually audited by appointed shareholders and were subject to frequent adaptation and amendment of form and terminology.

Essential to the successful operation of a steamship company of the period, apart from ensuring that capital was adequate to meet operational requirements and a sufficient return was made to satisfy shareholders, was the sensible review of potentially profitable but untried routes and the careful management of financial resources. Vital elements in this management process were ensuring that cash was readily available for ship and establishment repairs and maintenance, for insurance and for a depreciation allowance against the value of assets.

The principle of setting aside an annual sum for depreciation in the value of the fleet (termed deteriorations at that time) was acknowledged by Royal Mail in the 1850s, the value of the fleet being written down in the annual accounts by an average 5 per cent based on an anticipated 20-year life of a vessel. The percentage of the fleet value allowed in this period ranged, as a rule, between 6 and 8 per cent, the amount varying according to profitability. In the period 1850 to 1854 no deterioration set-aside was noted in the accounts, although, exceptionally, 6 per cent was allowed in the accounts for 1855, in respect of 1853 and 1854, and 10 per cent for 1855, an exceptionally profitable year.

The Company self-insured its vessels when at sea, the decision being made in the 1840s on the grounds that the level of insurance premiums was too high and, presumably, on the basis that the board, rightly or wrongly, was confident of the competence of its shipmasters. As a rule, 5 per cent of the value of the fleet was set aside in an insurance fund, which, on occasion, paid a dividend to shareholders. Before 1861, insurance cover was purchased for the fleet when it was in port.[26] When ships were hired to the government, as during the Crimean campaign, the Company appears to have allowed for only a proportion of the insurance risk, the rest being carried by the hirer. As with depreciation, the amount set aside annually for insurance very much depended on the state of the business. In 1851 only £25,000 was set aside on a fleet valued at £470,612. The insurance contribution was regarded as a cost, along with coal, stores and so on. The accounts for 1855, a very profitable year with over £400,000 receipts from government hire, show that a total of £80,783 was allocated, including £35,783 for a 'proportion of insurance for ships employed as transports'. This was an 8 per cent allowance on a fleet valued in the accounts at £962,003. A general reserve fund was maintained to meet costs for repair and other work. The intention was to transfer 8 per cent annually to the fund but, again, that was not always achieved. When profit was sufficient, the several funds were topped up to meet prior deficiencies.[27] In 1850 the fund stood at £149,283: in 1851 there was no record of the fund, which was, presumably, fully expended in the new building programme.

Through the early 1850s the Company paid the usual £2 dividend per share from profit at each half-year, an annual return of 7 per cent on the £60 paid up on the £100 shares. As revenues increased in the middle of the decade, larger sums were allocated to the insurance fund, up from £25,000 in 1851 to £45,000

---

26 RMSP, Annual Report to Shareholders, 24 April 1861. Following a fire on board *La Plata* in Southampton, the insurers proposed to increase cost of cover by 50 per cent. The Company declined and established a separate fund for that purpose.

27 RMSP, Annual Report to Shareholders, 10 April 1856.

in 1855. At that time the practice developed of paying a bonus from the 'excess' of the fund, no doubt to the satisfaction of the shareholders. The figure of £200,000 was considered to be the minimum requirement, so that in 1856, when the fund stood at £254,663, a bonus of £1 10s was paid.[28] The payment of bonuses from the insurance fund was not universally approved, then or later. The essential point was the directors' assessment of the sum required to meet calls on the fund. With new ships costing in excess of £100,000 and a succession of accidents and losses, it is arguable that the fund was inadequate. However, the £200,000 figure was maintained throughout the decade, increasing in the 1860s to nearer to £300,000.

Passenger and freight revenues, both outward and homeward, were essential for the profitability of the service. Records of the period, including the Company's, are rather vague about the weight and volume of cargo carried in ships built in the 1840s and 1850s, although the passenger and specie figures were invariably noted. Cargo was certainly carried outwards from the outset: typically *Teviot* left Southampton in October 1851 with 106 passengers, specie to the value of £115,000, and 'a very full cargo', which may have amounted to no more than 100–200 tons. *The Times* noted that *Medway* sailed from Southampton for Brazil earlier in the year with 27 passengers and a 'fair cargo of woollens, corahs, silks, silver plate, wines and plain and printed cottons ... and specie value £57.990 sterling'. The article also discussed in some detail already evident scheduling problems that caused the outward steamer to leave Southampton five days before the inward mails were received in London.[29]

The Company invited potential shippers to offer cargo and published freight rates: the rate outwards was £5 per ton measurement plus 5 per cent primage. Heavy goods were £4 per ton weight plus 5 per cent primage, quicksilver 2 per cent of value.[30] Specie was charged at 1 per cent of value outward. Specie (bullion, coin as opposed to paper money) and plate homeward, delivered to the Bank of England, rated 1.125 per cent on value, precious stones, 1.625 per cent. £5 per ton was usual for other products such as coffee.[31] Anticipated homeward freights included coffee and cocoa (5s per ton), spices (ginger, £7 per ton), essences and fruit and vegetables loaded homewards in Lisbon.

---

[28] RMSP, Annual Report to Shareholders, 16 April 1857. In 1855, an exceptionally profitable year, a bonus of £5 was paid, for a total in the year of 9.6 per cent.

[29] *The Times* (London), 11 March 1851.

[30] Primage was an additional charge, originally said to be a gratuity to the master. In time it became an inducement to shippers, who received half or more of the payment back for regular business.

[31] *The Times* (London), editorial, 31 December 1850.

Coal-burning Paddle-steamers

The building specifications for steamships of the period tended to refer to space in the lower decks being available for coal and/or coal and cargo. In Royal Mail's transatlantic ships, passengers were accommodated in the two decks under the top/spar, or main deck, with officers and crew towards the forward end of the vessel. Space available for cargo was dependent on the quantity of coal required for the passage. Despite this limitation, the indications are that, in regular service, given the facility to top up bunkers at specified coaling stations (St Vincent in the Cape Verde Islands was regularly used on the South American route), Royal Mail's 1840s-built steamers were capable of carrying in the region of 200 tons of cargo, the newer ones rather more. Stability was a problem in ships carrying little cargo and low on bunkers: the ships might become top heavy and be inclined to roll in even moderate seas or to list, sometimes referred to as 'coal-fever'.[32]

Cargo tended to be in packages, parcels or sacks of limited size, suited to loading and discharging through the small hatches available for access to the lower decks and then being dragged across the low-ceilinged spaces for safe stowage. This procedure was labour-intensive and time-consuming, an important factor when ships were anchored some distance from the shore for only a few hours and mail transfers determined the period in port. Mail, letters, newspapers and parcels, and specie were carried in secure lockers.[33]

The limited access for cargo was due, in part, to the design of the passenger spaces, with passenger accommodation across the full width of the vessel. Within a few years, as ship design altered to take advantage of the move from wood to stronger iron construction and smaller and more fuel-efficient engines, the disposition of the passenger spaces altered. Cargo hatches were installed in the centre of the hull with access by crane or derrick, passenger accommodation being moved to the sides of the vessel and to the spaces between the hatchways.

A typical paddle-steamer of the period was three-masted and carried a full set of sails, with square sails on the foremast used in favourable wind conditions to supplement the ship's speed and to reduce coal consumption, or in an emergency.[34] Navigation and lookout were effected from an open, raised passageway, later termed a bridge, built between the paddle boxes. This primitive structure was

---

32 Denis Griffiths, *Brunel's Great Western* (Wellingborough, 1985).

33 Ewan Corlett, *The Iron Ship: The Story of Brunel's S.S. Great Britain* (London, 1975) pp. 71, 72, 87 and 99. With benefit of involvement in the recovery and reconstruction of the vessel, the writer estimates that, with the available space two-thirds full she carried 360 measurement tons, about 200 tons weight of cargo on her maiden voyage. *Great Britain*, screw-propelled and of iron, was of 3,500 tons as compared with Royal Mail's three 1851-built wooden paddle-steamers of just under 3,000 tons.

34 The rigging of steam vessels with sails for emergency or other use was usual into the 1870s–80s. Bushell notes, p. 140, that in 1880 *Neva*, a 12-knot ship, used her square sails for 803 hours and her fore-and-aft sails for 285 hours in 42 days of steaming.

sometimes placed behind the funnel, a less than desirable position for the purpose. The available aids to navigation – charts, magnetic compasses, chronometer and sextant – were less than wholly reliable. A sounding machine, essential in coastal waters, was fitted in all vessels.[35] Lifeboats were carried in davits, usually in the after part of the main deck, although, almost invariably, they were heavy and of insufficient capacity for all aboard.

In the 1850s, and for many years later, there were no government regulations concerning the number of lifeboats carried. The directors considered the matter at some length, recognising the need to reassure passengers as to safety, especially after the *Amazon* disaster in 1852, and conscious of the stresses imposed on the wooden upper structures by the weight of heavy boats.

Figure 2.2 *Thames* (1841). From T.A. Bushell, *Royal Mail, 1839–1939* (Trade and Travel Publications Ltd, London, 1939)

A report by the marine superintendent some years earlier favoured two large lifeboats each capable of carrying 100 people and stowed in a manner that would, in theory, permit of safe launching. The boats proved to be heavy and difficult to handle, and inadequate for more than 200 passengers and crew. Four additional workboats were proposed, one of which, as required by contract, was used to

[35] RMSP, Cost and Outfit of Steamships from 1839–1912. The vessels of the first fleet were each fitted with a 'Massey's Sounding Machine' at a cost of £4 each, no doubt merely a development of the hand lead line in use then and for many years after.

provide a 'suitable boat manned by not less than four oars' to convey the naval agent and the mails to and from the shore.[36]

Ships were designed with a flush spar (main) deck, essential when sails were in use. This frequently resulted in water being shipped over the decks in heavy weather, with flooding of the engine-room and other spaces below, and damage to boats and other deck structures. Typically, the accommodation for passengers in the two 'tween decks was arranged with the promenade saloon in the upper, the dining saloon in the lower, both with cabins along the ship's side opening directly on to them. The saloons, particularly those for first-class passengers, were extravagantly decorated, although the cabins were small with barely space for two bunks.[37]

Lighting by day was from a number of large skylights placed in the main deck above and by night by candle lamps. Ventilation was poor: although there were shipside scuttles, these were closed in bad weather and at night. Important for the additional comfort of passengers was a supply of fresh meat: live animals, cows, sheep and pigs, suitably screened, were carried in pens with stocks of corn and hay.

Developing Markets in South America: Brazil

Brazil and, to a lesser extent, Argentina were established import–export markets in 1850. The value of British exports to Brazil in 1850 totalled £2.5m, with imports from that country slightly less. Five per cent of Britain's cotton and sugar came from Brazil and 27 per cent of her hides, whilst Argentina supplied 40 per cent of the demand for hides and 2 per cent that of wool.[38] Relatively small and slow sailing ships were the only means of transport, so that to Royal Mail the opportunity to take over, in time, a part of the trade of those countries was commercially attractive. Brazil was the Company's main focus: it offered the prospect of profit from increased shipments of manufactured goods southbound and export goods, mainly coffee, cotton and spices from the southern states, homewards. The exports funded the country's imports and provided essential government revenues. Sea communications were vital: Brazil lacked its own ocean shipping fleet, and regular and fast steam communication with Europe was immensely attractive.

By 1850, European countries, including Britain, already had strong commercial and diplomatic links, and well-established British mercantile houses contributed to the development of the business interests of Brazil, despite political and

36 RMSP, Special Reports to the Court, vol. 1, 14 January 1841.

37 *P.P., 1839, XLVII, 'Accidents'*, p. 110, quoted in Sarah Palmer, 'Experience, Experiment and Economics: Factors in the Construction of Early Merchant Steamers', *Proceedings of the Conference of the Atlantic Canada Shipping Project*, March–April 1977 (St John's, Newfoundland), p. 233. A witness to the investigation implied that (some) owners attached more importance to luxury accommodation than to safety.

38 D.C.M. Platt, *Latin America and British Trade 1806–1914* (London, 1972), p. 67..

economic uncertainties. Yet Brazil was a 'backward country in 1850', according to Richard Graham, with virtually no industry.[39] His comparison was with Britain of the period, already well into the process of industrialisation and modernisation, against which most countries of the world appeared backward.

Nevertheless, he well illustrates the situation of that country, only just achieving some small measure of political order and stability, although conditions would remain turbulent for many years. Brazil was vast and its potential largely unexploited due to poor to non-existent internal and coastal communications and a relatively small population. Investment was essential to enable produce to reach the main ports at economic prices and imported goods to reach the expanding population. Only then would Brazil become a serious player in international commerce.[40]

The directors, before making a very considerable financial commitment, had, no doubt, assured themselves of the potential of the new markets, in both freight and passenger terms. High-level contacts were made, including British diplomatic representatives, and agents were appointed in every port of call. A Mr Macauley was established in Rio in August 1850. The agents, most of them merchants engaged in the shipping business, were mainly British. They maintained essential contacts with port authorities, Customs and cargo shippers, and were vital sources of commercial intelligence, alert to freight available for shipment and freight rates current, and would, where possible, obtain a contractual commitment from the shipper. They also performed the vital service of making arrangements for a vessel's stay in port, liaising with port authorities to facilitate the loading and discharging of cargo and the disembarkation/embarkation of passengers. As a rule, payment to them was by commission on goods and passengers shipped from their ports, and at a lesser rate on incoming freight and passengers.[41] Many years later Royal Mail established its own substantial offices in Rio and Buenos Aires, a measure of the importance of local representation.

British capital and goods had flooded into Brazil for years under a tariff preferences agreement: in 1827, by commercial treaty with Britain, the preferences were abolished and tariffs were limited to 15 per cent. The treaty expired in 1844 and was not renewed, despite persistent British pressure for free trade, allowing the Brazilians to adjust tariffs to protect local manufactures and to ensure that government income revenues were maintained at a satisfactory level. The importation of cheap cotton goods inevitably eliminated many hand-craft industries, and other imports affected local production with damaging affects on employment. Nevertheless, in the context of protective tariffs, in 1857 Consul

---

[39] R.Graham, *Britain and the Onset of Modernization in Brazil 1850–1914* (Cambridge, 1968), p. 1.

[40] Platt, *Latin America*, pp. 65–7.

[41] RMSP, Agents' books, 1876–1884. Commissions varied by port. In 1882 the agent in Buenos Aires was appointed to succeed his father with commissions of 5 per cent for passengers and goods booked from his port and 2.5 per cent for cargo landed there.

Cowper reported from Pernambuco that the country's commercial laws were 'extremely liberal'.[42]

Between 1845 and 1849, half, by value, of all the country's imports were from Britain. In January 1850 all the ships arriving in Rio direct from Britain were British-flagged, as were a large number of those arriving from other countries. British merchants exercised considerable influence: they imported goods, mainly textiles and textile manufactures (about 70 per cent of the total), consumer goods and hardware, which they then sold on to retailers or bought products for export from middlemen, many of them, again, British.[43]

The country's key exports were coffee, which accounted for nearly half of the total, cotton, sugar and tobacco, products attractive to Britain's expanding economy, with an increasing population and rising wages creating demand for consumer products. In 1850, 5 per cent of Britain's expanded demand for cotton and 27 per cent of her hides were from Brazil. Platt notes that sugar and tobacco imports to Britain were adversely affected by preferential duties afforded to British colonies, and it was only when the duties were removed in 1851 (coffee) and 1854 (sugar), that the British market was fully opened to the Brazilian products. Much of the coffee received in British ports was re-exported to the Continent, in part because the British did not have much taste for it. Other products from South America were similarly disadvantaged in some measure throughout the nineteenth century as British importers favoured products from less distant parts and from the colonies.[44]

A practical problem was the primitive nature of most ports in South America, and elsewhere, in the mid-century. Through to the end of the nineteenth century, Rio de Janeiro, Brazil's largest port, required vessels to anchor in the wide, protected, bay. Loading and discharge were by lighter, then by trolley to the Customs quay, to elevators, then to deposit facilities, with heavy charges on each occasion. Cost was certainly a consideration, but so was time: although the 1850s schedule allowed for four days in Rio, overnight only in the other Brazilian ports, late arrival, not unusual, meant something of a scramble to unload southbound and load northbound cargo. Vital, of course, was the safe and timely loading and discharging of mails outwards and homewards, with, still, a mail agent in charge.

The business outlook appeared to be sound, but there were other problems: although Brazil benefited from relative political stability for 15 years from 1850,

---

42 Platt, *Latin America*, p. 80.

43 Graham, *Britain and the Onset of Modernization*, pp. 82–6 and Appendix C on p. 330, which values British exports to Brazil in the period 1850–54 at £16.1m, of which £11.7m was textiles or textile manufactures. The source for the statistics was the Board of Trade Statistical Office, 'Annual Statement of the Trade of the United Kingdom with Foreign Countries and British Possessions' (London, 1853–1909). Manchester, *British Pre-eminence in Brazil*, p. 262. Brazil's first two railways, inaugurated in 1854 and 1858, were built with British capital.

44 Platt, *Latin America*, pp. 36–7.

relations between the British and Brazilian governments were strained, to say the least, in 1851 and would remain so for some years. As Royal Mail was in the process of investing considerable capital in new ships for its extended service, Britain, frustrated by the Brazilian government's failure to end the slave trade (a matter of dispute between the two countries since 1845), ordered its warships to enter Brazilian ports to seize or destroy ships involved in the trade. The order was rescinded in May 1852, by which time 90 Brazilian ships had been seized by British cruisers, some of the crews being referred to British Admiralty courts for punishment.[45] Britain's actions, considered by the Brazilians to be arbitrary and arrogant, led to a cooling of relations between the two countries and threatened to undermine the considerable influence of British merchants, although Brazil still relied heavily on trade with Britain.

Throughout this period and further disputes in the 1860s, the British merchants continued to exercise great influence and were responsible for many aspects of the swift growth of imports and investment into Brazil and exports from it. Despite the bitterness of the Brazilians, the traders appear to have viewed the diplomatic uncertainties as little more than a distraction from their everyday activities, and they do not appear to have been adversely affected within their own business communities. Importantly, the trade developments led to greatly increased government revenues and a strengthening of the country's credit. Even so, in 1854 the Brazilian minister in London noted that

> the commerce between the two countries is carried on with English capital, on English ships by English companies. The profits … the interest on capital … the payments for insurance, the commissions, and dividends from the business, everything goes into the pockets of Englishmen.[46]

This situation would prevail to the end of the century. A commentator noted much later that, until late in the nineteenth century, 'All commercial transactions between Brazil and foreign countries, whether Britain or another, were conducted through London. Brazilian importers', he added, 'consistently turned to Britain to fulfil their wants of manufactured goods (and coal).' Manchester contends that the aim

[45] Manchester, *British Pre-eminence in Brazil*, p. 255. Naval activity continued, but not in Brazilian waters. The Brazilian government later argued, unconvincingly, that British involvement in the slavery issue hindered its own efforts to end the trade; see ibid., pp. 263–4. Manchester acknowledges that the Brazilians passed a law in 1850 making the slave traffic illegal. Slave importations fell from 54,000 in 1849 to only a few hundred by 1852. A further matter of contention was the still-unsettled claims of British subjects (totalling £250,000) dating back to losses sustained in the 1820s at a time of revolutionary activity in Brazil, and also the Brazilian blockade of La Plata in 1825–27; see ibid., p. 269.

[46] Graham, *Britain and the Onset of Modernization*, p. 73. Manchester, *British Pre-eminence in Brazil*, p. 286.

of the Brazilians was not to end British involvement but to free themselves from restrictions imposed by Britain in order to permit competition from other nations.[47]

Foreigners were a significant proportion of the business elite in the country's major centres, with British representatives and other Europeans included on the boards of the many influential commercial associations, Brazilians commonly being in the minority. The commercial associations were stronger than interest bodies in Britain at the time: the London Chamber of Commerce was established only in 1880 for a similar purpose. There were associations in all Brazil's centres of trade and they exerted considerable influence in facilitating commerce, perhaps reflecting the failure of central government to effectively manage the development of trade and the essential communications and infrastructure.

A measure of the associations' range of influence was the initiation of Brazil's first coastal steamer services by the Rio de Janeiro Association in 1840 and its involvement in 1854 in the organisation of the country's first railway line, vital to the movement of coffee to the coast and infinitely quicker than a mule train. There were restrictions on foreign vessels in the coastal trades, but these were gradually lifted in the 1860s, resulting in the virtual disappearance of Brazil's merchant marine by 1875.[48]

Ports vied with each other to attract steamship services, emphasising the importance of their trade and pledging the support of association members. And with good cause: the new services contributed to significant growth in the 1850s and a continuing steady increase. The Rio de Janeiro Association was party to persuading Royal Mail to make the commitment to the new service.[49]

Whatever view Royal Mail's directors may have had of the political atmosphere in 1850, their contacts with the business community were sufficiently persuasive to overcome any concerns the political situation may have caused. The mail subsidy apart, clearly there was the prospect of enhanced passenger revenues connected with the small but influential British communities in South America as well as from the improved connection between Lisbon and Brazil, beneficial to the Portuguese and the Brazilians. The shipment of specie, on occasion in large quantities, was an obvious source of income, much of it in payment for goods imported, a reflection of the trade imbalances of both Argentina and Brazil.[50]

---

47 *The Siren and Shipping*, special issue, 1916, p. 29: 'Brazil Commercially Considered'.

48 Eugene Ridings, *Business Interest Groups in Nineteenth Century Brazil* (Cambridge, 1994) pp. 36–43 and 250–51.

49 Ibid., p. 252.

50 Robert Walsh, *Notices of Brazil in 1828 and 1829*, vol. II (London, 1830), pp. 194–201, quoted in Platt, *Latin America*, p. 36. An example from a few years earlier: in 1828 Brazil paid for $24.5m of imports with $10m of produce and $14m of specie.

Argentina

The prospects in Argentina were less attractive. The period from 1850 to 1870 was one of uncertainty, of political unrest and war, together with Brazil and Uruguay, against Paraguay for five years from 1865. The country was disunited: the Confederation of Provinces, which included those on the important Parana River, was in constant dispute with the Province of Buenos Aires. The Confederation, determined not to cede power to Buenos Aires, sought to begin the process of developing railways and port facilities at Rosario, on the Parana River, bypassing Buenos Aires. It also attempted to attract overseas investment, in particular from Britain, which was already diplomatically involved in seeking a peaceful solution to the dispute. In 1855 an unsuccessful approach was made to British investors offering a concession for the building of a railway line from Rosario to Cordoba, 246 miles to the north. The British government was also petitioned, again unsuccessfully, to subsidise Royal Mail to enable it to operate direct sailings from Europe to Rosario and other river ports.[51]

In the 1850s the city of Buenos Aires was the principal centre of population and commerce. Most of the vast land area of Argentina was uninhabited, in part due to relentless war with the indigenous Indian population that continued into the late 1870s and inhibited the development of communities away from the coastal areas around Buenos Aires and the river port of Rosario. Transportation from the interior was primitive and expensive: ox carts, capable of carrying two tons of freight, might take a month to travel the 200 miles between the cities of Rosario and Cordoba, and were constantly at risk of attack from native Indians.

In 1862, a unifying president, Bartolomé Mitre, was appointed. He encouraged the establishment of internal communications and immigration, capital investment and overseas trade in, mainly, agricultural products all essential to the opening up of the vast interior of the country. Progress was slow but within a few years British businessmen, long established in the country, mainly in Buenos Aires, as import and export merchants, had facilitated the establishment of London-based banks, railway companies and a range of public utilities. These contributed greatly to trade between Argentina and Britain for very many years, with much of the materiel and machinery needed, for instance, for the railways being shipped from Britain.

The development of the economy was slow; it relied on improved railway communication with the interior to facilitate the movement of labour to work the land and to speed up the transport of, especially, export and import freights. A further important benefit of the railway system was the unification of the assorted provinces within the Confederation. The progress made hardly indicates urgency: the first railway, reaching six miles from Buenos Aires to a western suburb, was part funded by the provincial government and completed in 1857. By 1867 two further lines, both British financed, were built. A milestone in the opening up of the hinterland was the inauguration in 1870 of the British-financed and built

[51] H.S. Ferns, *Britain and Argentina in the Nineteenth Century* (Oxford, 1960), p. 312.

Central Argentine Railroad from Rosario to Cordoba, 246 miles to the north. The inducements offered to the builders of the Central Argentine and the Great Southern railways were considerable: they included three-mile grants of land on either side of the line, a guaranteed dividend of 7 per cent for a 40-year period and immunity from taxes.[52]

The development of the vital rail network was haphazard: several different companies were involved, some privately financed locally, some government owned; most employed overseas capital. A number flourished, especially those radiating from the capital. Finance for railway building originated mainly in London: in 1873 more than 70 per cent of the £5.2m invested in the railways was British capital.[53]

The River Plate passenger and freight prospects for Royal Mail were limited at the outset. *Esk*, first used on the Rio to Montevideo and Buenos Aires service, was too small to carry more than a few passengers, specie and mail.[54] She was withdrawn after less than a year and replaced by the 398-ton *Prince*. These small vessels reflect, perhaps, the Company's view of the limited cargo opportunities. By 1859 the newly built, larger *Mersey* (1,039 tons), a 10-knot paddle-steamer with increased passenger accommodation and still only limited cargo capacity, was employed. It is likely that by this time some cargo was being carried to and from Rio.

Argentina's main export was 'jerked beef', a low-freight, salted and dried beef product, tough and tasteless, which never found favour in Europe. Other cattle by-products, for example hides, tallow and bones, were shipped to Europe in large quantities. Although the prospects for cargo shipments from Britain to the Argentine may well have been a source of optimism for management, most available produce for export from that country was less than ideal for carriage in a passenger liner.

The value of imports into Britain from Argentina in 1854 was £1.3m and of exports from Britain in 1850 it was £0.8m (for Brazil the comparable figures were £2.1m and £2.5m).[55] These figures reflect a substantial movement of cargo in the

---

[52] James R. Scobie, *Revolution on the Pampas. A Social History of Argentine Wheat, 1860–1910* (Austin, TX, 1964), pp. 36–7. Winthrop R. Wright, *British-Owned Railways in Argentina. Their Effect on Economic Nationalism, 1854–1948* (Austin, TX, 1974), pp. 28–9.

[53] C. Lewis, 'British Railway Companies and the Argentine Government', in Platt (ed.), *Business Imperialism*

[54] Howat, *South American Packets*, p. 120. An announcement in *Commercio del Plata* of Montevideo advising that *Esk* 'will take passengers and freight of treasure' for Rio de Janeiro.

[55] Platt, *Latin America*, Appendix I, pp. 316–19, 'Exports of Produce and Manufactures of the United Kingdom to Latin America, 1850–1913', and Appendix II, pp. 320–23, 'Imports of Latin American Produce into the United Kingdom, 1854–1913'. Note that the UK imports statistics began in 1854.

small sailing vessels of the period that were better suited to the shallow waters of the Rivers Plate and Parana. Throughout the period of this study, passenger calls were regularly made at Montevideo in Uruguay and some cargo was discharged and loaded in, initially, an open anchorage. However, the country was never a major factor in Royal Mail's considerations, even into the twentieth century, although considerable quantities of meat products and grains were produced.

Freights Develop Slowly

The freight rates available to steamships were, predictably, higher than those for sailing ships, but they were subject to seasonal fluctuations and recession and depression within South America and in Europe, as well as the effects of disease. Freight rates on the South American routes were generally buoyant between 1852 and 1855. They declined from 1856 to 1859, due, in part at least, to the rapidly increasing level of steamship building. In 1860 steamship tonnage accounted for 10 per cent of the shipping between the UK and the east coast of South America.[56] And rates were subject to competitive factors: steamship companies vied for cargo shipments, as did the larger and faster sailing vessels that continued to offer regular services. A speedy, safe and reliable liner service might yield a higher rate than a slower vessel and in this respect Royal Mail's agents had some advantage when booking cargo.

Although new tonnage was built in 1852–53 to service the revised mail contract, most of the Company's ships continued to be employed on the West Indies services with its complex inter-island route structure. The first three sailings to South America were made by *Teviot*, *Tay* and *Medway*, all of which entered service in 1842 and were smaller and slower than the new ships, with less space for passengers and cargo, hardly a reassurance of the importance of the service. Later *Thames* and *Great Western* made sailings to Rio. These vessels appear to have coped adequately with the demands of the trade, although an 1856 Special Report to the Board noted that 'in certain seasons the packets are crowded with passengers and that outwards they are mostly filled with passengers'.

A typical homeward run was that of *Teviot* in late 1851. She arrived in Southampton on 10 September, precisely on schedule, and, having landed 30 passengers in Lisbon, she brought 77 into her home port. Cargo included 26 packages of ipecacuanha, a root used for medical purposes, and 15 barrels of coffee from Brazil and specie valued in excess of £30,000. In addition she carried over 400 boxes of grapes, chests of lemons, cases of tomatoes and sundry packages loaded northbound in Lisbon, a regular homeward cargo.[57]

---

[56] Juan E. Oribe Stemmer, 'Freight Rates in the Trade between Europe and South America, 1840–1914', in L. Bethell, V. Bulmer-Thomas and L. Whitehead (eds), *Journal of Latin American Studies*, Vol. 21, Part 1, February 1989, pp. 41–3.

[57] *The Times* (London), 11 September 1851.

Inward cargoes in the early days are variously and vaguely described as 'a large general cargo', or a 'full general cargo', with no indication of weight or freight earned. In 1854 *Great Western* brought into Southampton 50 barrels of tapioca, 390 bags of cochineal, 40 packages of ipecacuanha as well as 376 half-chests of oranges, 197 boxes of potatoes and sundry general merchandise. These two shipments, while acknowledging the space limitations, reflect the limited range of cargo shipped in Brazil at the time, although by the end of the 1850s bales of tobacco and cotton and bags of coffee were regularly carried in increasing amounts. Very little detail has been found of outward shipments to South America, although these may have been more substantial and profitable, bearing in mind the great production of textiles and hardware in this country and the demand for these products in South America. *Tay*, in 1851, loaded outwards a 'very large cargo of British manufactured goods' and specie to the value of £232,319, of which £185,905 was destined for Rio. The specie was described as 'capital contributed by British banks towards the establishment of a commercial bank at Rio'.[58]

From the earliest days of steamships, much more expensive to operate than sailing ships, the carriage of cargo, as well as of passengers, was essential in order to return a profit, even with a government subsidy. However, cargo capacity was limited by the great bulk of the engines and boilers, and, particularly on transatlantic routes, by the need to carry large quantities of coal to ensure safe passage between coaling stations strategically placed along the routes. Southbound from Southampton, St Vincent in the Cape Verde Islands was the last coaling station before Rio de Janeiro, a run of about 13 days. Royal Mail maintained a coaling station there, regularly importing coal from South Wales by chartered sailing ship. No reference has been found to Company facilities at Bahia and Pernambuco, although emergency supplies were most probably available, so that a minimum coal requirement on leaving St Vincent was in the region of 600 tons. The fleet of the period had total coal/cargo capacity of about 800 tons, leaving only limited space for cargo, although the situation improved throughout the 1860s and 1870s as larger tonnage was built and engines became smaller and more efficient.[59]

The loading and discharging of cargo was, inevitably, slow and was made still more difficult by the fact that most of this work was done with the ship at anchor, with barges or lighters alongside and subject to wind and weather. Progressively, from the early 1860s, steam winches were introduced to facilitate the handling of cargo, expensive but essential as freight capacity increased.

Specie, a mainstay of freight revenues, was stored in a secure bullion room on the upper decks, although some might be stowed in the holds when large shipments were carried. Captain Woolward describes one such shipment in *Teviot*, in 1859, of around 160 tons, valued at approximately $3.5m. On arrival in Southampton

---

58 S. Nicol, *Scrapbook*, Miscellaneous 2, p. 1054.

59 The figures are, at best, estimates only as no precise information has been found for the period. The run from Southampton to St Vincent was also of about 12 to 13 days, but coal was available at Madeira and Tenerife.

the specie stowed in the hold was manhandled on to the main deck and then lifted ashore, stowed in railway wagons and shipped to London.[60]

Trouble in the Boardroom

Royal Mail's directors enjoyed some measure of success in the 1850s. The establishment of the new route to Brazil proceeded relatively smoothly, very much to their credit, although schedules were frequently not adhered to. The most erratic sailings were those returning from Rio, due, at least in part, to delays in the arrival of the mails from Buenos Aires. Unfortunately, these failures gave further ammunition to those parties critical of the Company and its 'privileged' position.

Reports to shareholders gave little information about the development of the service other than a brief comment on trading conditions. Likewise, they seldom dwelt on the details of the accounts, referring only in general terms to the sources of receipts with a brief explanation of reasons for the increase/decrease. Rather more information was given on what were termed disbursements, costs of coal, stores and so on, and allocations made to funds such as insurance and general reserve.

The figures in Table 2.2 fairly reflect the very substantial development of the Company's overall business throughout the decade. Receipts rose from £566,284 in 1851 to £768,624 in 1860, up 36 per cent. Especially satisfying were the increases of freight and passage money, which reduced dependence on the mail subsidy, down from 52 per cent in 1850 to 35 per cent in 1860. Receipts of £418,124 from the hire of seven vessels to the government during the Crimean campaign meant that receipts in 1855 were substantially from that source. Although this was a subject of criticism in some quarters, shareholders enjoyed a dividend of £9 in the year, 15 per cent on their investments. Disbursements, however, increased even more sharply, up from £369,299 to £532,724, 44 per cent. Coal costs increased dramatically as larger vessels were added to the fleet and more frequent sailings were required by the new contract. Substantial additional costs were incurred for the purchase and shipment in chartered sailing vessels of coal to the new bunkering stations established in the Cape Verde Islands and in Rio.

---

60 Robert Woolward, *Nigh on Sixty Years* (London, c. 1894), pp. 179–83. Woolward describes how he, with five officers and eight senior crew members, who had already supervised the unloading of the freight, accompanied the train to Nine Elms Station, London, transferred the specie to 18 Pickford's four-horse wagons and accompanied it to the Bank of England. Quite why Woolward and his men personally accompanied the specie to London on this occasion is uncertain, although the reason may well have been the value of the shipment. Company Regulations required that all the ship's officers be in attendance when specie was loaded or discharged, the captain included, each with a designated duty, the specie being handed over to a treasure clerk who was responsible for the shipment once ashore.

No debentures were in issue in the 1850s, but debts were incurred through 1852–54 and 1858–60, both periods of heavy expenditure on new ships. No reference has been found in the annual reports to the intention to borrow cash or consideration of alternative means of raising funds. The 1854 balance sheet noted 'By Cash borrowed ... £235,000'. The report affirmed the intention to eliminate the debt, on which a high rate of interest was being charged, in the course of that year, and was achieved.[61]

The half-year accounts in 1859 show cash borrowed of £165,000. The accounts for the year-end indicate that that figure was increased to £200,000 and reduced to £100,000 in the following year, at which time the debt was cleared. The annual reports make no direct comment on this unusual situation, although it was most probably related to the failed Australian venture, of which more later.

Trade with Brazil developed slowly but there can be little doubt that the longer-established West Indies services contributed the greater part of revenues over the next 20 to 30 years. Certainly, in that period, judging from the many references in the annual reports and the allocation to it of the new, larger, tonnage, the directors were preoccupied with the further development of that service, understandably since it was the source of the greater part of the mail subsidy.

Table 2.2 Receipts, disbursements and capital, 1850–60 (including South American service figures from 1851)

	1850	**1851**	**1855**	**1860**
Receipts (£)				
Mail contract	240,000	270,000	270,000	269,243
Freight	84,607	105,856	118,529	183.377
Passage money	132,653	190,428	233,704	307,660
Hire to transport service	–	–	418,124**	8,345
Total receipts	457,260	566,284	1,040,357	768,625
Disbursements*	313,897	369,299	576,402	532,724
Operating surplus	143,363	196,985	463,955	235,901
Dividend	59,360	59,360	60,000	60,000
Capital	890,400	890,400	900,000	900,000

Source: Reports and Accounts.

* Includes coal, wages, provisions, insurance, repairs and office costs.

** Vessels used as troop and store ships during the Crimean War.

Table 2.2 confirms the absolutely essential nature of the mail subsidy. Receipts in 1850 less contract money were £217,260. Disbursements, including insurance

[61] RMSP, Annual Report to Shareholders, 12 April 1855.

and repairs, totalled £313,897. Add to this figure a 5 per cent charge for deteriorations, £39,108, total £353,005, a substantial deficit of £39,108 *before* dividend payments are considered. The incentive to battle for continuation of the subsidy and to build passenger and cargo receipts quickly was paramount, commercially a matter of survival. The annual allocation to the insurance fund was increased at this time from £25,000 to £45,000, a prudent measure, if not entirely consistent with the stated values of the fleet. The change reflects, perhaps, the adjustments being made in the accounts at that period. This was very much a time of creative accounting and surely reflected disdain for the shareholders, a minority of whom expressed concern on occasion.

By as early as 1860 the changes in the balance of the sources of income were becoming evident, no doubt to the great satisfaction of management. Between 1850 and 1860, as already noted, the percentage of mail contract income was reduced from 52 to 35 per cent. Freight income increased from 19 to 25 per cent, while passage money increased from 29 to 40 per cent. These figures merely confirm that Royal Mail's business was moving in the right dircction, with passage money particularly strong. The government subsidy, however, remained vital.

During 1854 and 1855 the directors were subjected to considerable pressure from shareholders who were critical of excessive expenditures. Serious defects were found in the newly built *Parana* (1852, Money, Wigram, Southampton), which cost £83,000. Repairs and alterations before she entered service amounted to an additional £76,000. Management inefficiency was blamed for this and other excessive costs, and it was proposed by shareholders that 'it would be desireable to introduce into the direction parties practically acquainted with shipbuilding and engineering'.[62]

In April 1856, in respect of the year 1855, the shareholders' report noted that, in addition to the usual £4 per annum dividend, a bonus of £5 was paid, with benefit of the windfall income from government hire of vessels, further bonuses being paid in 1856 (£1 10s) and 1857 (£1). Thereafter, dividends reverted to a consistent £4 per annum. At the annual meeting in April 1858 (for 1857) the directors indicated that there was an insurance fund excess that would justify a bonus of £1, but advised against the payment. Surprisingly, they then left the decision to the shareholders, who, predictably, opted for the bonus.[63]

This was a very odd procedure and reflected, at the very least, a measure of uncertainty within the board of directors, which had only recently undergone some dramatic changes. Richard Colville, chairman since 1846, died in early 1856 and was replaced by Captain C.E. Mangles. At the April general meeting a number of shareholders objected to the chairman's report and demanded a ballot. The specific shareholder demands are not recorded, although the report was not approved. The outcome was that all 10 of the directors immediately offered their resignations. Within weeks a number of new appointments were made. Six long-time directors

---

[62] *The Times* (London), 13 April 1854 and 13 October 1855.

[63] *The Times* (London), 22 April 1858.

resigned or were not reappointed, They were replaced by Messrs Baring, Ellice, Shepherd, Hibbert, Masterman and Captain Nelson.

Four directors retained their seats: Chairman Mangles, Colonel C.W. Short, deputy chairman, (who died a few months later), Thomas Baring and Captain Whish RN, with, in addition, newly appointed John Greenwood and T.R. Tufnell. In came Russell Gurney QC, George Thornton, Eden Colville (son of Richard) R.N. Captains H.B.Young and G. Redman. A useful, and overdue, addition was J.F. Gruning, who was said to have involvements with trade to Brazil and Pacific ports.[64]

The records do not make clear the specific reasons for the shareholders' concerns, other than cost over-runs, in what was, after all, a profitable period for the Company. General criticisms of management's performance and concerns regarding the failed attempts to establish services to Australia were no doubt factors. Chairman Mangles and his colleagues were most certainly given notice that there were those among the shareholders who were active and influential and who would, periodically, hold the directors to task.

The management structure, the board of directors apart, consisted of a board of management, chaired by a director, and a number of committees, each of which included several directors. Responsibilities included finance, freight and, oddly, wine. One or two of these met regularly, others only 'when summoned'. Notable in 1850 was a report to the board by the secretary suggesting that four committees be abolished as 'they have never acted more than once or twice'.[65]

Opportunities for Expansion

Although the opening of the new service to South America was a very considerable commitment for Royal Mail, the directors were consistently alert through the decade of the 1840s to opportunities for expansion elsewhere. From 1845 the Company had been closely involved with the development of the very difficult overland route, by mule and canoe, connecting Chagres (later Colon), its western terminus in the Caribbean, with Panama on the Pacific side, a three-day trek. In 1847 a service connection was made with the Pacific Steam Navigation Company, which held the contract for the carriage of mails from the UK to the west coast of South America, previously delivered by the long and difficult route via Cape Horn. The prospect of developing trade with the American west coast was a further attraction: an agent visited ports from California to Chile seeking business opportunities. At the time of the first Californian gold rush in 1848, large numbers of prospectors sailed from Gulf ports to Chagres in Company vessels before journeying northwards from Panama. Plans for an American-financed railway across the isthmus were soon

---

64 RMSP, Letter dated 11 April 1856 to proprietors and hand-written note dated 22 May 1856 following a special meeting on that day.

65 RMSP, Special Reports to the Court, 20 June 1850.

in hand and the Company made a substantial debenture loan of $125,000 to the Panama Railroad Company, which completed the line in 1855.[66]

The supplementary Royal Charter granted to the Company in 1851 permitted extension of its services, in addition to the new South American route. Soon afterwards the directors advised shareholders that, in their view, even without a mail contract, steam vessels would soon be established on the route between Panama and Australia. The majority of the directors were, it would seem, satisfied that a trans-Pacific mail service was viable, although some considered the move to be undesirable.

In 1852 a joint venture arrangement was agreed with the Pacific Steam Navigation Company and the Australian Pacific Mail Steam Packet Company; this was incorporated by Royal Charter. The route was researched, a manager was despatched to Sydney, the intended terminal, and coal stocks were established along the route. Five new 1,800-ton screw steamers were ordered at a cost of £200,000. As the first vessel, *Emeu,* was about to sail from Southampton in February 1854, the venture was wound up and three of the vessels sold at a handsome profit, at a time of shortage of tonnage due to the Crimean campaign, the two others being chartered to the government before sale. Bushell surmises that the service was abandoned because no mail subsidy was granted.[67] This was a serious, if perhaps marginally profitable, misjudgement by the directors and their partners. Despite their stated enthusiasm for the scheme, they must surely have recognised that a subsidy was essential in order to maintain a profitable steamship service over such great distances. Regardless of this setback, the directors maintained their interest in an Australian service.

In 1857 a further ill-considered partnership was entered into with the European and Australian Company (E&A) for a service via Suez. Royal Mail was responsible for the UK to Alexandria portion of the service. E&A ran into financial difficulties and consideration was given to amalgamation of the two companies, but when the extent of the losses became clear, Royal Mail shareholders vetoed the deal.[68] E&A became insolvent. Royal Mail briefly maintained the full service with generous government subsidy until the contract was awarded to the Peninsular & Oriental Company. It is uncertain what, if any, losses or gains were incurred in these excursions, although two ships were acquired in the process. For the time being, at least, the directors concentrated their attention on existing services.

They had been somewhat more alert in the previous year when approached by a representative of the Chilean government who offered the prospect of a £30,000 per annum subsidy and other inducements for a mail service from Valparaiso via

---

[66] RMSP, Annual Reports to Shareholders, 12 April 1855 and 10 April 1856. Bushell, *Royal Mail*, pp. 86–9.

[67] Bushell, *Royal Mail*, pp. 91–2; Nicol, *Scrapbook*, Reports of Directors 1843–99, pp. 517–18. Nicol surmises that a mail contract *may* have been awarded later, on completion of the railroad in early 1855.

[68] *The Times* (London), 22 April 1858.

the River Plate to Rio. Bearing in mind the dangers of the transit of the Magellan Strait (the Pacific Steam Navigation Company had lost two steamers on the route in the past two years), and the risk of that company, an associate on the Panama/west coast route, viewing the new service as hostile, the managers advised the board not to proceed.[69]

Competition

Liverpool's concerns were met in some measure when the South American and General Steam Navigation Company was formed in 1852 by Liverpool and Manchester merchants. Their offer to carry the mails for payment of £700 per monthly voyage was not accepted at the outset, although the Post Office was clearly under pressure to extend the service. The first sailing was made in August 1853 by *Brasiliera* (1,100 tons), newly built of iron and screw propelled, following a route similar to Royal Mail's, with extension to the River Plate. The ships were faster than Royal Mail's paddle-steamers: *Brasileira* completed the homeward run to Liverpool in 26 days (against a contracted 32 days) compared with *Severn*'s 31 days.

The following year a mail contract was awarded for monthly departures from Liverpool with payment per voyage of half the amount of British postage chargeable, rather less attractive than Royal Mail's annual guarantee. Time allowed for the outward voyage to Rio was 30 days, 32 for the homeward run, slightly slower than Royal Mail's contracted 29 and 30 days. *Lusitania* made the first contract sailing in August 1854 However, only three round voyage sailings were made before the Company withdrew from the contract on the grounds that its ships had been chartered by the government for use in the Crimean War, no doubt a more lucrative prospect.[70] It is more likely that General Steam found that business prospects in South America were rather more limited than anticipated. The ships were sold after the end of the war. It would be another 13 years before a second British packet service to Brazil was established. Bonsor notes that in the 1850s a number of speculative attempts were made to develop services from Europe to the east coast of South America by British, French, Italian, Portuguese and German companies: he comments that of the nine companies that attempted to establish steamer services to Brazil between 1854 and 1859, none lasted more than a year or two.[71]

Within government there was much dissatisfaction throughout the 1850s with Royal Mail's close association with the Admiralty, which was based from the

---

69 RMSP, Special Reports to the Court, Vol. 2. The recommendation was dated 18 August 1856.

70 Howat, *South American Packets*, pp. 147, 153, 158; *The Times* (London), 15 February 1854.

71 N.R.P. Bonsor, *South Atlantic Seaway* (Jersey, 1983), p. 53.

outset on the availability of Company vessels for naval service. The concept was challenged as unworkable, the vessels being unsuited to the purpose. An 1859 Select Committee accused the Admiralty of administrative failures and was critical of the methods for allocating mail contracts.[72] The outcome of much parliamentary and commercial pressure was that from 1860 the Post Office became responsible for the negotiation and enforcement of contracts with final approval from Parliament.

Criticism was never far from the boardroom, whether external or internal. In the matter of the government charters during the Crimean War the Company was taken to task by an MP and shipowner, Mr N. Lindsay, who alleged in the House of Commons that it, a monopoly, was being paid twice over for its services, as mail contractor and transport provider. He repeated his allegations in *The Times* and was firmly rebutted by the Company secretary, Captain Chappell, who pointed out that the mail contract required that 15 ships be available for service, which they were, and that a number of the vessels hired to the government was surplus to requirement, some having been earlier offered for sale.[73]

Other considerations for management in the years ahead were the effects of disease (cholera and yellow fever as a rule) and political unrest in South America. In 1854 an outbreak of cholera in Northern Spain resulted in Vigo being declared an infected port, with vessels touching the port being subject to quarantine. Outbreaks of seasonal yellow fever in Brazil were all too common: in the June to August period of 1854, ships touching Brazilian ports were quarantined in Montevideo and Buenos Aires for several days. Although these matters are only infrequently commented upon in the Company reports, the effect on service schedules and costs was appreciable.

Royal Mail's mail contract was again revised in 1858 when the Company was required to provide a significantly faster service on the South American route by increasing the average steaming speed to 9.5 knots and eliminating calls at Madeira and Tenerife, ports now served by the West Africa packets. The outward schedule was reduced by three days to 26 days, the revision ensuring that the homeward vessel arrived in Southampton several days before the next departure. In 1859 two larger and faster vessels, *Oneida* and *Magdalena*, the former a screw-steamer, were introduced to help speed up the service (*Oneida* was capable of 12 knots). Also agreed was the introduction of a new, larger, paddle-steamer for the Rio to Montevideo route. The Post Office contract was extended to January 1864.[74]

Bushell, commenting on the fact that mail companies were still building paddle-steamers into the 1860s, noted: 'All subsidised companies tend to remain static during the term of their contracts, for these usually specify the type of ship and

---

[72] *PP 1860 XIX, Report of the Select Committee into Packet and Telegraph Contracts*, in Greenhill, 'British Shipping and Latin America', pp. 36–7.

[73] *The Times* (London), 2 and 3 March 1855. *Severn*, *Medway* and *Great Western* were offered for sale in 1854, price £70,000. Following government service, *Severn* and *Great Western* were sold for breaking up in 1856.

[74] Howat, *South American Packets*, pp. 116–17.

the standards of performance required.'[75] In the increasingly competitive situation of the time, such an attitude was surely excessively cautious, especially when the March 1840 contract specifically required Royal Mail to update its vessels to keep pace with technological changes. It stated:

> That the Company shall and will, from time to time and at all times during the continuance of this contract, make such alterations or improvements in the constructions, equipments and machinery of the vessels which shall be used in this contract, as the advanced state of science may suggest and the said Commissioners, parties hereto, may direct.

It may well be that certain of the West Indies routes were best suited to paddle-steamers, in particular those involved with inter-island services and, of course, ships were switched from one service to the other as required. Nevertheless, P&O and Cunard, whose mail contracts were akin to Royal Mail's, had begun building screw-propelled ships in the early 1850s, although these were not used for the mail services at the outset. The Company, by contrast, introduced screw propulsion only when it acquired *Oneida* and *Tasmanian* in 1858–59 in the aftermath of the Europe & Australian Company's demise. Both operated successfully with up to 250 passengers and good cargo capacity, while Royal Mail did not build a transatlantic screw-driven vessel, *Douro*, until 1864.

---

[75] Bushell, *Royal Mail*, p. 104.

Chapter 3
A Decade of Contrasting Fortunes

In 1860 the court of directors was largely unchanged from the 1856 reshuffle: Captain Mangles remained in the chair, Russell Gurney his deputy, with nine others, including the three Royal Navy men, Captains Young, Redman and Whish.

At the year-end meeting in April 1862 the chairman referred confidently to the fact that the working account showed receipts (for 1861), up by £30,000 while costs were down by £5,000. Referring to negotiations soon to begin with the Post Office for the renewal of the mail contract, he stated that it was his view that government could not dispense with so important a service. 'Very little', he said, somewhat enigmatically, 'was known of what subsidised steamers did for the country.'

He then referred to the French Compagnie des Messageries Impériales (later Messageries Maritimes), which operated on the South American route with a 20-year government mail contract with subsidy equivalent to 12s 3d per mile against Royal Mail's 9s 10d per mile. He noted that, if Royal Mail were to lose the mail contract, 'the entire service will be necessarily given up to France'. Such publicly made remarks were unlikely to contribute helpfully to the forthcoming negotiations.[1]

The new mail contract, the first made with the Postmaster General, was agreed in July 1863 to be effective from January of the following year. The annual payment for the Brazil/River Plate service was marginally increased to £33,500, the contract to run for seven years, although in 1868 it was extended until the end of 1874. Regardless of the chairman's comments, this was a very satisfactory outcome for the Company in light of determined attempts by the Post Office to tighten the schedules. Cunard was less fortunate: its North Atlantic contract was altered in 1868 to payment by weight and category of mail carried. The effect was to almost halve the value of the subsidy.[2]

The intention was to speed up both the outward and homeward schedules by reducing the time spent in port in order to cut more than two days from the round trip. It can be safely presumed that the Post Office pressure in this matter was vigorously countered by the Company on the grounds that movements of passengers and cargo, especially the latter, were inevitably slow when ships were anchored off the ports and subject to wind and weather. By now cargo revenues were vitally important to the Company and sufficient time for loading and discharging was needed. The schedules remained largely unchanged, although penalties were

---

1 *The Times* (London), 17 April 1862, Chairman's Report to Shareholders.

2 Howat, *South American Packets*, p. 118. Duncan Haws, *Triumph of a Great Tradition, 1840–1990. A souvenir history of the Cunard Line* (London, 1990), p. 18.

introduced for performance failures. In 1866, at the request of government, it was agreed that homeward-bound vessels would call at Plymouth to land the mails and that a facility would be made available on board ship to permit the mails to be sorted before arrival there. Nicol comments that the changes resulted from pressure from manufacturers for a speedier service.[3]

The Post Office's total revised subsidy was now £215,300 per year for the seven-year period, down from £270,000. So began the progressive reduction of the mail subsidies with shorter contracts that were increasingly subject to competitive bids. The Post Office was concerned to eliminate the very considerable deficits in its subsidy programmes as the shipping companies increased their revenues from other sources: the subvention of £270,000 to Royal Mail in 1860 yielded postage income of only £80,000.[4]

The Company continued to rely heavily on the mail subsidy to supplement income from passengers and cargo, although both were improving steadily. In 1860, receipts less £269,243 subsidy and income from government hire of two vessels were £491,037. However, voyage costs were £535,724. Without the mail subsidy, a deficit, before allowing for repairs, new tonnage and a range of other costs, was inevitable.

Commenting on the new contracts and acknowledging the subsidy reduction, the directors' report to shareholders in May 1863 noted that the mileage for the West India service had been reduced by 41,304 miles, with two routes discontinued, and expressed the view that the contract would prove to be profitable, 'notwithstanding the competition of several new lines of steamers, including the highly subsidised French mail services'. A recognition, perhaps, of the increasing competition was the introduction by Royal Mail of five new steamers in 1864–65, two of them, *Douro* (2,824 tons) and *Rhone* (2,738 tons), screw-propelled. They each cost nearly £90,000. The others, *Eider*, *Arno* and *Danube*, were paddle-steamers. All were of iron build and capable of 10 knots in service. The chairman would later comment that the newer ships had been made more comfortable 'compared with any ships in the world'.

Competition and Slow Reactions

By 1860 the number of British steamships in overseas (as opposed to coastal and short-sea) service was 447 of average 620 tons, up from 86 vessels of average 525 tons in 1850. But the sailing ship was still very much in competition. There were 6,876 sailing ships operating on the high seas of average 400 tons. The number and size of steamships increased progressively: in the 1860s to 935 of

---

[3] Nicol, *Scrapbook*, Reports of Directors, 1843–1899, p. 549.

[4] *PP 1860 X IV, Packet and Telegraph Contracts*, quoted in Greenhill, 'British Shipping and Latin America 1840–1930'.

average 813 tons. The number of sailing ships was unchanged in 1870, although it declined nearly 40 per cent by 1880.[5]

Notices in *The Times* in 1864 confirm the heightened level of competition for cargo and passengers on the services to Brazil and Argentina: Royal Mail advertised its monthly service from Southampton. The Liverpool, Brazil and River Plate Steam Navigation Company Ltd (managers Lamport & Holt) offered a monthly through service to Buenos Aires from Liverpool via Lisbon. Davison Brothers' regular sailing packet, *Gustav and Marie* (600 tons), advertised sailings from London. The increasingly active French Messageries Maritimes left Bordeaux monthly for Montevideo.[6]

A particularly worrying source of competition was Liverpool-based Lamport & Holt, which was, with Messageries Maritimes, instrumental in causing Royal Mail to dispense with its inconvenient, to the Company and passengers alike, extension service between Rio de Janeiro and Buenos Aires in 1869. Lamport had started passenger and freight services to Brazil and the River Plate in 1863 with the newly built *Kepler* (1,500 tons), a screw-propelled iron steamer capable of carrying 113 passengers. The company exhibited a much more flexible approach to developing the Brazil trades with a service to Pernambuco and, later, to smaller ports. By 1866, 12 ships operated with three monthly sailings, two of them continuing through to Montevideo and Buenos Aires. Other services followed, including, by 1869, a lucrative trade in coffee to New York. Lamport & Holt would continue to be a strong competitor, and later a collaborator with Royal Mail, over very many years, although its priority would be cargo liner services.

Having applied considerable pressure on the Post Office, Lamport was offered a payment-by-weight contract in 1868 for the southward service only to Brazil and the River Plate, extended the following year to include the northbound sailing. Royal Mail's monopoly of the mail services was broken.[7] At the time of Lamport's negotiations with the Post Office it proposed that its ships should continue through from Rio to Buenos Aires, eliminating the need for trans-shipment. The Post Office approved the change and the first direct sailing was made by *Hipparchus* in August 1868.[8]

A further inducement to Royal Mail to protect its interests was the instigation in 1868 by the Pacific Steam Navigation Company (PSNC) of a monthly service from Liverpool to Rio de Janeiro and Montevideo, via St Nazaire and Lisbon, continuing through the Magellan Strait to Valparaiso and the west coast of South America. Four new 13-knot steamers were built for the trade, each capable of carrying over 500 passengers and offering serious competition, particularly to Rio.

---

5 Glover, 'On the Statistics of Tonnage', p. 228.

6 Nicol, *MacQueen's Legacy*, Vol. 1, p. 76. The Directors' Minutes for 14 July 1870 indicate that a Royal Mail representative would visit Paris to discuss with Messageries Maritimes schedules to and from the River Plate.

7 Bonsor, *South Atlantic Seaway*, pp. 86–7.

8 Howat, *South American Packets*, pp. 161–3.

In 1869 PSNC was awarded a payment-by-weight monthly contract for mails to Rio and Montevideo.[9] In 1870 the contract was revised to fortnightly sailings with extension through to Valparaiso.

Figure 3.1 *Great Western* (1838). From T.A. Bushell, *Royal Mail, 1839–1939* (Trade and Travel Publications Ltd, London, 1939)

Royal Mail's service, as required by contract, was by now appreciably slower than that of its competitors, and the Company was obliged to extend its service through to Buenos Aires, perhaps under pressure from the Post Office. Quite why it had failed to defend its situation when Lamport's initiative clearly suggested that the extension was by now viable and very much in the interests of passengers and cargo shippers is not known. It was a full year before the Company's service began, at which stage the small connecting steamers became redundant. The final sailing from Buenos Aires to Rio was made by *Arno*, an iron paddle-steamer of 1,038 tons.

In October 1869 *Douro* made the first through sailing. She had accommodation for 313 passengers, of whom 253 were first class. On her first departure from Southampton *Douro* carried 120 passengers and 634 tons of cargo. Thus began a service that extended for 100 years: *Aragon* (20,362 tons), built in 1960, made the final voyage under Royal Mail colours in 1969.

9 Ibid., p. 189; Pacific Steam Navigation Company, Minutes, 9 June 1868, quoted in Greenhill, 'Shipping 1850–1914', in D.C.M. Platt (ed.), *Business Imperialism 1840–1930* (Oxford, 1977), p. 127. Recognising an intrusion, Royal Mail proposed a meeting for 'the discussion of mutual interests'. The outcome is not known.

The schedules were tight: *Douro* sailed from Southampton on 9 October and arrived in Buenos Aires on 9 November, three days ahead of schedule. This gave her a little more time to disembark/embark passengers and discharge/load cargo from the anchorage some miles offshore using small boats and barges. She left on 14 November, a day ahead of the timetable, arriving back in Southampton on 15 December, again ahead of schedule. Her next departure from Southampton was not until 10 January.[10]

The Company persisted with its practice of using mainly older tonnage on the Brazil/Argentina service, new vessels being, almost invariably, allocated to the West Indies routes. In 1865, for instance, *Oneida* (1855), *Parana* (1851) and *La Plata* (1852), two of them wooden paddle-steamers, made the majority of sailings. An exception was the newly built *Rhone*, which made her maiden voyage on the route before switching to the West Indies service in 1867 and being wrecked in a hurricane in the same year. *Oneida* and *La Plata* made most of the sailings as late as 1870. There was occasional criticism of the use of older and slower vessels: it may well have been the view of the directors that the service was of only secondary interest, a view reflected in the various Company records, including the reports to shareholders, or it may be that they considered that the ships used were well able to cope with passengers and cargo available.

Finances

The tone of the directors' reports in the early 1860s was confident. In 1863 the chairman congratulated shareholders on large profits due to increased cargo and passenger traffic via Colon to British Columbia, where gold had been discovered, large specie shipments to South America and increased emigration to British Columbia. In 1864 shareholders were advised that the continued success and progress of the Company were such that it would not be necessary for him 'to trespass on their time', adding that the reduction in the mail subsidy would be more than compensated for.[11]

But the decade was to be one of contrasting fortunes: depression in Brazil, war in several South American countries, disease in Argentina, Brazil and the West Indies, ever-increasing competition and uncertain economic circumstances in Britain. R.A. Church, while acknowledging that the British economy had expanded between 1850 and 1873, offered the view that expansion in the period was erratic, as were the prices of raw materials and manufactured goods.[12]

All these factors, beyond the control of management, adversely affected profitability from about 1866, the situation made worse by the reduction of the

[10] Howat, 'Sailing Schedules of the Royal Mail Steam Packet Company', in *South American Packets*, p. 137.

[11] *The Times* (London), 26 October 1864.

[12] R.A. Church, *The Great Victorian Boom 1850–1873* (London, 1975), pp. 76 and 14.

mail subsidy. Receipts increased from £768,901 in 1860, peaked at £856,575 in 1862, before easing to £595,629 by 1868, at which stage the results were described as 'not satisfactory', with freight and passage money well down on the preceding year. In the decade, receipts fell from £768,901 to £646,207 in 1870 (see Table 3.1). However, in the interim shareholders enjoyed levels of dividend they would not see again. Payment for 1862 was £7.00, rising to £14.10s. in 1864, more than 21 per cent on a £60 share, at which stage revenues were already showing signs of decline.

Table 3.1 Receipts and disbursements, 1860–70 (£)

Receipts	**1860**	**1865**	**1870**
Mail contract	269,243 (35%)	207,589 (27%)	215,534 (33%)
Freight	183,377 (25%)	229,646 (29%)	184,170 (29%)
Passage money	307,660 (40%)	349,284 (44%)	246,503 (38%)
Hire, transport service	8,345	–	–
Total	768,901	786,519	646,207
Disbursements	535,724	526,804	446,024
Operating surplus	235,901	259,715	200,183
Dividend	120,000/8	187,500/12 10s	120,000/8
Capital	900,000	900,000	900,000

Source: Reports and Accounts.

Further financial pressure was applied by ship losses in severe weather. Three vessels were wrecked at St Thomas in a hurricane in 1867, *Derwent*, *Rhone* and *Wye*, with a further three being damaged and requiring substantial repair, as did wharves and other facilities. Two ships were immediately purchased in partial replacement. The insurance fund was debited appropriately, leaving only £134,452 rather than the usual minimum of £200,000. The chairman, having announced a dividend of only £1 for the half-year with no bonus, for a total return to shareholders in 1867 of £4 (following four to five years of generous dividends and bonuses), reminded them that the deficit in the insurance fund meant that no bonus could be paid.[13] Worse was to come: the dividend for 1868 was zero. In the difficult years through to 1870 all revenues slumped, that from passengers falling dramatically due to the adverse circumstances overseas.

[13] RMSP, Report and Accounts, 28 April 1868. The payment of bonuses from the 'excess' in the insurance fund was standard procedure for Royal Mail. Shareholders were well aware of the operation of the fund but were not always happy to accept the bonuses offered.

The Introduction of Screw Propulsion

In 1860 the fleet numbered 24 vessels of 47,408 tons, well in excess of the 15 ships required by the mail contract. Seven of them were built in 1841–42 and their operating and repair and maintenance costs made their profitability questionable. By 1865, eight of the older vessels were out of service. Nine ships were built or purchased between 1861 and 1870, six of them iron-screw vessels. In the same period 16 ships were wrecked, sold or scrapped.

Royal Mail's reluctance to embrace screw propulsion during the 1850s is attributed by Bushell to cautious adherence to the terms of the mail contract; in Royal Mail's case it seems that passenger preference for paddle-steamers was a factor. These considerations were hardly commercially sound, especially in view of the marine superintendent's advocacy of the screw from the 1840s. He notes that the 1864 building of *Douro* was 'in accordance with the terms of the new mail contract'. He does not, however, make clear if a dispensation was required from the Admiralty for the use in the mail service of the screw-steamers *Oneida* and *Tasmanian*, purchased in 1858–59.[14]

Cunard, with a North Atlantic mail contract, cautious by comparison with the competing Inman Line which had already demonstrated the advantages of iron-screw construction, built its first iron-screw steamer, *British Queen* (772 tons), in 1851. It was closely followed by 10 iron-screw steamers by 1855, although these were used on other services. It was not until 1862 that the Admiralty agreed to the building of *China*, a screw steamer, for the North Atlantic mail service.[15]

A most important factor was that the ships built in the 1860s had much-increased passenger and cargo capacities. *Douro* and *Rhone*, built in 1864–65 with compound engines, were notable for their much-reduced consumption of coal: they averaged 1,600 tons used per voyage, as compared with the older,*Oneida*'s 1,950 tons.[16] Reduced requirement for coal cut costs substantially and increased the space available for cargo. Other developments were the progressive introduction of steam super-heating apparatus and the fitting of steam winches to speed up the loading and discharge of cargo and baggage.

Neva (3,025 tons), built for the German Norddeutscher Lloyd, was acquired on the stocks of Caird & Co. in Greenock in 1868 as a replacement for *Rhone*, lost the previous year. She was of iron, screw-propelled and capable of carrying 272 passengers in first class, 58 in second and 42 in third. Bushell comments on her extravagant and luxurious fittings and, a novel feature, cowl ventilators to pass air to the passenger spaces below. She had four decks and 10 water-tight

---

[14] Bushell, *Royal Mail*, p. 104. He notes, p. 110, that the Company's marine superintendent, Captain Chappell, 1841–56, was an advocate of screw propulsion even before he was appointed in 1841.

[15] F.E. Hyde, *Cunard and the North Atlantic 1840–1973*,(London, 1975) pp. 29–30, Appendix, pp. 326–9.

[16] *The Times* (London), 26 April, 1866, Report of Annual Meeting.

compartments, the latter an important safety consideration not common at the time.[17] This was another case where Royal Mail improved the general standard of vessels in the fleet by necessary acquisition of replacement tonnage rather than by forward planning.

A specification for *Nile*, iron-built in 1868, indicated a cargo capacity of 800 tons measurement and required that cargo and coaling ports (doors), three on each side, be fitted on the main deck, which was a passenger deck, with moveable planks for walkways. It was only with the introduction of the much stronger iron hulls that cargo doors and ports in the ship's side were possible. The doors enabled cargo to be carried to and from the ship with ready access to the cargo spaces, considerably speeding up the process. In the absence of ship plans it is uncertain how cargo and coal were moved in and out of the hold spaces. Vitally important throughout this period was the continuous, and expensive, programme of updating existing tonnage, with boiler replacements, superheating apparatus and other engine improvements, maintenance of passenger facilities and extensions of cargo carrying capacity and working arrangements.

Danube (2,039 tons), built by Millwall Iron Works, London, in 1865, was the Company's last transatlantic paddle-steamer. Her delivery was much delayed and the quality of the work so inferior that the directors, threatening legal action against the builders, considered refusing to accept her.[18] No further orders were placed with the yard. The smaller *Eider* and *Arno*, built by Caird & Co., Greenock, in 1864–65, were also paddle-steamers.

Trade Expansion

Political and diplomatic considerations as well as periodic outbreaks of disease, mainly in Brazil, continued to affect trade. Manchester, referring to the difficult relations between Britain and Brazil, largely a holdover from Britain's forceful actions in the restriction of the slave trade, states: 'in the early 1860s relations were so strained that a relatively minor incident would precipitate an explosion of serious proportions'. Two such incidents occurred in 1861 and 1862, leading to the suspension of diplomatic relations between the two countries: a Glasgow vessel, the *Prince of Wales*, was wrecked on the Brazilian coast and there were vigorous protests of murder of the crew and robbery of the cargo and, later, three officers of a British naval vessel were arrested in Rio de Janeiro. The port was briefly blockaded by British warships, and King Leopold of the Belgians was brought in as arbitrator in 1863.[19] The matter was not finally resolved until late 1865. Thereafter, although friendly relations with Britain were maintained, Britain's

[17] Bushell, *Royal Mail*, pp. 123–4.

[18] Nicol, *Scrapbook*, Report of Directors, p. 546.

[19] Manchester, *British Pre-eminence in Brazil*, p. 274. *The Times* (London), 30 June 1863. The king determined, tactfully, that no offence was intended towards the British

political influence in Brazil was much diminished for a time. In that same year Brazil and Uruguay, allied with Argentina, became embroiled in a frustrating five-year war with Paraguay.[20]

Despite these very considerable difficulties, relationships at a commercial level between the two countries do not appear to have been greatly affected. Brazil continued to rely on British capital and imports/exports vital to the development of its national interests. In the mid-1860s British companies continued to be involved with railway construction and with the building of gasworks in Para and in Pernambuco and other major developments.

The historic Portuguese connections with Brazil were a useful bonus for Royal Mail. Although freight and passenger traffic was inevitably affected at times in this difficult period, transatlantic passenger numbers were an important revenue consideration. On a homeward run in 1865, *Oneida* landed 127 passengers at Lisbon and 89 in Southampton, and cargo may well have been shipped in both directions.[21]

Royal Mail chose not to burden its shareholders in the annual reports with references to difficulties in South America. Indeed, trade details were discussed only in terms of revenue increases or losses across the broad spectrum of Company services, the increases being accounted for by 'the continued success and progress of the Company' (October 1864), the losses to poor trading conditions, disease or competition.

Brazil remained the more lucrative of the South American destinations, although trade with Argentina slowly increased. Press reports from Rio de Janeiro reflected activity in coffee, cacao, cotton, tobacco and sugar. Those from Argentina, still troubled by internal conflict and war, were concerned with cattle products, hides, tallow, barrels of tongues and salted or dried meat and meat extracts. Wool and cotton were developing exports, as were agricultural produce, including wheat. Total wool exports in 1860 were 17,317 metric tons, increasing to 65,704 tons by 1870. *The Times* of the period carried regular market reports as well as political and social news in a column headed 'The Brazil and River Plate Mails', a measure of the value of the regular mail steamer services. Typical was the issue of 5 October 1863: 'The market closed, however, very firm at the departure of the *Estramadura*, a vessel of the French line Messageries Maritimes.'[22]

The 1860s through to the mid-1870s was a boom period for the British economy and for investment in Latin America, after which Britain fell, at least

---

officers. It was not until 1888, after years of political argument, that slavery was finally abolished in Brazil.

20 *The Times* (London), 5 June 1865, reported reassuringly for those involved in trade with Argentina 'that the great distance of the scene of war from Buenos Aires renders it a matter of slight importance to foreigners in the Province'. This, despite the fact that a Brazilian fleet was active in the mouth of the River Plate.

21 *The Times* (London), 4 August 1865.

22 *The Times* (London), 5 October 1863.

temporarily, into what was referred to as the Great Depression.[23] British banks and insurance companies were strongly represented in Brazil and Argentina, and much involved in the import–export businesses. Those governments relied largely on loans raised in London to meet revenue shortfalls brought about, in part at least, by falls in export duties.[24] Investments in Brazil and Argentina in railways and other infrastructure resulted in large exports to those countries of materials, rails, rolling stock, iron and coal, most of it from Britain and carried in British ships. Exports to Britain of primary products, raw materials and foodstuffs, from Brazil, rose strongly in the 1860–70 period, those from Argentina only marginally and unsteadily (see Table 3.2).[25]

Table 3.2 British exports to/imports from Brazil and Argentina, 1850–70 (£m)*

	1850	**1854**	**1860**	**1870**
Brazil				
Exports to Britain	–	2.1	2.3	6.1
Imports from Britain	2.5	2.9	4.4	5.4
Argentina				
Exports to Britain		1.3	1.1	1.5
Imports from Britain	0.8	1.3	1.8	2.3

Source: Platt, *Latin America and British Trade 1806–1914*, p. 317.

* Exports to Britain figures available only from 1854.

Vital to the economic development of the vast interior of Argentina were railway construction and mass immigration. In 1862, only 18 miles of railway line were open and 5,000 migrants arrived in the country. In 1872, over 700 miles of line were in use, with many more under construction, and the number of immigrants

---

[23] Gary B. Magee, 'Manufacturing and Technological Change', in Roderick Floud and Paul Johnson (eds), *The Cambridge Economic History of Modern Britain, Vol. II: Economic Maturity, 1860–1939* (Cambridge, 2004), table 4.5, p. 81. The writer contends that the 'depression', cyclical until 1890s, reflected the easing of Britain's situation as the world's largest manufacturer as other countries, America and Germany, increased theirs. The situation is certainly reflected in Britain's exports to and imports from Brazil and Argentina in the period.

[24] Graham, *Britain and the Onset of Modernization*, pp. 97–9.

[25] Platt, *Latin America and British Trade 1806–1914*, Appendices I and II, pp. 316–17 and 320–21.

increased to 40,000.[26] The incoming labour, mainly from Spain and Italy in that period, was essential to work the rich lands, from which the native Indians were being progressively and cruelly expelled, for the production of wheat, sugar and other crops as well as great numbers of sheep and cattle.

In the 1860s an increasing range of cargo was shipped from the River Plate and Brazil ports in Royal Mail vessels: the wooden paddle-steamer *Tyne* (1,603 tons, 1854) arrived in Southampton in January 1860 with, in addition to specie valued at £41,394, '165 barrels of tapioca, 494 bales of tobacco, 244 boxes of oranges, and sundries'. *Magdalena,* also a wooden paddle-steamer (2,318 tons, 1852), arrived in May 1863, with 176 passengers, specie and 1,300 bags of coffee and 30 bales of cotton.[27] Shipments of fruit from Lisbon were common. Other products brought in included cases of extract of beef and barrels of tongues from Argentina. Cotton was usually from Brazil. The specie carried northbound was, at least in part, payment for exports.

The great increase in the tonnage available for the carriage of general cargo on the South American routes, both to and from Europe and the USA, inevitably affected freight rates, despite the increasing volumes of cargo. Rates in the period were flexible and varied by product and the volume of cargo offered. Regular shippers benefited from reduced contract rates.

Political and economic uncertainties added to the problems. The result was a general decline through to the end of the century.[28] Freight rates were also affected by the seasonal nature of some of the products, such as wool and coffee; Brazilian coffee exporters succeeded in controlling the flow of their product to the market in order to better manipulate the price.

In 1860 steam tonnage accounted for only 10 per cent of the UK trade with the east coast of South America.[29] In the next 20 years, increased liner steamship services progressively excluded sail from the general cargo and passenger trades, largely due to their speed, frequency and reliability. Sail thrived in the bulk trades, along with steam tramp ships. A typical outward cargo for the tramp ships was coal from South Wales or the northeast of England. Homeward shipments, frequently destined ultimately to continental ports, were much more difficult to fix and might consist of raw cotton, wool or grains from the east coast in season, guano from Peru or Chilean nitrates.

---

[26] Ibid. The writer notes, p. 67, that in the 1830s the cost of moving a ton of goods by mule or ox-cart from Salta, in the interior of Argentina, to Buenos Aires was 13 times that from Buenos Aires to Liverpool.

[27] *The Times* (London), 5 January 1860 and 6 May 1863.

[28] Stemmer, 'Freight Rates', pp. 26–7. The writer notes that freight rates for bulk and general cargoes showed a 'long-term downward trend'. He cites the rate for coffee in 1847 as £2.75; in 1906 it was £1.30; outward rates for, for instance coal, also fell.

[29] Ibid., p. 43. The figure of steam tonnage leaving ports in the UK for Central America and the Caribbean was 1 per cent.

Pacific Service Aborted

Despite the failure of earlier attempts to enter the trade to Australia and New Zealand, the Company again became involved in a trans-Pacific venture, influenced by the increase of through traffic via Panama of freight and passengers in combination with the Panama Railroad Company and the Pacific Steam Navigation Company. Chairman Mangles attributed a large portion of the increase in freight revenues to that source.[30]

In 1865 the Panama, New Zealand and Australian Royal Mail Company Ltd (PNZA) obtained a mail contract covering UK to Australia via Panama. Shareholders were advised of the plan for PNZA to handle the trans-Pacific crossing from Panama using newly built tonnage, Royal Mail providing the already well-established transatlantic service to Colon. No detail was given at the time of any financial involvement with the new company, though a Royal Mail director, Eden Colville, sat on the board. Nicol speculates that, mindful of the costs incurred in previous Australian ventures, the directors chose not to give full details of the Company's involvement with PNZA.[31]

Atrato made the first sailing from Southampton in June 1866. Despite initial optimism, by 1867 problems were evident and, unable to return a profit, in 1869 the company went into liquidation. Royal Mail held debentures in the value of £20,000 and had advanced further sums against mortgages on some of the ships. Final negotiations, including legal action, were protracted but by late 1869, three 1,500-ton vessels were reported to be lying in Southampton.[32]

Their futures were uncertain; sale was considered but no acceptable offer was received. In the event, the ships were refitted, two of them being equipped with compound engines, and they entered service on the Brazil/Argentine route in 1871.

A successful Pacific service would have been greatly beneficial to Royal Mail, offering the prospect of increased freight and passenger traffic. When PNZA folded, the Company and other creditors explored the possibility of restoring the service but concluded that the prospect of profit was remote. The directors' minutes make clear that from the outset there had been dissension within the board, two directors, Messrs Mathieson and Greenwood, arguing that the Company was over-extending itself financially. An attempt to refer the matter to an extraordinary shareholders' meeting was defeated and they resigned. Once again the directors had displayed

---

[30] *The Times* (London), 25 April 1861. He noted that the discovery of gold in British Columbia was expected to lead to further revenue improvements.

[31] Nicol, *Scrapbook*, Reports of Directors. 1843–99, p. 544.

[32] Bushell, *Royal Mail*, pp. 96–7. *Rakaia, Ruahine* and *Kaikoura* were substantially refitted and re-engined. They entered Royal Mail service in 1872 as, respectively, *Tiber*, *Ebro* and *Liffey*. A smaller ship, *Phoebe*, was sold. *The Times* reported a meeting that took place in October 1866 to hear a report by a Captain Pym RN of his plan for a railway route through Nicaragua to connect the Caribbean with the Pacific. Some Royal Mail directors were present. Perhaps fortunately for the Company, the matter did not proceed.

poor judgement: although the sum of the loan may have been recovered, at least in part, in the value of the mortgaged vessels, the exercise probably proved costly.

A Disappointing Decade

The 16 per cent collapse of receipts from £768,901 in 1860 to £646,207 in 1870 was more than unsatisfactory; it was a disaster. The dividend was passed in 1868 for the first time since 1843, the directors' report noting only that they would 'continue to use every exertion to improve the affairs of the Company'. Shareholders, seemingly, remained largely uncomplaining, judging by the Company's hand-written meeting records, a more reliable source than the reports to shareholders and press comments. However, they must have been very far from happy: the value of the £100 shares, £60 paid up, was £120 in 1865 and by 1868 it had fallen to £39.[33] As the *Stock Exchange Year Book 1876* notes in respect of Royal Mail, 'The dividends undergo rapid and considerable fluctuations.' Dividend payments resumed in 1869 and the share price recovered.

The record was abysmal. Messrs Mathieson and Greenwood, the directors who resigned in 1869, claimed that the board's dealings with PZNA were outwith the authority of the board and not in the best interests of shareholders. This was a serious charge, worthy of vigorous action by shareholders. Yet the majority – and the remaining directors – failed to register disapproval, so far as can be established from the archive material.

Questions must be asked about the calibre and capabilities of directors and of the board of management, which, chaired by a director, reported to the main board. The directors, probably preoccupied with business matters elsewhere, relied on the guidance of the managers based in Southampton and overseas in operational matters, those concerning services, ships, structure and so on, but policy was decided around the boardroom table.

Through the 1850s and the 1860s – Mangles was in the chair from 1856 – the Company became embroiled in three schemes to extend its activities to Australia. The directors were, quite rightly, ambitious to extend the activities and the profitability of the Company in the best interests of the shareholders. But sound business sense was absent, a matter argued by the two directors who felt obliged to resign. In each situation, judgement of the potential for profit was unsound and the choice of partners was flawed. It is impossible to gauge the financial losses of these excursions, but they were appreciable, almost certainly greater than shareholders were given to understand.

More damning still was that, while seeking opportunities to enter the Australian service, the directors failed to anticipate and respond to pressure in

[33] *The Stock Exchange Year Book, 1876*. In this, the first issue of the publication, the Royal Mail entry included a brief summary of dividends and share prices in the 1860s and early 1870s.

existing trades and services. Preoccupation with the collapse of the PNZA venture resulted in a delayed reaction to developing competition on the South American route, particularly that of the rapidly expanding Liverpool-based Lamport & Holt Company, which clearly identified business opportunities in territory once the preserve of Royal Mail and aggressively pursued them.

The declining receipts in the latter part of the decade distorted the positive move in the earlier years towards reduced reliability on the mail contract as passenger and freight income developed. Table 3.2 illustrates the collapse of revenues through to the end of the decade so that the very much reduced subsidy of 1870, £215,543, still contributed 33 per cent of the total, up from 27 per cent in 1865.

More positively, the new tonnage added to the fleet in the 1860s, nine ships in all, reflected an overdue move towards screw propulsion. The number of ships operated was also appreciably reduced, 19 in 1870, just sufficient to maintain services and permit of regular repair and maintenance schedules while containing costs. It is noteworthy that, after 1865, no ships were ordered and it was not until the loss of three vessels in 1867 that two replacements were quickly purchased and two further ships ordered for delivery in 1869–70. As the decade ended, the directors must have been very conscious of the need to defend and consolidate their existing services in light of still increasing competition and indications that the Post Office was intent on further cutting mail subsidies.

Chapter 4
The Second Epoch

Bushell notes that in the early 1870s the days of Admiralty control and large mail subsidies ended and the Company was required to operate on strictly commercial lines, 'with the carriage of passengers and cargo a primary instead of a secondary consideration'. A period of expansion lay ahead, described by him as 'the second epoch of the Royal Mail story'.[1] His views are to be questioned in that they imply that, before 1870, the Company had failed to maximise its opportunities in the passenger and freight trades. True, progress had been uncertain from 1851, in part due to management's unfortunate attempts to extend the Company's operations, yet income from freight and passengers had developed appreciably, even allowing for passenger and freight-rate increases.

Nevertheless, significant changes took place in the years that followed. Larger ships with more efficient compound engines burned less coal, cutting costs and allowing greater space for passengers and cargo, thereby reducing the reliance on mail subsidies. The economies of Argentina and Brazil expanded, although there were difficulties along the way, with the numbers of passengers increasing and greater movement of cargo in both directions.

The board in 1870 was still headed by Captain Mangles, with Russell Gurney, QC, MP his deputy. Changes were not unusual, vacancies being due to business or political commitments, or death, and there was an overdue attempt to introduce businessmen with knowledge of the trades. The Royal Navy presence remained strong, with two admirals, Whish and Young, and Captain Redman. Additional were Messrs Tufnell, Colville, Chapman, Berens and Barlow. In 1873 Captain Mangles, chairman since 1856 and a director for 30 years, died.[2] He was replaced by H.C.E. Childers, MP, who occupied the chair until 1880 when he resigned; Eden Colville took over with Admiral Whish as deputy.

---

1 Bushell, *Royal Mail*, p. 125.

2 F. Boase, *Modern English Biography* (London, 1965). The entry for Captain Mangles records his naval rank, that he was an MP from 1857 to 1859 and that he was chairman of the London and South Western Railway from 1859 to 1872. The latter was vitally important to Royal Mail for the carriage of both passengers and cargo to and from London. Oddly, no reference is made to his lengthy involvement with the Company.

Mail Contract Cutbacks

The 1863 mail contract was extended to the end of 1874 following pressure from the Company. The new 1874 annual contract for the West Indies was sharply reduced to £84,750, a shock for management yet a relief that it had been retained. The directors advised shareholders that they had considered the matter and concluded that 'it would be well worth while' to continue to carry the mails. (The rate was further reduced in 1880 to £80,000.) Whether or not this seeming reluctance was an attempt to pressure the Post Office, the decision to continue was never in doubt, whatever the payment offered.

The annual fixed rate arrangement for Brazil and Argentine mails was scrapped, payment by weight being introduced: 1s 3d per ounce for letters from Southampton, 1s for letters from other European ports to South America and 6d for mail carried on the coast. The contract was now for a fortnightly service and it was cancellable by either party at six months' notice. There were lesser payments for packages. The Post Office was clearly concerned to take better control of the costs of its services. At the same time it was in the process of closing its packet agencies in South America, which required that mail be taken to British consulates for transmission to England. The Buenos Aires Agency had closed in 1873.

A concession in the new contract was that the Southampton to Buenos Aires schedule was extended by two days, important in that it permitted additional time in port and/or speed reductions at sea that could result in reduced costs. The original 9th of the month sailing was unaffected in terms of ports of call. The Company's already operating second service was now included within the contract. The sailing from Southampton on the 24th was required to call at Corunna and Carril before Lisbon outwards and, from 1876, at Vigo after leaving Lisbon homewards.[3]

A further contract in 1876 appreciably reduced the weight payments for letters from 1s 3d per ounce to 10.5d, 3d per pound of newspapers and 5d per pound of books or trade patterns. From European ports to South America the payment was 1s per ounce and, between ports in South America, 6d per ounce. The new contract further sought to limit the responsibility of the Post Office to the carriage of outward mails only. Portugal, Brazil and Argentina, having become members of the General Postal Union, were required by the first international postal convention to pay for the mails originating in their countries. At this time the Post Office contract with Lamport & Holt was terminated.

It was 1878 before all three countries signed agreements with the Company for the shipment of mail from South America to Europe at the same rate as the Post Office. In 1876 Royal Mail carried 88,000 letters from Argentina to Europe, 28 per cent of the total: Messageries Maritimes carried the greatest

[3] Howat, *South American Packets*, pp. 123–4.

share, 100,000 letters, 31 per cent of the total. Lamport & Holt was responsible for only 10,000 letters.[4]

A contract was agreed with the Brazilian government in 1876 for the carriage of its mails to Europe, to the River Plate and between Brazilian ports on a poundage basis. (From 1900 payment ceased, although the Company was still required to carry the mails.) In 1878 an additional five-year contract was agreed requiring a monthly call at Maceio, between Pernambuco and Bahia, with subsidy of £2,500 per annum. The arrangement was twice extended, although the precise termination date is uncertain. A similar service to Europe was arranged with the Argentine government in 1877 with payment by weight. The payment was withdrawn in 1888, after which time the mails were carried free.[5] The effect of these several changes on the Company's Post Office mail revenues was dramatic: income from the outward journeys only were £33,100 in 1874, £16,967 in 1876,, £6,438 in 1878 and, £5,538 in 1880.[6]

Trade Depression Worldwide

Until the 1870s Britain's predominance in the South American markets was not in doubt. However, a severe and cyclical worldwide depression in trade affected most countries from 1873 through to 1893. S.B. Saul contends that this was a time when prices across a wide range of products fell steadily, inevitably creating serious problems for industry and commerce, with periods of severe unemployment and suffering for workers.[7] During this period Britain ceased to be the 'workshop of the world' and became merely one of its three greatest industrial powers. British export values in the early 1870s were not surpassed until the second half of the 1890s, although, it should be noted, volumes increased. These crisis conditions inevitably affected trade and investment in South America and the ability of countries to service debt. Periods of downturn were followed by uncertain recovery, with direct consequences for the movement of import and export goods, inevitably affecting the Company's business. (See Table 4.1.)

Argentina's economy suffered in the early years of the decade. Demand for its export products, hides and wool, declined, and import revenues, essential to government finances, collapsed. It was 1876–77 before national revenues began to recover. The crisis occasioned some reaction against Britain's monetary influence

---

4 Ibid., pp. 125–6. Table 6 reflects the reduction in contract income through the 1870s.

5 *A Link of Empire or 70 years of British Shipping*, pp. 61–2. The book was published by Royal Mail in 1909.

6 Annual Reports of the Postmaster General in Howat, *South American Packets*, p. 128. It is not possible to separately identify receipts from other countries.

7 S.B. Saul, *The Myth of the Great Depression, 1873–1896* (London, 1969), p. 55.

within the country and began a lengthy debate about the development of the nation's resources in order to reduce the dependence on imports.[8]

The value of Brazil's exports to Britain declined in the 1870s, due in part to financial crises in mid-decade. Cotton exports more than halved, while sugar and rubber also declined. Railway mileage increased, mainly in the coffee provinces, to 3,387 km in 1880, and the construction of harbour facilities in the main ports began, although the process would take a further 30 years. By 1878, Santos, the main coffee export outlet, had a pier that could accommodate seven ships and by 1892 new quays were built. The development of modern port facilities and improved rail communications was vital for the economy of the country. Industry began to serve the requirements of an increasing population, with the establishment of iron foundries, breweries and textile mills.[9] A further boost was the inauguration of telegraph communication directly between Rio and Europe in 1874.[10]

Both countries continued to be reliant on overseas investment, mainly from London. By 1870, in addition to substantial government and commercial loans, four major Anglo-Latin American banks were established with substantial resources. The assets of the London and River Plate Bank totalled £3.7m in 1870, increasing to over £12m by 1890.

In the decades through to the end of the century British manufacturing industry came under pressure as other nations, the USA and Germany in particular, increased their output and their share of international trade. Nevertheless, Britain's output continued to rise, as did total world production, and it would dominate the rapidly increasing South American markets for some years to come. Table 4.1 reflects the uncertain trade situation in the 1870s of Brazil and Argentina, the latter, especially, affected by the adverse economic situation, although the Argentine was slowly developing its agricultural output as immigration helped open up the interior.

[8] D. Rock, *Argentina, 1516–1987* (London, 1986), pp. 147–9. A considerable volume and value of imports to South American countries was of South Wales coal carried in sailing and tramp ships, many of which continued to Chile for return cargoes of nitrates.

[9] Graham, *Britain and the Onset of Modernization*, p. 33.

[10] E. Bradford Burns, *A History of Brazil* (New York, 1993) p. 159. *The Times* (London), 28 October 1875. A report of a general meeting of shareholders in London of the Brazilian Submarine Telegraph Company reported that lines were open between North and South America.

Table 4.1 British exports to/imports from Brazil and Argentina, 1870–80 (£m)

	1870	1875	1880
Brazil			
Exports to Britain	6.1	7.4	5.3
Imports from Britain	5.4	6.9	6.7
Argentina			
Exports to Britain	1.5	1.4	0.9
Imports from Britain	2.3	2.4	2.5

Source: Platt, *Latin America*, pp. 317–23.

The 1870s opened with the directors still, with good cause, preoccupied with the winding up of the PNZA, judging by the reports to shareholders, although revenues from both freight and passengers had developed very satisfactorily. Chairman Mangles noted, in April 1871, a continued improvement in the Company's position, with much-improved receipts and reduced costs, despite war on the Continent, which, inevitably, affected passenger and cargo traffic. Dividend for the year 1870 was £7 per share.

In March 1871 *Douro* arrived in Southampton with 116 passengers, a mixed cargo of specie, small shipments of wool, tobacco, tapioca and 5,352 sacks of coffee, the last at good freight rates, £2.50 and 5 per cent, rather better than sailing ships, which were being paid £1.80–£2.00 on consignments to the Continent.[11] Other cargo being brought in by Royal Mail ships included cases of meat extract, tapioca, hides and fruit. A press article refers to a severe outbreak of yellow fever at Buenos Aires, with vessels subject to 12 days' quarantine at Montevideo.

Having salvaged three ships from the wreckage of the PNZA, the Company considered selling them and received offers, while, at the same time, seeking suitable terms for their conversion and re-engining. A directors' minute of 11 October 1871 stated that if no suitable offer to purchase was received within a few days the prior offer of Messrs Day & Co. for the conversions was to be accepted. No offer was forthcoming.

Meantime, requests had been received from shippers in Manchester that the South American service be increased to two sailings per month (directors' minute, 26 July 1871) and a similar proposal came from Messrs Benn & Co., the Company's Buenos Aires agent, who suggested that calls be made at Spanish and French ports. The agent had in mind, most probably, the development of the

[11] Stemmer, *Freight Rates*, p. 44.

migrant trade from Europe.[12] The outcome was an additional monthly sailing using the PNZA vessels. *Ebro* inaugurated the service in August, leaving Antwerp on the 17th for Southampton, Cherbourg, Lisbon and Brazil and the River Plate. Sailings were scheduled for the 9th and 24th of each month. The directors noted merely that the service operated 'in a satisfactory manner'.

At the April 1874 shareholders' meeting (for 1873), with Admiral Whish temporarily in the chair, the mood was cautious. Receipts from passengers and freight were up on those of 1872, from £532,000 to £621,000, he said, and he hoped that they would continue to increase so that 'they might not feel the loss of the [mail] subsidy at some future period'. (Income from the mail subsidy in the year was £225,000.) Revenues were up again in 1874, at £860,282, the highest-ever figure, with vessel hire charges disregarded. Costs were well contained. The chairman, H.C.E. Childers, MP, reminded shareholders that the (total) mail subsidy was now reduced by £100,000 and advised that he had visited the West Indies and consulted with managers and agents concerning possible increases in trade in the face of great competition.[13] No doubt he was also looking for opportunities to cut costs. Clearly the board was far from confident that the possible loss on the mail contract could be made good, even in favourable trading conditions, and dividend payments maintained.

The year 1875 was not a good one: passenger and cargo receipts were only slightly up on those of 1874, and the mail contribution was down by more than £100,000, as expected. Total receipts were £757,660, a fall of £102,622. In addition, two ships were lost, *Boyne* running aground on the French coast, near Brest, and *Shannon* stranding when approaching Jamaica from Colon. Replacements were hastily purchased from the Pacific Steam Navigation Company and renamed *Para* and *Don*. At just over 4,000 tons they were the Company's largest vessels.[14]

Throughout the remainder of the decade cargo receipts made slow progress, up from £292,938 in 1875 to £335,802 in 1880, in difficult trading circumstances. Passenger revenues, however, declined, from £358,030 in 1875 to £274,354 in 1880. Considerable sums were spent on vessel purchases, conversions and maintenance, and additional expenditure was incurred by the introduction of the second service on the South American route. Dividend payments were, inevitably, affected: the directors were under very considerable pressure. At the October 1876 shareholders' meeting, the chairman, acknowledging the improvement in freight income, referred to 'great competition' and the 'very depressed state of trade all over the world'.[15] This condition persisted through to the end of the decade.

---

12 Nicol, *Scrapbook*, Reports of the Directors, pp. 890–91.

13 Childers was in the chair in October 1874, although he was not a board member earlier in the year. His appointment is not commented upon in the reports.

14 The master of *Don* on her first voyage to the West Indies in 1876, Captain Woolward, remained in the vessel for 81 voyages: 18 years.

15 *The Times* (London), 19 October 1876.

Competition and Conferences

Despite the difficult economic circumstances, the number of steamships in service increased substantially in the 1870s, cargo space outstripping the rise in the volume of trade. British vessels in foreign trades increased from 935 of average 813 tons to 2,193 of just over 1,000 tons by 1880.[16] On South American routes Lamport & Holt alone built further 30 small vessels, usually around 1,500 tons, for its now extended Liverpool, London, Antwerp and Glasgow (mainly cargo) services in the decade. It was particularly active in the smaller ports in Brazil. The Pacific Steam Navigation Company built 18 ships for its west coast services, which included the Liverpool to Chile via Rio and Montevideo line. In fact it overbuilt due to concerns regarding its competitive situation and by 1873–74 its services were drastically revised, 11 steamers being expensively laid up, two being sold to Royal Mail.[17] Booth Line continued to serve Amazon ports out of Liverpool and Lamport & Holt and Harrison were active on the Brazil coast from the same port. Continental companies flourished, notably the French Messageries Maritimes and Compagnie des Chargeurs Réunis and the German Hamburg-Sud Line, all of which remained in competition with Royal Mail over very many years.[18]

British shipping continued to dominate trade with South America, with the French in second place. The USA maintained significant traffic while the Germans, from the 1870s, were an increasing threat, particularly to Brazilian ports where significant numbers of German migrants were established.

A means for shipping companies to protect their interests in a particular trade was what came to be known as a conference, or cartel. This was an association of two or more companies operating regular services on a particular route(s): it attempted to limit competition between members and exclude competition from rival companies and tramp ships and others who took advantage of seasonal shipments, such as Brazil's coffee harvests. Conference members charged similar rates, limited the number of sailings and strictly observed arrival and departure dates. Cargo shippers and agents were encouraged to deal exclusively with conference companies, by means of reduced freight-rate inducements. For the conference companies, regulated freight rates, share of loading and discharging rights and agreement on sailing schedules were among the benefits. The first of these organisations is generally agreed to have been established in 1875 for the UK to Calcutta route. In 1871 a steamship conference was held that involved companies in the South American trade.[19] It is likely that it was some years before the South American conferences were firmly established.

---

16 Glover, 'On the Statistics of Tonnage', p. 50.

17 Arthur C. Wardle, *Steam Conquers the Pacific* (London, 1940), p. 130.

18 Bonsor, *South Atlantic Seaway*, passim.

19 B.M. Deakin and T. Seward, *Shipping Conferences: A Study of their Origins, Development and Economic Practices* (Cambridge, 1973), pp. 3–5.

An interesting development before this was a visit to Paris in mid-1869 by a Royal Mail manager to discuss with Messageries Maritimes the coordination of sailings of the new through service, beginning in October, to River Plate ports for the benefit of the Post Office.[20] This was hardly a conference agreement but it did indicate that some companies were willing to make mutually beneficial informal arrangements covering certain matters.

With so much competition it was essential to maintain flexibility in order to ensure a share of the trade and, progressively, the Company extended its outward and homeward services beyond Southampton to continental ports. In 1877 the directors, reminding shareholders that one of the Brazil services now called at Antwerp after Southampton each month, announced that a monthly call at Le Havre was added to the schedules. A waybill dated 31 March 1876 notes the arrival of *Mondego* at Southampton with a small amount of cargo, the largest shipment 1,043 packages of meat. She carried, in addition, 5,405 packages of merchandise 'for exportation in the same ship', indicating the extension of the homeward service to a continental port.[21]

Yellow fever and cholera in Brazil, a continuing problem, caused serious difficulties and increased costs intermittently in 1878–80. Quarantine restrictions imposed by Argentina and Uruguay could result in ships being held for several days on arrival, entirely disrupting the service schedule. (*Mondego* arrived in Montevideo from Rio on 24 May 1878, and was delayed for three days, arriving at Buenos Aires on the 26th.) Mails were, on occasion, trans-shipped in Montevideo to a smaller vessel in order to avoid delayed arrival in Buenos Aires. Royal Mail attempted to overcome this problem in some measure by, in November 1878, starting a third service that left Southampton on the 27th of the month via Cherbourg, Carril and Vigo direct to River Plate ports, the Brazil services terminating at Santos.[22] This unanticipated demand on resources required that two vessels, *Trent* and *Tamar*, be purchased. The quarantine restrictions were lifted as fever conditions changed, sailings being altered accordingly, and the Brazil ships continuing through to the Plate.

---

[20] Nicol, *Scrapbook*, Directors' Minutes, various, June to September, p. 888, The implication is that the Post Office was, at that time, shipping mail with the French company.

[21] Southampton Customs and Revenue Waybills are held within the London records at the Liverpool Maritime Museum. The record is far from complete. It must be presumed that the meat was shipped from Lisbon.

[22] This is the first reference to the use of the port of Santos, to the south of Rio, by then Brazil's main port for the export of coffee. In time, and for very many years, Santos was regularly scheduled by Royal Mail, both northbound and southbound. Howat, *South American Packets*, p. 127. In 1879 Lisbon began to feature regularly in Company schedules, the direct River Plate service calling there both outward and homeward. *The Times* (London), 6 July 1871, p. 6. The River Plate countries were also subject to disease, not so severely or frequently as Brazil but sufficient to disrupt business, although the directors' reports make no reference to it.

The deputy chairman, Admiral Whish, officiated at the annual general meeting in April 1880. He shed an interesting light on Royal Mail's alertness, or lack of it, when speaking of the additional direct line to Buenos Aires. Noting that the service was established, in the first instance, due to the quarantine difficulties, he added: 'They [the Company] also found that their various competitors on that line had started a direct line to the River Plate. This Company, therefore, followed suit and hoped they would get a very fair share of the traffic.' Chairman Whish then indicated that it was intended to withdraw the additional service (in 1880), 'which they could do with perfect ease', in anticipation of the easing of the quarantine difficulties. Much more importantly, he indicated that the results had been unsatisfactory.[23] Over the next two years the service resumed intermittently, as made necessary by further outbreaks of disease.

During 1880 the directors considered a report by Company Chairman Childers who had made an extended visit to the West Indies in November 1879. Action was taken on some of his proposals and it was agreed to transfer tonnage to the West Indies services on the grounds that profits on the River Plate route were disappointing. It is uncertain whether or not this was done, bearing in mind the need to maintain the mail service. Certainly Bushell makes no reference to it. Subsequently, the chairman resigned. Nicol speculates that the resignation may have been due to the failure of his colleagues to fully accept his advice.[24]

More Efficient Tonnage

In 1870 the fleet numbered 19 vessels, eight of them 15 years old, with still two wooden paddle-steamers, *La Plata*, 1852, and *Conway*, 1846, although both were out of service by the following year, sold to builders in part settlement of the cost of new tonnage. Of the seven remaining iron paddle-steamers five were out of service early in the decade.

Casualties were few: *Boyne* (3,318 tons, 1871) was wrecked off the French coast in 1875, all passengers and mails being saved. *Shannon* ran aground and became a total loss in the same year. Altogether 13 replacement ships were built or bought within the first five years of the decade, some of increased tonnage, cargo and passenger capacity. The three ships taken over from the PNZA were renamed *Tiber*, *Ebro* and *Liffey*. All three, with accommodation for over 200 passengers, were placed on the South American run. *Ebro*, in 1872, inaugurated the new, second, service calling at Cherbourg outward bound and then, homewards, continuing to Antwerp after Southampton.

All new tonnage was single-screw, compound-engined. John Elder of Govan built three ships of around 3,200 tons in 1870–71, *Elbe*, *Moselle* and *Tagus*. Each was capable of a service speed of 12 knots and had accommodation for 100 first-

23 *The Times* (London), 29 April 1880.

24 Nicol, *Scrapbook*, Reports of Directors, pp. 581–2.

class, 50 second-class and some third-class/migrant passengers, and, importantly, capacity for 1,000 tons of cargo.[25] It is likely that the contract for these three vessels was given to the Elder yard because of its considerable experience with compound engines. The reductions of per voyage coal usage and costs produced in 1870, shown in Table 4.2, illustrate the benefits of the compound engine and screw propulsion. *Shannon* was converted to single screw in 1875, halving her coal consumption and giving an estimated 1-knot speed increase.

Table 4.2 Reduced costs, increased cargo space and speed

Ship		Coal (tons)	Cost (£)	Av. speed (knots)
Shannon	1859/paddle/3,609 tons	3,604	4,468	9.45
Elbe	1870/screw/3,109 tons	1,411	1,582	11.83
Nile	1868/screw/3,025 tons	2,244	2,698	10.62

Boyne (3,318 tons), built in 1871 at the Dumbarton yard of Denny Brothers, was allocated to the South American route almost immediately, one of three vessels that maintained the original monthly service.[26] *Minho* and *Mondego* (2,500 tons), both built in 1872 for the Ryde & Co.'s Belgian mail service, were acquired in 1874 when that company went out of business. They were described as being fitted with steam cranes and carrying 80 passengers in first class, 30 in second and 500 in third.[27] The purchase of two ships with reduced first-class and extensive third-class accommodation affirms that Royal Mail was involved in the migrant trade from Peninsular ports to Brazil and Argentina, although no comment was made to shareholders. Three more ships were acquired or built in 1873 to establish a new service to the West Indies.

Perhaps surprisingly, considering her age, the 1855-built *Tasmanian* was fitted with compound engines in 1871, halving her fuel consumption and increasing her cargo capacity from 300 to 1,000 tons. On trials she made 14 knots, rather more than required in service. On her first crossing, Southampton to St Thomas in 338 hours, she used 466 tons of coal whereas a previous crossing took 466 hours

[25] *The Times* (London), 1 June 1871. *Tagus* exceeded 14 knots on trials. Bonsor, *South Atlantic Seaway*, pp. 145–6. Elder was prominent in the development of the compound engine. He fitted an efficient compound engine in Pacific Steam's *Valparaiso* in 1856 with dramatic reduction in coal consumption.

[26] Howat, *South American Packets*, p. 120. *Boyne* was advertised in the Buenos Aires *Standard* in June 1873 with first-class fares of £35 (and upwards) to Southampton, second-class £20 and third-class £15. The service was described as: 'Direct and Quickest Route to Europe'. The advertisement confirmed that calls were made at Antwerp.

[27] Bonsor, *South Atlantic Seaway*, p. 177. Ryde was a British firm operating out of Antwerp and, mainly, London to the east coast of South America from 1870 to 1874.

using 1,088 tons.[28] In 1877–78 four vessels were added to the fleet: *Medway* and *Solent* were built to Company order while *Trent* and *Tamar*, both built in 1873, were purchased in 1878. In 1879 *Derwent* inaugurated a West Indies cargo line, her two sister ships following in 1880.

Finances

The decade started brightly, receipts rising very substantially from £646,207 in 1870 to £860,000 in 1874 before easing to £708,406 in 1880. Disbursements decreased up to 1872, which, noted Chairman Mangles, 'showed the advantage of the directors introducing ships of large capacity for cargo and speed, having compound engines, by which the consumption of coal had been greatly reduced'. However, costs rose from 1873, still supported by strong receipts of £846,672. The level of receipts peaked in 1874 before beginning a progressive decline through the decade. Dividends reflected the situation: the payment in 1872 of £10 15s per share was followed by a general decline over the next 30 years.

Table 4.3 starkly illustrates the dramatic fall in the total mail income, from 33 per cent in 1870 to 14 per cent in 1880. Freight revenues were, however, particularly resilient, rising steadily throughout the decade while passage money peaked in 1875 before declining through to 1880.

Table 4.3 Receipts and disbursements, 1870–80 (£)

	1870	**1875**	**1880**
Receipts			
Mail contract	215,534 (33%)	117,264 (15%)	98,250 (14%)
Freight	184,170 (29%)	292,938 (38%)	335,802 (47%)
Passage money	246,503 (38%)	358,030 (47%)	274,354 (39%)
Total	646,207	768,232	708,406
Disbursements	446,024	597,369	523,973
Operating surplus	200,183	170,863	184,433
Dividend	150,000 (10)	37,500 (2 10s)	45,000 (3)
Capital	900,000	900,000	900,000

Source: Reports and Accounts.

The item that most excited the interest of shareholders at the bi-annual meetings was discussion of the insurance account. The reasons were twofold: the Company continued to self-insure its vessels so that costs related to accident or total loss of a ship were carried straight to the insurance fund. Importantly, the fund was

[28] *The Times* (London), 27 April 1871.

frequently the source of shareholders' bonus payments, provided the total was in excess of a prior agreed sum, in the 1870s usually in the region of £250,000, although some shareholders considered £300,000 to be a sounder figure. However, in a time of fairly relaxed accounting procedures, funds could readily be transferred from elsewhere to improve the appearance of the accounts and to keep shareholders happy. The cost to the insurance fund resulting from the loss of three ships in 1875–76 was estimated at £150,000. These costs and other lesser accidents much depleted the fund and required that a loan of maximum £150,000 be secured to purchase new tonnage.[29]

Shareholder frustration became evident during 1876 when Chairman Childers presented a none too impressive set of accounts, noting the 'very depressed state of trade all over the world'. He added, in an attempt to reassure those present, that, although freight rates and business generally were worse than in the previous year, public confidence was such that the weight of traffic was maintained. A Dr Beattie was so concerned that he suggested that Parliament should be approached in an attempt to reduce shareholders' liability, still £40 on the £100 shares, and, in theory, subject to a cash call. Another shareholder, Mr Carpenter, thought the position of the Company was very serious and that there were 'defects in the management somewhere'. He was especially concerned that other similar companies were paying good dividends, despite the depression in trade. The reason for this aggressive intercourse was the absence of a bonus from the insurance fund, down from £3 10s in 1873, £1 7s 6d in 1874 and nil from 1875 to 1877, although a dividend of £2 to £2 10s was paid in the final three years of the decade. There was a small group of shareholders always ready with trenchant criticism when their bonuses were under pressure, although the proposal to approach Parliament for permission to amend the Charter in order to reduce their liability does suggest a very positive concern.

The depression of the latter years of the 1870s affected most countries, with severe unemployment, uncertain demand for goods and services, and generally falling prices. Freight volumes and rates were affected. A press report in 1879 comments that in the previous two years the general opinion in shipping circles was that the freight rates and ship prices were so low that, without an improvement, shipowners and builders would be forced out of business. Things did not improve but, despite production cutbacks and many business failures, there were few casualties amongst shipowners and shipbuilders, many of whom were building speculatively and selling at rock-bottom prices just to stay in business.[30] Royal Mail suffered as much as any, the directors' reports making frequent references to the difficult trading conditions. The total values of imports and exports from/to Brazil and Argentina did not alter greatly in the 1870s, while liner competition increased dramatically.

---

29 Bushell, *Royal Mail*, pp. 130–31; RMSP, Directors' Minutes, 24 November 1875.

30 *The Times* (London), 4 July 1879.

Twenty vessels were added to the fleet in the decade but the preoccupation of the directors remained with the West Indies services. Most new ships were still built with that service in mind. The introduction, in 1872, of the second Brazil and River Plate service was a measure of some confidence in the trade prospects, although it imposed considerable demands, not least the financial requirement to provide additional three vessels to maintain it. The confidence of the directors

Figure 4.1 *Elbe* (1870). J & M Clarkson Collection

early in the decade was, inevitably, damaged by the increasingly difficult economic conditions throughout the decade.

The route on the Brazilian coast altered hardly at all. The directors, preoccupied with matters in the West Indies, failed to maximise the Company's predominant situation, largely due to the board's persistent view of Royal Mail as a passenger and mail service, one that prevailed until the early 1900s. Lamport & Holt, operating generally smaller ships carrying fewer passengers, developed additional cargo services to Paranagua and Rio Grande in Southern Brazil and Rosario in the Argentine as well as participating actively in the triangular coffee trade to New York.[31] It offered greater flexibility to cargo shippers by adding Glasgow and London as loading and discharging ports and began a service out of Antwerp

---

[31] Robert G. Albion, 'British Shipping and Latin America, 1806–1914', *Journal of Economic History*, Vol. XI, No. IV (Cambridge, 1951), p. 371. Albion notes that more cargo was carried outwards to Brazil than homewards in that period, so that some ships loaded for Brazil, then, homewards, carried coffee to New York (America was the biggest importer of Brazilian coffee), shipped American goods to the UK, then loaded outwards again for Brazil. Lamport & Holt was active in this trade. *Halley* carried the first New York shipment in 1869.

carrying the Belgian mails. Likewise, Pacific Steam continued to expand its services to the west coast via Rio and Montevideo.

In the very difficult prevailing circumstances the directors came under heavy pressure from shareholders, few of whom knew anything about the management of a shipping company but were very knowledgeable about the nature of their investments. One disgruntled shareholder, a Mr Carpenter, complained that the situation of the Company was 'very serious', to which the chairman was obliged to deny 'that the Company was in a disastrous and lamentable condition'.[32]

After a dividend slump towards the end of the 1860s, improved trade resulted in payment for the year 1870 of £10, a very acceptable 17 per cent on capital invested. At that stage the share price was £57. Good dividends were paid until 1875, the share price rising to a heady £88 in 1874. Dividends then slumped, as did the share price, respectively £2 10s and £54 in 1878. A measure of the directors' predicament was their announcement in 1875 that they would be unable to make dividend payments from the insurance fund 'for some time'.

---

[32] *The Times* (London), 19 October 1876.

Chapter 5
Difficult Trading Conditions

H.C.E. Childers MP continued in the chair with Admiral Whish his deputy. Other directors were Messrs Barlow, Berens, Chapman, Colville, Curtis, Edelman and Tufnell. The representation of ex-naval personnel was by now much reduced. The precise experience of other directors is uncertain, although, on appointment, Messrs Curtis and Edelman were described as having business connections with Brazil and the West Indies. In early 1880 Eden Colville became chairman when Childers resigned, probably as a result of disagreement with his colleagues over his recommendation that ships be withdrawn from the South American service and allocated to the West Indies. At Colville's first shareholders' meeting as chairman, most unusually, no reference was made to Childers's departure. An interesting addition to the board in 1883 was Captain Richard Revett, a former commodore of the fleet.

In 1882 Royal Mail obtained a further supplemental Royal Charter enabling it to, among other things, raise additional funds by issue of debentures as and when it was thought necessary. (Funds had previously been raised by loans, which were not always readily identifiable in the accounts.) Capital available remained at £900,000, 15,000 × £60 paid on £100 shares issued. The main purpose of the Charter extension was to incorporate the route extensions already made. The West Indies mail contract was extended for five years from 1880, at a rate of £80,000 per annum. The arrangement for the South American service was continued with payment by weight, as before. At this time the Company arranged, whenever the opportunity arose, mail contracts with individual governments, mainly in the West Indies, which yielded some additional revenue.

The decade began with a sober assessment of prospects by Deputy Chairman Whish at the April 1880 shareholders' meeting. He announced that no dividend would be paid from the working account for the latter part of 1879 (a small bonus of £1 15s was paid from the insurance account) in the course of recording depression in the South American trade. He also made reference to what he described as a transition in the carrying trade of the country, in that steamers were now used where sailing vessels were previously employed and they were active in every port. The increase in steamship numbers and their greater carrying capacity and speed (over sailing ships) resulted in a significant reduction in freight rates.[1] Much of the increased tonnage operated as tramp ships carrying bulk cargoes: liner services with their frequent, scheduled sailings were protected in some measure

[1] *The Times* (London), 28 April 1880.

by agreements with regular shippers, but increased competition of whatever nature inevitably adversely affected freight rates.

This development was highlighted in 1882–83 when a press report quoted the chairman's reference to the Company carrying cargo from the River Plate 'at the absurdly low rate of 15s per ton', about half of the rate of the previous year. He added that such was the volume of goods being carried that a very small increase in the rate would make a marked difference in receipts and profits.[2] The low rates also affected cargo carried between ports in Brazil, Uruguay and the Argentine.

Despite the difficult economic conditions, in April 1882 *The Times* carried an advertisement for three South American services per month out of Southampton (see Table 5.1). The 1st of the month service, taken by *Mondego*, departed from London, Victoria Dock, on the 27th of the previous month for Southampton. No vessel was named for the two subsequent sailings. Fares to Lisbon, Vigo and Carril were from £8 first class, £5 in second. Equivalent fares to Montevideo and Buenos Aires were from £35 and £20.

Table 5.1 Three South American services out of Southampton

Date of month	Ports of call
1st	Lisbon, Pernambuco, Maceio, Bahia, Rio de Janeiro and Santos
9th	Cherbourg, Lisbon, St Vincent, Pernambuco, Bahia, Rio de Janeiro, Santos, Montevideo and Buenos Aires
24th	Carril, Vigo, Lisbon, Pernambuco, Maceio, Bahia, Rio de Janeiro, Montevideo and Buenos Aires

It is clear that spare tonnage was available to take advantage of opportunities that arose. An advertisement identified a fourth service sailing on the 27th of the month for Carril, Vigo, Montevideo and Buenos Aires. This additional service was scheduled when quarantine difficulties were anticipated in Brazil or when profit opportunity arose. The ports of call suggest that the carriage of emigrants from Spanish ports was a major consideration.

The chairman, under pressure to cut costs, advised shareholders in 1883 that he considered it very unwise to sell ships engaged in unprofitable trades at that time, as it would mean withdrawing from certain ports and the Company might find that it took a long time to re-establish itself in those ports when business improved.

Throughout the 1880s services were, on occasion, revised to take account of fever outbreaks: at one stage the north Brazil ports were briefly excluded for this reason. A press report of the 31 May 1884 shareholders' meeting refers to additional voyages made, noting that prevailing conditions required management to exercise greater flexibility in order to maintain revenues. A factor referred to

[2] *The Times* (London), 26 April 1883 and 1 November 1883, Reports of shareholders' meetings.

frequently in shareholders' reports was extra mileage sailed in pursuit of cargo, not always a profitable exercise. Nevertheless, the chairman was able to advise shareholders in 1888 that they had 'every reason to congratulate themselves on the South American trade'.

British companies continued vigorously in competition on South American routes. Pacific Steam operated fortnightly services from Liverpool/Birkenhead via Bordeaux, Spanish ports and Lisbon to and from Brazil and the River Plate en route to the west coast.[3] Lamport & Holt advertised weekly services from Liverpool to Brazil as well as weekly services direct to the Plate, some terminating in Rosario, increasingly important for grain and wool exports. Every 10 days one of its vessels left London for Antwerp, proceeding to Brazil and the River Plate. It was also much involved with the coffee trade between Brazil and the USA. A range of UK and continental discharge ports was offered, with occasional calls in Southampton, no doubt a matter of particular concern to Royal Mail.[4]

The Allan Line and the Donaldson Line operated from Glasgow to the Plate. Throughout the 1880s French and, increasingly, German shipping lines continued to offer competition. No fewer than six Italian lines began services from the Mediterranean in this decade, the majority withdrawing fairly quickly. One, the Veloce Line, sailing out of Genoa, advertised the 'Best, Quickest and Cheapest' route to South America from London with three sailings a month. At this time increasing numbers of European countries were offering subsidies to their merchant shipping companies in one form or another, for mail services or for the construction of new tonnage.

The Directors under Pressure

The continuing difficult trading conditions and their effects on dividend payments predictably caused dissension among shareholders. In 1883 there were complaints about increased operating costs and ship losses. A Mr Dence suggested that 'the Company would be better by the infusion of a little fresh blood at the board'. Dispute over a vacant seat on the board resulted in the appointment of Captain Revett, an experienced Company shipmaster, against the wishes of all but one director, a Mr J. Gatley.[5] A modest victory, it may be said, for shareholder power and one guaranteed to cause some discomfort in the boardroom. On another occasion the 'extravagant management of the affairs of the Company' was criticised and Gatley expressed concern at the failure to contain costs in a very difficult trading period, commending reductions in commission rates to agents and shippers. At the 1886

---

[3] *The Times* (London), 29 September 1883. Unusually, the 1st of the month sailing for Brazil is routed via Bordeaux. No reference to this has been found in the Company archives.

[4] *The Times* (London), 9 January 1882. Lamport & Holt's *Archimedes* was reported as due in Southampton with the mails from the River Plate and Brazil.

[5] *The Times* (London), 26 April 1883, Report of shareholders' meeting.

meeting a suggestion that the directors were overpaid, at £3,000 per annum, was not welcomed by the chairman, who responded that he did not think they were overpaid. (Some captains received £500 per month, the commodore £1,000.)

A series of unfortunate ship losses added greatly, and expensively, to the Company's difficulties and to the discomfort of management. It was determined in 1884 to begin a triangular service whereby the steamer leaving Southampton on the 1st of the month for Brazil and Argentina returned via New York to Southampton and London. The intention was to capitalise on the increasing trade with New York, especially with northbound coffee shipments. Disaster followed: three ships were lost and the service was suspended.

There was further disagreement when a director, Mr Alderman Savory, indicated that he would not approve the adoption of the report and stated, 'the dual system of control was absolutely fatal to the proper administration of the Company's affairs'. It can only be speculated that the reference was to differences between the board of directors and the board of managers. It was proposed that a committee of inquiry be set up. The chairman and two other directors indicated that if a committee were established they would resign.[6] An agreement was negotiated but criticism, indeed antagonism, continued with a further demand for a committee of inquiry in 1886.

Political Tensions in South America

Brazil experienced internal political turmoil in the 1880s, with tension between rival groups, disaffection within the army and a movement towards removal of the old social and political order and the establishment of a republic. Active to this end was a new breed of entrepreneurial coffee planters and industrialists of the southeast of the country who sought progress through modernisation. The modernisers demanded the end of slavery, a move reluctantly agreed by Emperor Pedro II in 1888. The following year he was deposed and a provisional Republican government was convened in 1890, a new constitution being introduced in 1891.[7] British interests soon adapted to the opportunities offered by the altered situation, as did the new Brazilian government, which was anxious to secure Britain's recognition of the Republic and access to loan funds to develop and maintain economic development.

Throughout this turbulent period Brazil's exports to Britain, still controlled largely by British merchants and shippers intent on profit regardless of the political distractions, decreased from £5.3m (1880) to £4.4m (1890), as total exports decreased marginally. Coffee still accounted for more than half of the total as

[6] *The Times* (London), 1 November 1883 and 1 May 1884, Reports of shareholders' meetings.

[7] Graham, *Britain and the Onset of Modernization*, pp. 39–43, and Joao Pandia Calogeras, *A History of Brazil* (Chapel Hill, 1939), pp. 276–7.

sugar production fell. Imports from Britain rose from £6.7m to £7.5m, a significant increase of 12 per cent.[8] Despite mounting competition from Germany and France, with the USA becoming increasingly active, Britain continued to dominate trade with Brazil and to be the major source of investment funds, which increased through the decade from £38.8m in 1880.[9]

Consular and diplomatic reports consistently noted that the manufacturers of competing countries were inclined to be more concerned with the wishes and inclinations of potential customers and sought to meet their requirements. British firms tended to employ salesmen or agents who did not speak the language, showed a disregard for customers' specifications and were of the view that their products were entirely suited to the market, as they had been for years.[10]

Argentina was also politically unstable, civil war prevailing for some months in 1880. The Argentine navy blockaded Buenos Aires, searching foreign ships for arms and closing the port for a time.[11] There was fighting and looting in the city. Peace was restored in October when General Roca was installed as president, although tensions within the country and with its neighbours continued throughout the decade. The directors' report to shareholders dated April 1881 offered no comment on the turmoil.

Rock comments that Argentina lifted itself out of the depression of the 1870s by simply increasing production of exportables. Confidence returned, as did British capital, which financed railway extensions, tramways, water and sewage systems, and gas and electricity services in Buenos Aires and other major cities. The companies operating the services not only imported vast quantities of machinery and equipment, but, in particular for the railways, many staff were brought in from Britain. Immigration increased by more than three times, mainly from Spain and Italy, and vast areas of land in the interior were developed for crop and animal production. A reflection of this new prosperity was the increase in shipping using Argentine ports, from 2.1m tons in 1880 to 7.7m tons in 1889, and the development of Buenos Aires's first dock.[12]

Exports, particularly cereals, increased rapidly with benefit of cheaper prices resulting from a necessary depreciation of the peso and reduced freight rates. From

---

8 Platt, *Latin America*, pp. 316–21.

9 Graham, *Britain and the Onset of Modernization*, p. 5. The nominal value of British capital in Latin America in 1880 was £179m.

10 Great Britain, 'Commercial Reports, Consular, 1881' (7–8), 1430, in Manchester, *British Pre-eminence*, p. 330. Subsequent reports through the 1880s and 1890s reiterated the failure of British manufacturers to adapt to a changing market and the progressive loss of share.

11 H.S. Ferns, *Britain and Argentina in the Nineteenth Centur*, pp. 388–91. Lamport & Holt's steamer *Plato* was stopped and searched. British interests were at risk. The resident British minister was party to an arrangement whereby 10 days' grace was permitted for the loading of discharging of cargo in the port before it was closed.

12 Rock, *Argentina, 1516–1987*, pp. 152–3.

£0.9m in 1880 the value of exports rose to £4.1m in 1890. As exports grew, so did imports, up from £2.5m to £8.4m in the same years (see Table 5.2).[13]

Table 5.2 British exports to/imports from Brazil and Argentina, 1880–90 (values in £m)

	1880	1885	1890
Brazil			
Exports to Britain	5.3	4.1	4.4
Imports from Britain	6.7	5.3	7.5
Argentina			
Exports to Britain	0.9	1.9	4.1
Imports from Britain	2.5	4.7	8.4

Source: Platt, *Latin America*, pp. 317–23.

Trade improved despite the financial crises of the national as well as provincial governments, which had over-extended themselves: the annual debt service more than doubled between 1885 and 1890, by which time it accounted for 60 per cent of the year's total export earnings. Government expenditure consistently exceeded revenues. British investors became alarmed by its heavy borrowing. Baring Brothers, the government's agent in London, failed to attract subscribers for a loan it had underwritten for public works in Buenos Aires. Panic resulted when it became clear that the government would default on its loans. Although Baring Brothers, one of the City of London's most prestigious merchant banks, was considered to have behaved imprudently and there was risk of bankruptcy, it was kept afloat by concerted action by City banks and the Bank of England. The peso was depreciated as the Argentine government took remedial action.[14] New British investment ceased for a time but was restored by mid-decade. Although the volume of exports increased, prices fell.

Foreign shipping still dominated the trade of both Brazil and Argentina, and Royal Mail continued to be a force in the trades. In 1880 nearly 40 per cent of foreign shipping entering Rio de Janeiro was British; Germany accounted for 16 per cent and France 19 per cent. In Santos, the main coffee-exporting port, British and German shipping each accounted for about 40 per cent of the total. Of 1.7m tons of foreign shipping entering Argentine ports in 1885, over half was British; France, at 34 per cent, was in second place. The situation in Montevideo was similar.[15]

[13] Platt, *Latin America*, pp. 316–21.

[14] P.J. Cain and A.G. Hopkins, *British Imperialism 1688–2000* (London, 1993), pp. 256–7.

[15] Albion, 'Capital, Movement and Transportation', table p. 373.

However, those factors that were clearly of benefit to Argentina and Brazil in terms of imports and exports were not of comfort to Royal Mail or to other liner companies as the numbers of tramp steamships greatly increased. These were designed for the carriage of cargo in bulk and operated without the constraints of schedules: a shipper might charter a vessel to carry a one-off cargo of 4,000 tons of grain from Rosario to London, infinitely more cost-effective to the producer than a number of smaller shipments by regular-service liners. There were two major advantages for the shipper: the charter agreement would require the vessel to be available on the loading berth on a specific day and the charterer was able to negotiate the freight rate at, invariably, less than the liner rate. It was this developing factor of supply and demand that adversely affected freight rates throughout the latter years of the century.

The Fleet Modernised

In 1880 the fleet numbered 27 vessels of 65,985 tons, of which only six were more than 10 years old. The Company's last two iron paddle-steamers, *Eider* and *Arno*, continued in the West Indies service but they were disposed of by 1883. Five more vessels were sold, all for further trading, usually for less than £10,000. One of them, *Minho*, had been laid up for a time and tenders were invited to expensively outfit her for the emigrant trade with new boilers and a triple-expansion engine. Oddly, perhaps as a result of considerations regarding planned new tonnage, within weeks she was sold for £7,500.[16]

A number of casualties added greatly to costs: *Douro* sank in 1882, following a collision with the Spanish *Yrurac Bat* off Cape Finisterre, when homeward bound from Brazil. Five passengers and 12 officers and crew were lost. In the same year *Tiber* was wrecked in the West Indies. Three further vessels were lost in 1884–85 when operating a new Santos–New York–Southampton service. The first, *Dart*, ran aground after leaving Santos and became a total wreck. The following year *Humber* disappeared in the Atlantic when homeward bound from New York to Britain in February. It was speculated that she may have encountered ice. Within months *Guadiana* was wrecked off the Brazilian coast. The service was abruptly ended.[17]

In the 1880s significant changes took place in the fleet as new building technologies developed: *Orinoco* (4,572 tons, 1886), the Company's largest vessel to date, was from the yard of Caird & Co. in Greenock. She was built of steel, stronger and lighter than iron, and had a more powerful and more efficient triple-expansion engine. She had improved electricity-lit accommodation for 257 in first class and 26 in second. So successful was *Orinoco*'s engine that all new

---

16 Nicol, *Scrapbook*, Directors' Minutes, 16, 30 November 1887, p. 907.

17 Bushell, *Royal Mail*, pp. 134–5.

tonnage was thus fitted and the Company began to convert all of its larger ships, an expensive exercise.

Further radical change took place in 1888: an order was placed with Napier's yard in Glasgow for four steamers, three of them intended specifically for the South American service and each in excess of 5,000 tons. The first delivered was *Atrato* (5,347 tons, 1888), which achieved 16 knots in trials. The structural changes were dramatic: instead of passengers being housed below the open spar deck, a substantial two-deck superstructure was built incorporating much of the passenger accommodation and public rooms, and featuring covered promenade decks. She was capable of carrying 221 in first class and 32 and 26 in second and third respectively. The new building techniques also allowed for increased cargo capacity: *Atrato* had space for approximately 2,600 tons of cargo. She made her maiden voyage to Buenos Aires in 1889 before reverting, as planned, to the West Indies service.

The three other vessels, *Magdalena, Thames* and *Clyde*, were delivered in 1889–90, the latter two slightly larger and more powerful. They were handsome vessels with twin funnels and clipper bows, and they added greatly to the increasing prestige of the South American service. They had accommodation for 174 first-class passengers, 44 in second class and 330 migrants in third class. Although the Company had been involved with the carriage of migrants from the Continent to Brazil and Argentina since the 1874 acquisitions of *Minho* and *Mondego*, the service warranted little comment in the directors' minutes or reports.

Six smaller vessels were built between 1880 and 1883: *Humber* (2,371 tons) and *Avon* (2,162 tons) entered service in the West Indies in 1880. The building and outfitting cost of the former was near to £50,000. (In the following year *Humber* was employed briefly as a troop ship, carrying 492 officers and men of the 2nd West India Regiment from Jamaica to Ashantee on the West Coast of Africa.) *La Plata II* (3,240 tons) was purchased in 1882. *Eden* and *Esk* II (both 2,145 tons) entered service in the same year and were allocated to inter-island services in the West Indies. *Dart* (2,641 tons) was bought in 1883 and was used on the Santos to New York run.

The programme of updating tonnage continued: *Tamar* and *Elbe* were given new boilers and the much more efficient triple-expansion engines in 1887; the engines of *Medway* and *Dee* were converted the following year. The directors noted that the considerable expense of these conversions was justified by the reduction in coal costs. Electric lighting was installed in all vessels as they were repaired or refitted. On the downside the chairman acknowledged in 1887, in response to shareholders' questions, that some Company vessels were 'a little obsolete but none of them were of wood'.

At this time the use of sail, still common into the early 1880s, was greatly reduced: yards were removed from all vessels, although some retained fore and aft sails for a time. In 1885 *Para*, a 13-knot vessel, was under canvas for 424 hours in 36 days of steaming time with resultant fuel savings. The development of accommodation superstructures late in the decade made the use of sails impractical. However, the benefits of substantially increased cargo spaces below deck, accessed through large hatches and with winches to speed the processes of loading and discharging, more than compensated.

Figure 5.1 *Magdalena* (1889). J & M Clarkson Collection

A Turbulent Decade

Revenues continued uncertain through the 1880s, following the decline to £708,406 in 1880, due to a combination of reduced mail and passenger income. Uncertain trading conditions in South America and increased competition resulting in ruinous freight rates were frequently cited by the chairman when addressing Company meetings. Receipts held up fairly well until 1884, when cargo and passenger revenues collapsed. An important factor in these losses was revolution in Colombia. During disturbances in Colon, the Company's terminus, its offices, stores and cargo sheds, were destroyed by fire. For a time, trade in the Western Caribbean was adversely affected.

Table 5.3 Receipts and disbursements, 1880–90 (£)

	1880	1885	1890
Receipts			
Mail contract	98,250 (14%)	100,185 (16%)	107,603 (14%)
Freight	335,802 (47%)	246,662 (39%)	315,430 (41%)
Passage money	274,354 (39%)	288,285 (44%)	345,171 (45%)
Total	708,406	635,132	768,204
Disbursements	523,973	477,860	558,313
Operating surplus	184,433	157,272	209,891
Dividend/bonus	48,750 (£3 5s)	22,500 (£1 10s)	71,250 (£4 15s)
Capital	900,000	900,000	900,000

Source: Reports and Accounts.

Table 5.3 reflects the drastic decline in freight income in the middle of the decade and the positive attempt to contain costs. The tenor of the directors' reports suggests that the problems were greatest in the West Indies services, although competition and cholera affected South American revenues. The situation improved progressively in the latter part of the decade, with passenger income up appreciably by 1890 and freight much improved but struggling to regain the revenues of 1880. In October 1888 and again in the following year the directors noted that the improved receipts were largely from the Brazil and River Plate services, where additional sailings were operated as opportunity offered.

Allocations to depreciation were made consistently: £40,000 (4 per cent) was set aside in 1880 against a written-down fleet value of £1,087,075. In 1890, £70,000 was set aside against a valuation of £1,140,113, 6 per cent. Inevitably dividends suffered: they averaged £3–£3 10s, mostly bonuses from the insurance fund, until 1885 when only £1 10s was paid, the lowest figure since 1868, despite reserves shown in the accounts. Payments improved to £5 15s in 1888 and 1889 a fair return of nearly 10 per cent. The share price was likewise volatile, falling dramatically to £51 in 1882, £38 in 1885, down from £60 10s in 1880, before recovering to £62 10s by 1887 and finishing the decade at £58 10s.

In 1888, in improved trading conditions, Chairman Eden Colville reassured shareholders that the financial position was very strong, with 'solid investments of £230,000 and in money £55,000 as well as a very satisfactory £242,900 in the insurance account'. He also addressed shareholders' heightened concerns (regarding the £40 outstanding on their £100 shares) at a time of 'extraordinary expenditure on fleet modernisation', reassuring them that no call was likely to be made. He said that the potential to raise additional shareholder capital enabled him to obtain short-term loans at very good rates, although these loans and repayments made are not identifiable in the accounts; nor are they commented upon in the reports. The board was merely acknowledging shareholders' pressure: they had no wish to be hit by a £40 cash call on their shares and sought to have the share value reduced to £60. It was pointed out that such a move would require alteration of the Company's charter and the matter was put aside.[18]

Good Progress

Despite adverse trading conditions and increasing competition, much progress was made during the 1880s. The fleet numbered 27 ships of 65,985 tons in 1880; these figures became 25 vessels of 72,910 tons by 1890. Eleven ships were lost or sold in the decade, replacements being, generally, of increased tonnage. The addition of three ships of more than 5,000 tons to the South American services was a solid measure of some increasing confidence in the development of the trade. In addition to the costs of new ships, many of the existing ships were expensively refitted with triple-expansion engines, improved accommodation for passengers, electricity and refrigerated spaces for the carriage of provedore stores. The operational efficiency of the fleet was increased and the improvements for passengers were much appreciated.

The obstacles were great: while services to the West Indies remained relatively stable, revolution in Colombia apart, Brazil and Argentina continued politically and economically in turmoil, with periodic disease outbreaks adding greatly to the difficulties. Despite this, exports, particularly from Argentina, continued to expand.

Nevertheless, management in the 1880s was conservative regarding services to South America, uncertain if the obvious potential would be realised. There were still opportunities to establish cargo services to the many other ports in the north and south of Brazil which were being developed by Lamport & Holt, Messrs Booth, Harrison's of Liverpool and continental companies. But Royal Mail continued to view itself as essentially a mail and passenger line, although, from 1880, it already operated a regular monthly cargo service to the West Indies from London's Victoria Dock with a call at Southampton for passengers and mail. Its move into the Brazil to New York coffee trade, with cotton, usually, home to Southampton, was a disaster.

Some shareholders expressed the view that the Company should move its headquarters and services to London, at Tilbury. At the annual meeting in April 1883 the chairman, while acknowledging that he was a director of the Southampton Dock Company (and might have some vested interest), argued against the move on the grounds of, among other things, cost. In 1886 a director, Captain Revett, who was of the view that the move should be made, produced a lengthy report for his colleagues. He cited the successful transfer of P&O to Tilbury and calculated that greater cargo volumes would result and, in what he called a costing exercise, that £65,000 per year would be saved. Revett's colleagues, with one or two exceptions,

---

[18] *The Times* (London), 25 October 1888.

remained unimpressed: it was not until some years later that the head office did move to London, and Victoria Dock became the Company's main terminal, although the larger passenger vessels continued to operate out of Southampton for many years.

Throughout the period of this study, at least from 1856 when six directors were unseated, it is noticeable that, despite sometimes vigorous complaints by shareholders and, on occasion, by directors, the situation of the board remained secure. From press reports, mainly in *The Times*, it seems clear that the numbers of complaining shareholders were relatively small and, as one noted, the chairman would, in any case, hold sufficient proxies to win a vote of confidence.

The most significant decision of the directors during the decade was to make a major investment in new tonnage for the South American service. From 1888 three larger, more efficient and faster steel vessels with triple-expansion engines were built for the South American service. They were capable of in excess of 15 knots and had large passenger and cargo capacities. A press report commented that the luxurious passenger accommodation was steam heated and had electric light.[19]

The building of a dock system in Buenos Aires had begun in 1884, the first dock opening in 1889. Vessels were by now able to anchor sufficiently close to the port for improved passenger and cargo movements. It is likely that at that time the maximum practical tonnage for the service was around 5,000 tons. The directors' decision to proceed with the new buildings was, no doubt, stimulated by the need to remain competitive with their European rivals, who were doing likewise.

[19] *The Times* (London), 4 July 1890, Report on the run from the Clyde to Southampton of *Clyde* before her maiden voyage to South America. The article referred to the vessel's ability, on trials, to achieve 17 knots.

Chapter 6
A Period of Uncertainty

Eden Colville remained in the chair when the 1890s opened, with Thomas Tufnell as his deputy. Of the other eight directors, three, Revett, Gatley and Savory, were recent critics of their fellow board members. Messrs Barlow, Chapman, Curtis and Russell completed the numbers. By now, added at the foot of the published list of directors, was the manager, Rear-Admiral A.J. Chatfield. In 1891 Chatfield was appointed a director and he remained the Company's manager. His appointment as director and manager, and later, in 1898, chairman, was extraordinary. He was a former naval officer with, so far as can be established, no prior experience of commercial shipping operations and finances.

Substantial changes were afoot: in 1892 John Gatley, one of the dissenters, resigned, due, it was said, to other commitments. He may have been forced out, although he had been a director since 1884. The chairman, announcing his departure, said that he was standing down as the government considered it incompatible to be a civil servant and a director of a public company. A replacement was Thomas Dence, a shareholder and businessman, who had a decade earlier been critical of the board's performance. Eden Colville died in 1893 after 37 years as director and chairman. He was replaced in the chair by his deputy, Thomas Tufnell, with by then Vice-Admiral Chatfield as his deputy. At that time no fewer than three directors were MPs. Edward Norton, described as 'having a considerable stake in the Argentine', was introduced to the board in 1898

In early 1896 Captain Revett was obliged, most probably under pressure, to resign, due, it was said, to ill-health.[1] He was replaced by Captain John Jellicoe, who had retired as commodore (senior master) of the Company in 1892. In 1898 Chairman Thomas Tufnell died, replaced by Chatfield, now Admiral Chatfield, who continued to occupy the position of manager. The rapid rise of Chatfield to chairman and his retention of the role of manager was noteworthy.

The mail contract for the West Indies was again extended in July 1890 for a further five years with annual payment of £85,000 for a fortnightly transatlantic and inter-island service. This arrangement was extended in 1895. The Company continued to make short-term contracts with individual island governments, covering mail and other services. *Tyne* (615 tons, 1891) began service for the government of the Leeward Islands in 1891. The arrangement with the Post Office for the South American mails is not referred to in the directors' reports, so that payment by weight continued at rates not specified.

---

1 RMSP, The Gatley Papers (RMS/52/15).

At the annual general meeting on 1 May 1890 the chairman was in buoyant mood, describing the report as 'very satisfactory', with passage money and freight income up, due, in part, to the additional profitable voyages made. With relief, no doubt, he pointed out that claims against the insurance fund were negligible. Soon, however, he spoke of 'extreme depression', and throughout the remainder of the decade shareholder reports continued in the same vein: political and financial instability and depressed trade. Argentina only slowly recovered from the crash of 1890–91 when the government applied severe fiscal measures, including taxes on exports, and some banks were wound up.[2] There was civil war in Brazil, the harbour in Rio de Janeiro being at one stage blockaded by naval vessels.[3] Disease and quarantine restrictions, and, in the early 1890s, strained relations between Britain and Portugal added to the difficulties, as did cholera in Europe. Inevitably, trade was adversely affected. At the shareholders' meeting in 1895 the chairman noted that the River Plate freight rate was 2s per ton, down from 25s in the previous year due to exceptional levels of competition in the difficult circumstances prevailing.[4] It was not until the latter years of the decade that freight rates and revenues began to recover, due to generally improved trade conditions and, in part, to the demand for chartered shipping in the time of the Spanish–American and Boer Wars.

In 1892 the need for further capital in light of increased expenditure on two recently ordered larger and faster ships and to rebuild cash reserves was highlighted. With benefit of the 1882 Supplemental Charter, which permitted borrowing to a total of £500,000, it was proposed to issue debentures not exceeding £250,000 in value. The first tranche, £150,000 of five-year debentures with interest at 4.5 per cent issued in July 1892, was fully taken up, mainly by shareholders. Security for the loan was the value of the fleet and other assets, which now exceeded £1m.[5]

References to the South American services became more frequent in the directors' reports and the building programme confirmed the substantial change of focus by the Company. New, larger ships were allocated to this route rather than, as had been the case over many years, to the West Indies. The migrant trades from Portugal and Spain to Brazil and Argentina, previously only hinted at by the directors, were now clearly a factor in revenue considerations. Most of the new liners carried 400–500 migrants, in addition to cabin passengers, and some of the older ones were refitted to carry migrants only.

2 Roberto Cortes Conde, 'The growth of the Argentine economy, c.1870–1914', in Bethell (ed.), *The Cambridge History*, pp. 346–7.

3 *The Times* (London), 26 April 1894. At the annual meeting the chairman expressed his thanks to Her Majesty's Government for the valuable assistance rendered by the man-of-war stationed at Rio, which had enabled them to land and embark all their passengers and cargo without any serious detention.

4 RMSP, Shareholders' meeting, 1 May 1895.

5 RMSP, Reports of Directors, 27 April 1892.

Migration contracts with the Brazilian and Argentine governments were arranged. The payment rate was related to the numbers carried and the range of ports at which they were disembarked.[6] The encouragement of migration was Brazilian and Argentine government policy throughout the 1890s. Agents were employed in Europe to recruit settlers to meet the labour demands of rapidly expanding agriculture bases and infrastructures. Governments paid a bounty to the shipowner for each passenger landed.

The flow of migrants and seasonal workers increased substantially in the late nineteenth century, curbs being applied by government in times of economic difficulty. In most years there was a return traffic of seasonal workers and migrants to Europe and, especially when the labour market dried up, the numbers were significant. Of the 110,594 who arrived in Argentina in 1890, more than 80,000 returned to Europe.[7]

The planning of services was a matter for constant consideration by management. Apart from commercial factors, disease, with quarantine restrictions, continued to affect the scheduling of services. Over the decade, for the most part two regular monthly sailings were made through to Buenos Aires. Additional services were added as opportunity presented and conditions warranted. On several occasions two ships left Southampton on the same day, one bound directly for Buenos Aires, the other for Brazil ports only. The European ports of call were subject to change: *Tagus* is recorded as extending the outward service in 1890 with calls at Rotterdam and London before final departure from Southampton.[8] Cherbourg was included at times, as were Corunna and Oporto/Leixoes, the latter a major departure point for migrants to Brazil. An additional service to Brazil was introduced in 1895. In *The Times* in early January of that year the services from Southampton shown in Table 6.1 were advertised.

---

[6] Nicol, *Scrapbook*, Directors' Minutes, 24 August 1892. The Company's agent in Rio, Mr Anderson, commended resumption of the calls at Maceio in north Brazil on the grounds that it would strengthen the prospect that he would obtain an immigration contract at a higher rate; p. 912.

[7] Ernesto Tornquist and Co., 'The Economic Development of Argentina in the Last Fifty Years', in Rock, *Argentina, 1516–1987*, table 5, p. 142. Eighty per cent of Argentine immigrants were from Mediterranean countries, half of them from Italy, a quarter Spaniards. Migrants to Argentina numbered 41,651 in 1880 and 260,909 in 1889, falling to 110,594 in 1890.

[8] *A Link of Empire*, p. 8. The publication was a souvenir published by the Company on the 70th anniversary of the incorporation of RMSP.

Table 6.1 Services from Southampton in 1895

Date	Vessel and ports of call
11 January	*Thames*, 5,645 tons. Vigo, Lisbon, Las Palmas, Pernambuco, Bahia, Rio, Montevideo and Buenos Aires
17 January	*Tamar*,* 2,591 tons. Vigo, Lisbon, Las Palmas, Pernambuco, Maceio, Bahia, Rio and Santos
25 January	*Nile*, 5,946 tons. Vigo, Lisbon, Las Palmas, Pernambuco, Bahia, Rio, Montevideo and Buenos Aires

* Third-class passengers only. *Nile* carried 215 in first class, 36 in second and 350 in third.

During 1894 consideration was given to the establishment of the additional monthly service to Brazil using *Tamar*, *Trent* and *Tagus*, much smaller and more than 20 years old. They were refitted for the carriage of cargo and migrants consequent to obtaining the migrant contract. The results must have been successful, as orders were placed for three new ships, which entered service in 1896–97, the older vessels being scrapped. The new tonnage was described as being for the 'Brazil cargo line' with extension to the River Plate and capable of carrying approximately 4,000 tons of cargo. This new development would become vitally important to Royal Mail over many years and was indicative of some considerable confidence in improving freight volumes with additional passenger revenues. On the return voyage, after the Southampton call, this service discharged and loaded cargo in Antwerp.[9] A significant development was the chartering of cargo vessels for the South American services.

Competition and Conferences

Competition on routes between British and South American ports remained fierce: advertisements in *The Times* in January 1897 listed Pacific Steam's fortnightly service to Brazil, Montevideo and the west coast, with outward calls at Peninsular ports for migrants. Houlder Line, Prince Line and Lamport & Holt advertised services from London to Plate ports, and North German Lloyd called at Southampton en route. Nelson Line also operated to Buenos Aires out of Liverpool, carrying general cargo outwards and, increasingly, some frozen cargo homewards. German, French and Italian lines were active from North European and Mediterranean ports. *Fairplay*, the weekly shipping journal, commenting on the European competition, urged that 'the concerted action of well-established shipowners who know the Plate' was needed.[10]

[9] Nicol, *Scrapbook*, Directors' Minutes, 24 October 1894 and 28 June 1895, pp. 915–16.

[10] *Fairplay*, 3 September 1896.

The directors' minutes make occasional references to informal discussions being held with other shipping companies on matters of mutual interest, the most pressing of which was the depression of freight rates due, in part, to increased competition as available cargo capacity, including tramp ships, increased more quickly than the import–export trades.[11] Although Chairman Chatfield had told Pacific Steam only the previous year that he 'declined to participate in arrangements with competing lines', in 1895 a significant development affected liner companies involved in the carriage of general cargoes through to the River Plate. British liner companies reached an agreement covering southbound general cargoes. In the following year the International River Plate Conference was established. It included continental companies' sailings out of the UK and continental ports between Le Havre and and Hamburg.

The conference agreements for central and north Brazil services were established in 1896. Most covered only a relatively small geographic area, so that Royal Mail would be a member of all three southbound conferences and, later, of those for northbound services.[12] Membership was extended to continental shipping companies. Additionally, confidential bilateral arrangements were made: Royal Mail and Pacific Steam agreed to regulate sailings to the east coast.

The conferences were, inevitably, controversial. They were intended to safeguard the interests of members who were committed to agreed arrival and departure schedules and freight rates were, arguably, beneficial to cargo shippers, and passenger fares. The objective was to minimise losses and maximise profits as freight rates fluctuated and progressively declined due to ever-increasing competition. Producers and shippers were resentful: they felt, with some justification, that they were being held to ransom by monopoly interests able to adversely affect their freedom to trade. The larger shippers were able to exert some considerable control over individual companies when they felt that their interests were not being safeguarded and they had the option to use non-conference companies. Greenhill notes that a major coffee shipper switched its Le Havre cargoes to Royal Mail and later threatened to move elsewhere in order to ensure that its interests were safeguarded.[13]

---

[11] B.M. Deakin and T. Seward, *Shipping Conferences: A Study of their Origins, Development and Economic Practices* (Cambridge, 1973), p. 21. The writers estimate that between 1873 and 1897 the volume of British overseas trade rose at 2.62 per cent per annum while the effective capacity of British ships rose at 5.33 per cent per annum, after allowances were made for increased speeds.

[12] Francis E. Hyde, *Shipping Enterprise and Management, 1830–1939. Harrisons of Liverpool* (Liverpool, 1967), pp. 57–9. Parties to the Central Brazilian Conference of 1896 were Royal Mail, Pacific Steam, Lamport & Holt and Harrisons, and three German companies, Hamburg-America, North German Lloyd and Hamburg South American Steamship Company. Hyde refers to a conference in the South American trades in 1880, which included Royal Mail, but no other reference to this has been found.

[13] Robert Greenhill, 'Shipping 1850–1914', in Platt (ed.), *Business Imperialism*, p. 139.

British exporters and importers would later, in 1909, air their complaints to a Royal Commission on Shipping Rings. The Commission expressed the view that the commercial relationship between shippers and conferences was justified and endorsed the benefits of a strong conference system. In South America the conferences were seen to protect British and continental shipping interests and, in effect, the commercial interests of their countries.

There were, however, contractual inducements for regular shippers: reduced rates and loyalty rebates based on volume were offered, the rebates, which might amount to 5 to 10 per cent, being frequently deferred for up to a year to ensure commitment. The inducements were resented by smaller businesses on the grounds that they were unable to take advantage of them. The important benefit to shippers was the availability of regular and efficient liner services, enabling them to plan confidently the movement of cargoes. The larger shippers, both in Britain and in South America, were able to exert some considerable influence on contractual arrangements, on occasion withholding cargo from specific shipping lines and favouring others or chartering their own tonnage.

Conference members vigorously expressed the view that the agreements were essential in order to mitigate the effects of depressed shipping rates and maintain some level of profitability.[14] The argument was predictable and had some merit in light of the very difficult years of the early 1890s and the ever-increasing output of British shipyards, with new companies eager for a share of developing markets. Shipping companies outwith the conferences were, unsurprisingly, far from happy. However, they and tramp-ship operators were still able to negotiate rates directly with shippers and their agents, usually for larger, irregular shipments. Importantly, the availability of substantial non-conference tonnage affected, in some measure, the rates charged by conference members.

Governments, national and local, in Brazil and Argentina adversely influenced the activities of shipping companies: harassment by petty officials caused costly delays due to berthing, quarantine and sanitary regulations, the last item important in light of frequent outbreaks of disease in the various ports. Royal Mail complained to the British minister in Rio in 1897 that the inspector in the custom house was 'only occupied in raising obstacles and imposing unjust fines'.

Argentina: Booming Exports

Despite continuing unsettled political and financial conditions and deep depression through the first half of the decade, Argentina entered a period of economic growth that lasted into the early twentieth century. David Rock comments that export prices were around 25 per cent higher between 1895 and 1900 than the average for 1890–95.[15] From 1893 a strict monetary policy was applied by the government

[14] See ibid., pp. 127–33 for details of the development of conferences.

[15] Rock, *Argentina, 1560–1987*, p. 165.

that, with increasing exports and improving commodity prices, led to agreements being reached to pay off foreign debt and the country was able to return to the gold standard.[16] Even so, a 1903 report by the British Chargé d'Affaires in Buenos Aires noted the unexploited potential of the country's agricultural and pastoral resources and cited the weight of taxation as an ongoing obstacle to prosperity. Developing home industries were favoured while high Customs duties inhibited the flow of imports.[17]

The value of exports to Britain multiplied nearly five-fold to £19.1m in 1903, meat and grain shipments being largely responsible, while imports, which initially fell sharply from the 1890 figure of £8.4m, eased upwards to £8.0m in 1903 (see Table 6.2). The process was not easy: crippling foreign debt and low world prices for export goods made the early years very difficult. Rock states that by 1896 the last traces of the depression were gone. In the second half of the decade economic growth was rapid, with export prices, higher by 25 per cent, supporting increased shipments of, mainly, wheat, wool and meat, all of which found ready outlets in international markets. Debt repayment schedules were met and the peso strengthened, all with the benefit of a continued inflow of migrants that enabled vast areas of farmland to be opened up.[18]

However, grain exports in particular were subject to volume and price fluctuations according to harvests in Europe and elsewhere, although low freight rates, constantly commented upon by Royal Mail's directors, combined with strong demand, supported the increases in production. Animal products, hides, tallow and so on continued to be major exports. A trade report in 1902 confirmed that Britain continued to be the country's major export market and source of imports, with Germany and France also significant trading partners and sources of substantial investment capital, although Britain remained the primary source of funds.[19]

Between 1890 and 1892 railways were greatly extended, amounting to nearly 8,000 miles of track. In 1900 the total mileage was 10,281, over 85 per cent owned by British companies, the majority of the rest Argentine-owned with a small involvement by French interests.[20] Work began in Buenos Aires in January 1901 on a new 3,000-mile rail connection with Rosario to connect with the existing narrow-gauge line to the north.

By 1891 the capital had two enclosed docks, Ensenada and Madero, which allowed greatly improved access to port facilities. A directors' minute in June of that year notes receipt of a telegram from the Argentine government decreeing that all steamers must use the docks. Other ports, Rosario and the developing Bahia Blanca in the south of the country, offered improved freight services. Even

---

16 Cortes Conde, 'The growth of the Argentine economy'.

17 *The Times* (London), 15 April 1903.

18 Rock, *Argentina 1560–1987*, pp. 163–5.

19 *The Times* (London), 27 October 1902. Report by the US Minister in Buenos Aires.

20 C. Lewis, 'British Railway Companies and the Argentine Government', in Platt (ed.), *Business Imperialism*, table 415.

so, such was the rate of expansion of agricultural and pastoral production that transport and other trade services were under constant pressure. Britain's heavy involvement in the development of the Argentine' railways and ports continued to drive imports and provided good outward cargoes for British shipping. Export and import figures are shown in Table 6.2.

Table 6.2 British exports to/imports from Brazil and Argentina, 1890–1903 (£m declared value)

	1890	**1895**	**1903**
Brazil			
Exports to Britain	4.4	3.6	6.7
Imports from Britain	7.5	7.3	5.6
Argentina			
Exports to Britain	4.1	9.1	19.1
Imports from Britain	8.4	5.4	8.0

Source: Platt, *Latin America*, pp. 316–18 and 321–3.

The Development of the Meat Trade

A new and most important addition to Argentina's export trade and to Royal Mail's increasingly profitable commitment to its South American services developed strongly in the 1890s. Both the Argentine government and the country's cattle and sheep breeders, with the supply of animals far exceeding local demand, had shown early interest in the development of a frozen meat industry as an economic and profitable alternative to the long-established drying and salting of meat. The production of hides and tallow and other products involved considerable wastage of the carcasses. The shipment of live cattle to Europe was another consideration, as was the production of meat extract and tinned meats. In the early 1880s several freezing plants (*frigorificos*) were established to supply frozen mutton for shipment to Europe, mainly Britain. Following small test shipments by other producers, in 1883 the London-based River Plate Fresh Meat Company shipped 7,571 carcasses of mutton from its Campana plant, initiating the export of small shipments of frozen meat on a commercial scale.[21]

The USA was by far Britain's major source of chilled beef into the early part of the 1900s, with the benefit of only a short sea passage of about 10 days. New Zealand and Australian shipments, necessarily frozen because of the long sea voyage through the tropics, increased significantly during the 1890s. The Argentine beef and mutton products were, at the outset, of inferior quality and not well

[21] Simon G. Hanson, *Argentine Meat and the British Market* (London, 1938), p. 53.

suited to the British market, fetching an appreciably lower price than those from Australia and New Zealand. Moves already well in hand to improve the quality of both sheep and cattle through the importation of British pedigree animals were stepped up. All imports to Britain, including the quality American product, had to contend with the premium prices obtained for top-quality home-produced meat, the supply of which was insufficient to meet increasing demand. Argentine frozen mutton and lamb exports to the UK, by 1900 2.3m carcases, compared well with New Zealand's 3.2m and Australia's 0.9m.[22] Frozen beef shipments also increased progressively from Australasia and from the Argentine.

Much of the capital invested in the early *frigorificos* was British, some of it from long-term residents in Argentina. In addition to the River Plate Fresh Meat Company, in 1886 Hugh Nelson of James Nelson & Sons, a Liverpool firm of cattle salesmen and retail meat outlets, moved to the Argentine and built the Las Palmas meat factory at Zarate, up river from Buenos Aires. The first shipment of frozen meat was in *Ranmoor*, a Lamport & Holt vessel. A steamer, *Spindrift* (3,060 tons), was bought in 1889, renamed *Highland Scot*, and fitted with insulated holds and refrigeration machinery. She was the first of many *Highland* ships owned by what became known as the Nelson Line.

It was usual in the early days for the *frigorificos* to install refrigeration equipment and ship meat to their own account in chartered tonnage. Messrs Turner, Brightman & Co. operated a number of ships chartered to the River Plate Fresh Meat Company and equipped in this way.[23] However, the shippers preferred to contract refrigerated space from independent shipowners. As the trade developed, the shipper would arrange for space to be available on a regular basis, paying for that facility whether or not he had sufficient carcasses to fill it.[24]

Houlder Brothers, which was to remain in the meat trade for very many years, chartered tonnage from 1883 to carry frozen meat and in 1890 built its first ship, *Hornby Grange* (2,356 tons), with 70,000 cubic feet of insulated space.[25] Houston Line operated for the Sansinena Frigorifico from 1884 and, in the same year, carried the first shipment of the many hundreds of thousands of live cattle and sheep shipped to Europe. (In 1890, 643,000 head of cattle were imported into Britain from the Argentine and, in 1895, 1,056,000 sheep.) The trade was terminated by the British government in 1900 because of an outbreak of foot and mouth disease that seriously affected British stocks. It was resumed for a few

---

22 J.T. Critchell and J. Raymond, *A History of the Frozen Meat Trade* (London, 1912), appendix IX, p. 422.

23 Ibid., pp. 140–43.

24 Royal Commission on Food Prices, QQ 6222–6, quoted in Platt, *Business Imperialism*, p. 314. Not all hold space was insulated: a ship was able to carry general cargo outwards in insulated spaces, if required. These spaces were then cleaned and prepared for the refrigerated cargo. Again, homeward bound, unused insulated space was available for general cargo.

25 Bonsor, *South Atlantic Seaway*, p. 329.

months in 1903 before being finally ended when the disease was again identified. Large numbers of live animals continued to be imported into Britain from the USA and Europe.[26] Royal Mail did not participate in the shipment of live animals at any stage: its vessels on the route, passenger carriers with limited deck space, were totally unsuited to the trade.

Most of the frozen meat shipped from the Plate through to the end of the century was lamb or mutton. By 1900 the trade was well established and competing effectively with produce from Australia and New Zealand, although the latter remained Britain's major source of frozen meat. Of the 32 British steamers involved in the Argentine trade in that year, six were owned by the Nelson Line, with Liverpool receiving the great bulk of imports. No Royal Mail vessel was listed.[27] By 1903–04, demand for Argentine beef, by then of improved quality, increased greatly, with exports nearing 100,000 tons in 1904.

The *frigorificos* were extremely profitable in the period, and their shareholders, who included some of the larger cattle producers, received excellent, if volatile, returns. The River Plate Fresh Meat Company increased trading profit from £67,822 in 1901 to £272,475 in 1902, paying dividends of 10 per cent in both years with an additional bonus.[28]

Chilled beef was considered to be a superior product to frozen and could fetch a higher price in a British import market still reliant on supplies from the USA. Shipment of the product was experimented with in the 1890s – *Highland Lassie* carried a shipment of sorts in 1893 – but it was not until the early 1900s that significant quantities reached the British market.[29] *The Times* in 1900 recorded the shipment of a few carcasses of bullocks and sheep from Buenos Aires to Liverpool in a Houlder Brothers' charter, *Southern Cross*, using a system of sterilised air without refrigeration. Although the experiment was claimed to be a success, the system was not developed.[30]

The chilled product (lamb and mutton were always carried frozen) was more expensive to carry, requiring refrigeration machinery capable of controlling and maintaining specific temperatures in the insulated hold spaces with air circulation around the carcasses, which were usually quartered and hung from the ceiling of the chambers rather than the solid stow used for frozen products. This shipment

---

26 Critchell and Raymond, *History of the Frozen Meat Trade*, pp. 75–6.

27 Weddell & Co., *Review of the Frozen Meat Trade, 1900*. The Weddell Company produced annual statistics of meat imports from all sources.

28 Roberto C. Gebhardt, 'The River Plate Meat Industry since c. 1900: Technology, Ownership, International Trade Regimes and Domestic Policy' (PhD Thesis, London School of Economics, 2000), pp. 136–7. Gebhardt notes that Uruguay's first *frigorifico*, the Frigorifico Uruguaya, was established in 1904 with local capital.

29 Weddell & Co., *Review of the Frozen Meat Trade, 1904*. Argentine chilled beef competed unfavourably, initially, with large quantities of American chilled beef and with home-killed beef in the British market.

30 *The Times* (London), 24 July, 7 August, 5 September 1900.

arrangement demanded greater space: frozen meat stowed at approximately 105 cubic feet to the ton while chilled beef occupied from 170 to 200 cubic feet to the ton. As a rule the freight rate for chilled beef was marginally greater per pound than that for frozen, requiring, for the shipper, a higher market price, something subject to supply and demand, in particular the availability of premium-price, home-killed British beef. Even in good conditions the cargo would safely survive for no more than 24/25 days, thereby excluding competition from Australia and New Zealand in the early years, although attempts were made to ship small quantities of chilled meat from about 1895, mostly unsuccessfully.

Critchell and Raymond and others, including Bushell, assert that Royal Mail was involved in the meat trade from 1883 when *Tagus* was fitted with 'refrigeration equipment'. *Tagus* was, indeed, fitted for the carriage of meat, but for provedore purposes only in that year; most other fleet passenger vessels were similarly equipped thereafter. The directors' report for that year noted, quite specifically, that she was fitted with 'a cold air machine and chamber for the better conveyance of Provisions in connection with the victualling of Passengers, and the plan has already met with expressions of approval'.[31]

The evidence regarding the start of Royal Mail's involvement with the refrigerated trade is inconclusive. A press report on the launch of *La Plata* in 1896 refers to 'chambers of 7,700 cubic feet capacity for the conveyance of frozen meat etc.'.[32] Such chambers would have been capable of carrying in the region of 50–60 tons of meat, hardly a commercial operation yet rather more than would be consumed by passengers and crew in the two months taken for the return voyage from and to Southampton. It may well be that small commercial shipments were carried in a number of Company vessels through the late 1880s and into the 1890s, although no mention of this has been found in reports to shareholders. Nor are Company ships listed in Weddell & Co.'s *Reviews* through to the 1900 list of 32 ships engaged in the frozen meat trade.[33]

A directors' minute of January 1898 refers, not specifically in the context of provedore supplies, to the cost of changing the cold air system of refrigeration in the 1890-built *Thames* and *Clyde* and the 1893-built *Nile* and *Danube* to the carbonic anhydride principle. This reference refers, almost certainly, to the installation or updating of provedore machinery to improve the standard of food on the ships following complaints from the Company's agent in Buenos Aires that passengers were deserting Royal Mail ships in favour of French and German lines because of 'bad victualling'.

However, in June of 1900, having completed arrangements with the River Plate Fresh Meat Company for the carriage of small, regular shipments of chilled beef, it was proposed, and agreed, that tenders be invited from refrigeration equipment

---

31 RMSP, Report and Accounts, 31 October 1883.

32 *The Marine Engineer*, 1 July 1896.

33 *Weddell & Co., Review, 1900*. Six of Nelson's *Highland* ships were included in the list. Nicol concurs with this view.

installation firms with a view to drawing up a five-year contract.[34] The directors noted later that the River Plate Company 'will consider using *Severn*, *Ebro* and *Minho* for chilled and frozen meat', although other vessels were outfitted for the trade and it is likely that shipments were made later in that year.

The first firm reference to a Royal Mail ship carrying refrigerated cargo was in 1901: *Danube* is credited with conveying the then largest shipment of chilled beef, 2,976 quarters, from the Plate to Britain for the River Plate Company, which then contracted with Royal Mail for regular space.[35] The contract was arranged by a Company director, later chairman, Thomas Dence, who was also a director of the River Plate Company.[36] The shipment was a modest one and required only a small insulated space. Weddell & Co.'s 1901 *Review of the Frozen Meat Trade* refers to a *Danube* voyage in August 1900 as a test of the possibility of developing a (chilled beef) trade with London, and notes that the experiment 'did not prove to be altogether successful'. It seems clear that there were initial difficulties with the machinery (frosting of the meat was a problem) before the successful 1901 voyage. Whether or not *Danube*'s refrigerated space was by way of a limited one-off experiment is uncertain, but 12 months later, in April 1902, it was reported that 'The Mail steamers on the South American route have been fitted for the conveyance of chilled beef from the River Plate to this country.'[37] The accounts noted that 'Cold Chambers and Refrigeration Engines' were installed at a cost of £42,905.

On 12 February 1902 an agreement was confirmed with the River Plate Company that all insulated space, probably a small proportion of the total cargo capacity at the outset, in four of the five mail steamers would be taken up at 38s 4d per ton of space, with, perhaps, *Magdalena* in addition. In 1903, a further contract was agreed with the River Plate Company for meat shipments to be made in the new cargo steamers, *Parana*, *Pardo* and *Potaro* (about 4,500 tons), which entered service in 1904. They were Royal Mail's first purpose-built refrigerated ships, two of the four holds being insulated, and they had, in addition, accommodation for a large number of migrant passengers. This sequence of events strongly suggests that Royal Mail's interest in the trade dated only from 1900, and that its initial interest was in the carriage of higher freight chilled meat, although the larger P-ships carried both frozen and chilled.

---

[34] Nicol, *Scrapbook*, Directors' Minutes, 30 June 1900, p. 924.

[35] Hanson, *Argentine Meat and the British Market*, p. 83. Nicol, *Scrapbook*, Directors' Minutes, 28 August 1901 refers to a satisfactory report by Captain Dickenson on the loading of this cargo; p. 927.

[36] C. Crossley and R. Greenhill, 'The River Plate Beef Trade', in Platt, *Business Imperialism*, p. 314.

[37] RMSP, Report and Accounts, 30 April 1902. The amount of refrigerated space is not specified but it is highly likely that only a small proportion of the cargo space was thus equipped. The Mail steamers at that time were: *Nile*, *Danube*, *Clyde*, *Thames* and *Magdalena*.

British imports of refrigerated Argentine beef (no separate figure was given for chilled meat) in the five-year period 1896–1900 totalled 40,250 tons, only 5 per cent of total imports. In the following five-year period, 1901–05, chilled imports were 61,500 tons, frozen 293,650 tons, total 355,150 tons, 33 per cent of total meat imports of 1,088,200 tons.

Brazil: Slow Development

The path of the new Brazilian Republican government from 1890 was not a smooth one. Political turmoil continued, culminating in military and naval revolts, the latter in 1893, and labour unrest due, it was said, to the influx of European settlers with socialist ideas.[38] Severe inflation resulted from the collapse of the currency, the value of the milreis falling by 50 per cent between 1889 and 1891. Inevitably, trade was adversely affected. A threatened bombardment of Rio de Janeiro by the navy was prevented by foreign warships anchored in the harbour that threatened to intervene on the grounds that such action would be in contravention of international law. Richard Graham notes that British merchants, already concerned about developing Brazilian/American trade arrangements, expressed unhappiness at the continuing adverse effect of hostilities on business, while the British government pursued an uncertain course of neutrality.[39]

Nevertheless, in the very difficult circumstances new industries developed, mainly in the large centres of population, Rio de Janeiro and São Paulo. Textile and cereal mills were built, as well as breweries, and many factories produced consumer goods, some of them items previously purchased abroad. Imports from Britain fell from £7.5m in 1890 to £5.6m in 1903, in some measure reflecting the confused political and economic state of the country. Despite the adverse figures, 27 per cent of Brazil's import trade was sourced from Britain, roughly twice that from the USA and Germany. Exports to Britain increased in the period from £4.4m to £6.7m, 18 per cent of the total, of which 40 per cent was destined for the USA.[40]

British firms continued to exercise great influence on the Brazilian export–import economy, handling the bulk of the coffee exports as well as owning some of the estates. Its shipping companies largely controlled Brazil's ocean-going trades and British firms continued to be greatly involved in the modernisation and extension

---

38 Ridings, *Business Interest Groups*, p. 274.

39 Graham, *Britain and the Onset of Modernization*, pp. 307–11. Numerous communications between Hugh Wyndham, the British minister in Rio, and the Foreign Office indicate that Britain had four men-of-war in Rio Bay at the time, protecting the interests of traders and some 75 British merchant ships. The Americans had five warships in attendance, protecting 12 merchant ships.

40 *The Times*, 31 August 1903. Report from the British Consul-General in Rio de Janeiro.

programmes of harbours, including Rio, railways and infrastructure. British banks were largely responsible for the country's foreign loans, which totalled £7.4m in 1895, down from £19.8m in 1889.[41] Brazil struggled through the 1890s. The correspondent of *The Times* reported at length in late 1897 on the dire situation of the country. 'The government', he said, 'is quite unable to meet the outstanding liabilities', which totalled over £7m. A funding loan of £10m to the Brazilian government was arranged by London City bankers in 1898: payment to cover debt servicing was over a three-year period and the terms demanded vigorous, and ultimately successful, action by government in order to avoid complete loss of credit.[42]

An Ageing Fleet

In April 1890 Royal Mail's fleet consisted of 23 vessels of 72,762 gross tons, with *Clyde* still building. Nine of them had triple-expansion engines and the four most recent were of steel construction. *Clyde*, delivered during 1890, was the last of the four-ship *Atrato* class, all of them in excess of 5,000 tons and with a service speed of 15 knots. In 1893 two larger and faster ships entered service on the Brazil and Argentine route, affirming the increasing importance of the trade: the twin-funnelled *Nile* and *Danube* (5,900 tons) exceeded 17 knots in trials, nearer to 15 knots in service.

Continental competitors were operating similar tonnage in the period. The French Messageries Maritimes built two 16-knot passenger vessels of over 5,000 tons in 1889 for its Bordeaux service to Brazil and the Plate. Two 6,000-ton vessels were built in 1895–96. North German Lloyd expanded rapidly during the 1890s, building no fewer than 16 vessels for its several trades, including four of just over 5,000 tons for its Bremen to South America service. Pacific Steam, having built no ships through the 1880s, launched five vessels in the 1890s, three of 5,300 tons, for its Liverpool to Valparaiso via Montevideo service. Lamport & Holt, an important competitor in the Argentine/Brazil trades, mainly in the cargo services, built 15 vessels in the 1890s, of which three of over 4,000 tons operated for a time via Brazilian ports to Valparaiso. Lamport was much involved in the transport of live cattle and sheep homeward from the Argentine.

Of Royal Mail's remaining 19 vessels, no fewer than 12 were more than 15 years old, the oldest being *Don* and *Para*, two of the Company's largest vessels, built in 1872 and acquired in 1875. Only four of these elderly ships were disposed of during the decade: *Moselle* was wrecked in 1891; *La Plata* was sold in 1893; and *Tamar* and *Trent* were scrapped in 1897. The directors were much criticised for failing to maintain competitive tonnage on the Company's services through the 1890s. A *Times* report of the 1899 shareholders' meeting records that Chairman

[41] Graham, *Britain and the Onset of Modernization*, table 5 on p. 100.

[42] Cain and Hopkins, *British Imperialism*, p. 265.

Chatfield acknowledged: 'the company has been a good deal hampered in the past few years by their old ships which were now being gradually disposed of'. He offered no comment on the board's failure to act more speedily.[43]

Significant additions to the fleet in 1896 were *La Plata (III)*, *Minho* and *Ebro* (of 3,445 tons), each with greatly more efficient triple-expansion engines. They were built specifically for the non-mail Brazil and Argentine cargo trades, a new development. Each was capable of carrying 4,000 tons of cargo and had accommodation for 135 in first class and 370 migrants. The Company literature gives no hint of the nature of the cargo carried, but it is likely that material was included for the major British harbour, railway and other infrastructure activities of the period. The entry into service of the three cargo ships coincided with severe depression in Brazil, with suspension of the migrant subventions and poor harvests in Argentina. The fact that *La Plata* was sold in 1900 for further trading, and the other ships in 1903, suggests that they were not suited to the service conditions of the time, a major and expensive miscalculation. Three larger vessels were added to the West Indies service in 1898/99. *Tagus* and *Trent* (5,500 tons) were capable of carrying 200 passengers in first class, 30 in second and 250 in third. *Severn*, a cargo ship of 3,760 tons, carried 400 passengers in steerage. In June 1898 a directors' minute recommended that cellular double bottoms, which permitted the speedy loading and discharging of water ballast, be fitted to the new steamers.[44]

An addition to the fleet in 1900 was *Eider* (1,236 tons), a replacement for the venerable *Larne*. She was built for the feeder service between Southampton and Bremen and Hamburg. No prior reference has been found to this connection, so that the date of its introduction is uncertain. A directors' minute dated 7 March 1900 records that orders were given that *Larne* and *Essequibo* should be sold at once and ships chartered to replace them.

The fleet in April 1900 numbered 24 ships of over 1,000 tons for a total of 91,741 tons, with one, *Tyne*, still building. (A directors' minute dated a few days before her launch in April 1900 instructed that she was to be sold if a profit of £10,000 could be obtained. No explanation was given and no suitable offer appears to have been forthcoming. *Tyne* remained in service until sunk in 1917.) No fewer than nine vessels were more than 15 years old. Seven ships were disposed of before 1903, all of them built between 1869 and 1873 and by now trading, most probably, at a loss.

Nine additional ships were built or acquired between 1900 and 1903, the largest, *La Plata*, formerly *Moor* (4,464 tons) built in 1882, was bought in 1901. One source describes her as being painted white for cruising. It is likely that she was employed in that role within the West Indies islands, although the cruises were, strictly speaking, connections with transatlantic services. In that year Royal Mail decided to paint

[43] A Directors' Minute dated 24 June 1891 agrees that the topsail yards on *Trent* and *Tamar*, both built in 1873, be dispensed with. Both survived until 1901, when they were scrapped.

[44] Directors' Minute, 8 June 1898.

all its vessels white with buff funnels, disregarding the inevitable mess (and cost) caused by frequent coaling. Perhaps embarrassingly, by 1903 the fleet reverted to black hulls with salmon-coloured boot topping and white upper structures, although some ships allocated to cruising duties continued to be painted white.

Most of the other new-buildings were small, usually for West Indies service. In 1900 and 1901 the directors' reports noted that some cargo vessels had been chartered, suggestive of trade opportunities not specified. At least one scheduled sailing from London to the West Indies was made by the chartered *Rosneath* in 1900. She was probably a replacement for tonnage in government service in the period of the South African War. In 1902, two cargo ships, *Tamar* and *Teviot* (each 3,700 tons gross), entered the South American service, each with capacity for over 5,000 tons of cargo. These vessels were most probably employed on a new service begun in late 1903 from Newport in South Wales to Rio and Santos in Brazil. The service was extended to include ports in Argentina when, in 1903, agreement was reached with other shipping companies permitting Royal Mail to lift cargo from London.

Debentures Finance New Buildings

Perhaps a measure of the increasing importance of the South American services was the chairman's statement at the annual meeting on 28 April 1892: he advised that, of the passage money increase of £55,000 in the previous year, £39,000 was attributable to the Brazil and Argentine route. (The increase was negated by increased costs of £65,000 due largely to extra mileage run because of yellow fever in Brazil.)

Figure 6.1 *La Plata* (1896). J & M Clarkson Collection

At the same meeting shareholders were advised that two fast steamers, *Nile* and *Danube*, would be built for the service, despite the fact that they, the shareholders, might consider that 'the directors were rather imprudent, in the present state of the Company's affairs, to contract for these steamers'. (Dividend for the year of 1891 was reduced to £3). Chairman Eden Colville, reminding those present that more than £1m had been expended in recent years in updating the fleet, confidently proposed that £150,000 of five-year 4.5 per cent debentures be issued.[45] The proposal was approved at a subsequent extraordinary general meeting and the issue was fully taken up. The 1892 debentures were duly paid off in 1897, as were all bank loans. In giving this information to shareholders at the annual meeting the chairman reassuringly stated that a 'respectable balance' stood to their credit.[46]

The 1890s were certainly difficult years for the South American services: reports referred to continued plague and quarantine regulations, which, unusually, affected ports in Spain and Portugal as well as in Brazil, further upsetting Company schedules and affecting receipts. Reduced outward cargoes with lowered freight rates due, in part, to competition added further to the difficulties and these conditions generally persisted throughout the decade. Brazil's financial situation in the same period was under constant pressure, especially affecting imports, although these increased in the latter years of the decade. Both Brazil and Argentina continued to experience political and financial upheavals with uncertain trading conditions.

In January 1898, an issue of £100,000 10-year 3.5 per cent debentures was made with a further issue of £150,000 at 4 per cent in May 1899. Shareholders were advised that the issue had been made to pay for the new steamer, *Severn*, now due for delivery and, if necessary, further issues would be made.[47] The 1900 accounts show that debentures to a total of £250,000 were in issue. Later in that year a further £100,000 of 4.5 per cent debentures was issued, for a total in the 1901 accounts of £350,000, still well within the total of £500,000 permitted by charter.

Table 6.3 Receipts and disbursements, 1890–1900 (£)

Receipts	1890	1895	1900
Mail contract*	107,603(14%)	106,472(14%)	n/a
Freight	315,430(41%)	253,491(33%)	n/a
Passage money	345,171(45%)	402,469(53%)	n/a
Total	768,204	762,432	868,068**
Disbursements	558,313	554,857	634,218
Operating surplus	209,891	207,575	223,850
Dividend and bonus	4 15s/8%	3.00/5%	3.00/5%
Capital	900,000	900,000	900,000
Debentures	–	150,000	250,000

Source: Reports and Accounts.

* Includes payments for government contracts and postal services.

** Breakdown of receipts no longer given. The total includes contract income for Boer War charters.

45 *The Times* (London), 28 April 1892.

46 *The Times* (London), 29 April 1897.

47 *The Times* (London), 27 October 1898.

The need to borrow such a large sum of money in a three-year period confirms that the requirement for expensive new and larger tonnage to meet a changing competitive situation was being impressed upon a management that was short of capital. The Company's nominal capital remained at £1.5m with, still, £900,000 paid up. This level of available capital was well below that of competitors: Pacific Steam's fully paid-up capital was £1,477,125 in £25 shares, whilst Cunard had £1.6m paid up of £2m and P&O operated with a total of £2.32m in a variety of deferred and preferred stock.[48] Very considerable expense was incurred through the reminder of the decade, from 1896, with the building of two large liners and three cargo ships, all for the South American services. Consistent allocations were made to the repair and renewal, insurance and depreciation accounts: in 1900, £80,000 was set aside against a fleet value of £1.27m, a prudent 6 per cent.

Revenues in the late 1890s were significantly improved, largely by virtue of income from government charters for service during the Boer War. At least five of the Company's larger ships, including *Nile* and *Tagus*, were in use for that purpose, the latter remaining in service for more than two years.[49] Disbursements were similarly increased so that operating surplus, at £223.851, was not exceptional, strongly suggesting that revenues from other sources were disappointing, especially those from freight (see Table 6.3),

Throughout the 1890s the carriage of migrants to, mainly, Brazil became a considerable income source, although it was frequently affected by outbreaks of disease. The Brazilian authorities were, it seems, hard bargainers and the per-person charge varied between £1 and £5 per person, much to management's frustration. The cargo ships involved in the trade, the *La Plata* class, were able to carry 600 migrants and they were were frequently full.

The main interests of shareholders did not change: their investments were made with profit in mind in terms of dividends and share value. The former was consistent, if modest, through the decade. After 1890, when a total of £4 10s dividend was paid, payments of only £3 were made every year, all of it from the insurance account, termed bonuses by the directors. This amounted to a 5 per cent return on capital investment of £60. The share price, however, was alarmingly inconsistent: in January 1890 it touched £73, easing during 1891–92 to nearer to £62 and to £45 in early 1894. There was some recovery, to £50, through to 1900 before it plunged to £28 10s in mid-1903, hardly figures to reassure investors.[50]

Reports, Company and press, of the bi-annual meetings of the period offer little indication of shareholders' attitudes, critical or otherwise, to the performance of the directors through the decade. At the October 1892 meeting there was

---

[48] Details from *The Stock Exchange Year Book*, various issues.

[49] Nicol, *Scrapbook*, Directors' Minutes, 3 January 1900, p. 923. The *Nile* charter was, initially, for three months at 27s 6d per month per gross register ton, £7,600. Details of the contract are not available.

[50] The share values quoted are end-of-year figures from *The Stock Exchange Year Book*.

discussion concerning allocations to the insurance fund and the rate of interest, 4.5 per cent, paid on the debentures issued, considered by some to be excessive. A shareholder raised, yet again, the proposal that the outstanding £40 due on the £100 shares should be cancelled. In the latter part of the decade, with dividends at a modest 5 per cent and further debentures being issued, shareholders questioned expenditure on new tonnage when the Post Office was granting contracts for the West Indies service of no more than five years.

Total receipts improved only marginally in the years to the end of the century, at £778,450 in 1899 and £868,068 in 1900, with the benefit of income from government charters in the period of the Boer War. The charter income balanced reduced passenger revenues in 1899/1900 due to disease in Spain and Portugal as well as in South America. From 1900, no breakdown of receipts was made available to shareholders.

Takeover

Although receipts improved to over £1m in 1902–03, still with the benefit of substantial income from government charters, costs also increased in very difficult trading conditions so that by 1902 the operating surplus was a mere £118,857, no dividend being paid. The figures, shown in Table 6.4, make it clear that without this additional income source the Company's situation by the turn of the century would have been dire. Efforts were made to cut salary and other costs, and to effect redundancies both ashore and afloat.

Table 6.4 Receipts and disbursements, 1900–03 (£)

	1900	1901	**1902**	**1903**
Receipts	868,068	822,731	1,015,414	1,034,320
Disbursements	644,218	663,460	896,557	864,000
Operating surplus	223,850	159,271	118,857	170,320
Dividend + bonus	3.00/5%	1 10s/2.5%	Nil	Nil
Capital	900,000	900,000	900,000	900,000
Debentures*	250,000	350,000	350,000	350,000

Source: Reports and Accounts.

* All debentures were due for repayment on 1 January 1908 or earlier at the option of the Company.

The difficulty in assessing the success, or otherwise, of the South American services remained, in that still no separate accounting information was available within the figures given to shareholders. However, for 1902, at the specific request of a director, individual ship voyage earnings were made available and they make interesting reading. Of the 26 mail-ship sailings to South America in that year, only 13 showed a voyage profit of average £1,000. The losses were largely attributed to *Nile*, which required expensive repairs on two occasions. The balance was a deficit of £9,369. Losses on the West Indies services were £14,160. The following year most South American voyages were profitable, average about £2,000, for a total of £21,901, whilst West Indies sailings showed a total loss of £26,500. Small wonder that no dividend was paid.[51]

Royal Mail, so long established in Buenos Aires and with first-hand knowledge of trade developments, was slow to involve itself in the developing refrigerated meat trade. However, by 1900 experiments with machinery suited to the carriage of chilled meat, a more difficult process than that required for frozen meat, had progressed, as had the Company's relationship with the London-based River Plate Company, which had an office in Southampton.

Frozen meat from Argentina, and from Australia and New Zealand, shipped into Britain in the 1880s and 1890s, as well as small quantities of chilled meat from the USA, was destined for, mainly, Liverpool and London, already well equipped with refrigerated storage facilities. From 1901 Royal Mail was unquestionably at the forefront of the potentially more lucrative, in terms of freight rates and profit potential, chilled meat trade.

A vital factor not to be overlooked when considering Royal Mail's seemingly tardy involvement in the trade was the non-availability, before 1901, of refrigerated storage facilities in Southampton. A 100-year history of Southampton Docks published in 1938 by the then owners, the London and South Western Railway, records that 'the Cold Storage building, the largest in Europe', was opened in 1901–02 as part of the expansion of the docks.[52]

Adding significantly to the problems of the Company was the gloomy trade situation in the West Indies trades, with sugar exports depressed. In the mid-1890s the Jamaican government, in an attempt to boost export trade, invited the Company to consider providing ventilated spaces for the carriage of bananas and other fruit to Britain. After due consideration the directors determined that the trade was 'not considered practicable'. The matter was later reconsidered and in 1901 *Para* was outfitted with a hold equipped with experimental equipment.[53]

The first voyage appears to have been satisfactory, although no details are known of the quantities and condition of the fruit shipped. On the second voyage, when homeward bound, an explosion killed the inventor of the system, Mr Lawton,

---

[51] Nicol, *Scrapbook*, Voyage Accounts, p. 1030.

[52] *The Railway Magazine*, April 1909, p. 296. An undated photograph, presumably taken before the cold store opened, shows a London and South West Railway train of flat-bed trucks, each one carrying two 'road meat vans' capable of carrying 34 beef quarters. The meat was loaded direct from the ship into the canvas-covered vans, which were then hauled to Nine Elms station in London, where the shafts of the vans were reshipped and the vans hauled by horses through the streets to the various markets, arriving three to four hours after dispatch from Southampton.

[53] Nicol, *Scrapbook*, Directors' Minutes, p. 916.

and his two engineers. The directors' reports refer to subsequent repairs to the vessel but there is no further comment at that time regarding the carriage of fruit.

In 1901 Elder Dempster & Co.'s Alfred Jones, with encouragement from the government, which sought an expansion of West Indies trade and hoped to, among other things, increase the price paid to the growers for bananas and other commodities, established the Imperial Direct West India Mail Service Company Ltd sailing between Avonmouth and Jamaica. Jones's company was granted a 10-year contract with an annual subsidy of £40,000. (The contract was not renewed.) Elder Dempster's incursion into Royal Mail territory was, without doubt, a considerable blow. Meantime Royal Mail had, in 1900, retained its West Indies mail contract for five years with an annual subsidy of £80,000. In 1902 the subsidy was increased to £85,000, when a call at Trinidad was introduced.

Others were aware of the Company's vulnerable situation: the directors confirmed on 9 June 1902 that they had been approached by unnamed interested parties who, with acquisition of the Company in mind, required asset valuation details. Whether the initial contact was made by the directors is uncertain. One of the approaches was from Sir Christopher Furness of Furness, Withy & Co., whose interest was in bringing Royal Mail into a consortium to include Cunard, Elder Dempster and Beaver Line. The directors agreed that, subject to government and shareholders' approval, they were prepared to entertain an offer on the basis of the value of assets, which they estimated at £1.92m.[54] Shareholders were advised that negotiations were in hand that might lead to the Company being included in a 'very large and important British Shipping Combination'.

A statuary notice was issued by a group of dissatisfied shareholders calling for a special general meeting. The notice stated that the directors had mismanaged the Company and no longer enjoyed the confidence of the proprietors, citing the depressed share price, £33, and the failure to pay a dividend; they also pointed out that some ships of the fleet were too old and unsuited to purpose. Apparently aware of the terms of the negotiations, they objected to some of the financial arrangements proposed. At the meeting a list of ten potential directors was circulated, one of whom was Owen Cosby Philipps. The Furness negotiations fell through in mid-July when he disputed the valuation.

The directors, who were not without their supporters, argued vigorously that dividends over the past 20 years had averaged 5 per cent and, regarding the charges of the condition of the fleet, that larger and faster ships, including cargo steamers, had been built funded by debenture issues and without any call on the proprietors.

Meantime, Chairman Chatfield met with John Philipps, a successful investment banker influential in City financial and business circles and with considerable railway interests in South America. His views were discussed at board level. Philipps, with his brother, Owen, controlled a small shipping company, King Line, and other related businesses. Together they established, in 1897, the London

---

54 Nicol, *Scrapbook*, Directors' Minutes, p. 929.

Maritime Investment Co. for the purpose of attracting funds for investment in shipping companies; they already controlled shareholdings in Royal Mail.

A measure of their aggressive methods was their attempt in 1901 to take control of the Tyne Steam Shipping Company through their King Line operation with a cash and share offer valued at £180,000. The company was also the subject of interest from Sir Christopher Furness. Owen Philipps and a colleague were, remarkably in the circumstances, appointed to the board of the Tyne company at an early stage, resigning in May of 1902 when their offer was withdrawn, leaving Furness free to acquire the company and the Philipps brothers free to concentrate on Royal Mail.

In late 1902 the Philipps brothers acquired further stock cheaply as Royal Mail's share price fell, placing them in a strong position to effect management changes. John again met with Chairman Chatfield and, shortly thereafter, following a special general meeting on 22 October at which he failed to win shareholders' support, Chatfield resigned, as did another director, A.O. Lumb, Thomas Dence taking the chair.[55] John Philipps then opened negotiations with the directors with a view to, with his brother, taking effective control of the Company.

At an unofficial shareholders' meeting in November John took the chair and urged that changes be made; he claimed 'that life and energy ought to be instilled into the company'. It is clear that at that stage he was the leading protagonist. However, at a special general meeting in January of 1903 Owen Phillips and a King Line colleague, James Head, were elected directors. In February John Philipps travelled out to South America in *Thames* with a letter of introduction to the Company's agents.[56] When Chairman Thomas Dence retired due to ill-health in March, Owen Philipps was appointed chairman with Sir James Ferguson as his deputy. Five of the directors in April 1900 remained on the board in April 1903.

Owen Philipps's first report to shareholders, in April 1903, for 1902, reflected the dynamic changes to come. He indicated that he had already made a visit to South America and met managers and made contact with a great number of people with whom the Company did business. He advised shareholders: 'I believe this Company can be pulled round.' 'But', he added, 'do not be in a hurry.'[57] Plans were already afoot to increase the capital by, among other devices, issuing preference shares and the draft of a supplementary charter for that purpose was made available to shareholders. The charter application was submitted later in the year, by which time the provision of new tonnage was under discussion by the board and operational economies had been effected. Some office and sea staff were made redundant and salaries reduced: a new schedule of captains' salaries resulted in a reduction from £1,000 to £850 per annum. Much more telling was the

---

[55] RMSP, Directors' Minutes, various, and Nicol, *Macqueen's Legacy, Vol. One*, pp. 89–90.

[56] Nicol, *Scrapbook*, Directors' Minute, 28 January 1903.

[57] *Fairplay*, 30 April 1903.

employment of staff to bring up to date arrears of voyage accounts, indicative of poor management controls.

Most commentators are critical of the directors' performance, particularly in the latter years of the 1890s. Nicol observes that 'such initiative as there was largely comprised catch-up measures against the progress of competitors'. An issue of *The Financier* in 1912, which might have been written by the Philipps brothers' press agent, describes the Company as being in 'very low water' in 1902, managed by 'those who had grown grey in the service'.[58] Without doubt, the dividend reductions from the usual £3, a fair percentage on the £60 paid up, to £1 10s in 1901 and the nil payment in 1902 plus the abysmal share price and debt of £350,000 were matters of very considerable shareholder disquiet.

The critics were on fairly solid ground: the performance of Chairman Chatfield and his colleagues had been woeful. Their function was to anticipate and adapt to changing commercial and trading conditions. To their credit they firmly established Royal Mail in the Argentine chilled and frozen meat trade, a vital revenue and profit source over the following half-century. They were, however, over-cautious and slow to appreciate the developing opportunities to establish cargo services in the South American trades. The two 1902 cargo ships were recorded in the April 1903 report as 'profitable additions to the fleet'.

Royal Mail, perhaps evidenced by the number of Royal Navy men employed over the years, regarded itself as a mail and liner company, while appreciating that freight revenues from those liners were essential to profitable operation. The notion of running efficient cargo services, other than the small ships operating around the West Indian islands, was only slowly absorbed, so that, by 1900, the demands of the Brazil cargo service required the chartering of vessels on occasion. The directors' minutes of the period are unhelpful in that they give no indication of management's intentions or concerns; over the years they recorded largely trivia, such as an injury to a man operating a winch, and the like, matters that should have been dealt with at a lower level of management.

But perhaps the most damning indictment was the failure to properly capitalise the Company. The directors yielded still to shareholder pressure not to call in the outstanding £600,000 due on the shares. Funds to meet the costs of badly needed new tonnage in the 1890s were raised by the issue of interest-bearing debentures; the first £150,000 at 4 per cent was largely taken up by shareholders in 1892. A further total of £350,000 was issued between 1898 and 1900 – this at a time when orders were placed for two ships to cost in excess of £150,000 each. The decision to even contemplate a sale of the Company, one of the country's oldest and most reputable businesses, was, surely, an admission of failure.

It should, however, be noted that in the early 1900s Royal Mail was operating a considerable network of steamers, the South American service apart, in the West Indies, connecting the many islands and with calls in Venezuela, Colombia and other Central American ports and through to Colon. From Colon there were

[58] Nicol, *MacQueen's Legacy*, Vol. 1, p. 89; *The Financier*, 24 May 1912.

connections, via the Panama Railroad, with the Pacific Steam Navigation Company vessels to the West Coast of South America, to North Pacific ports and to Japan and China using the Pacific Mail Steam Ship Company.

The Philipps brothers, although their background in the shipping business was modest, viewed Royal Mail's situation as a potentially profitable opportunity. Green and Moss note John's reputation in the City, his disciplined approach to investment and his shrewd appreciation of the benefits of the manipulation of shareholders' voting powers. The brothers, by the end of 1902, completed arrangements to take control of the Company without being obliged to make a formal bid or even a promise to inject fresh capital.[59] This was a form of management new to Royal Mail, and to most other shipping companies. By March 1903, when Owen Philipps became chairman of the board, control by the Phillips brothers was complete and they very quickly imposed their authority on the Company.

[59] Edwin Green and Michael Moss, *A Business of National Importance. The Royal Mail Shipping Group, 1902–1937* (London, 1982), pp. 19–22.

Chapter 7
Focus on South America

The report to shareholders for 1902, 29 April 1903, listed eight directors, with Owen Philipps in the chair and Sir James Ferguson his deputy. New to the board was James Head, a director of the Philipps' King Line, and newly appointed manager, Alfred Williams. Perhaps surprisingly, directors Curtis, Jellicoe, Norton, Savory and Lubbock survived the change in control: or, they had been party to the change-over. Along with the chairman, directors Head and Williams brought useful shipping management experience to the board, something sadly lacking in years past. Messrs Edelman and Dence resigned in early 1903 and were replaced by W.C. Kenny and Alfred Williams, who continued as manager.

The board remained unchanged until, in 1907, Deputy Chairman Ferguson was killed during an earthquake in Jamaica while attending a conference related to the development of trade. He was replaced by Alfred Williams. It is likely that when directors retired in rotation each year they were returned by a shareholder majority controlled by the Philipps brothers and their supporters. The 1910 report recorded the knighthood conferred on the chairman and a new name, James Cameron-Head, appeared on the list of directors. By 1913 no fewer than three general managers were identified in the annual report. Spencer Curtis, a director for 34 years, died in 1913, having retired the previous year, and Captain Jellicoe died in September 1914 at the age of 89, having joined Royal Mail as a midshipman 73 years previously.

Addressing his first meeting as chairman in April 1903, Phillips spoke only in general terms, noting the continuing depression of trade and low freight rates, and commenting that the fleet was not working economically. He then advised shareholders that the directors considered it desirable that the Company obtain further powers to enable it to make alterations to its capital and to issue preference shares. Additionally, authority would be sought to enable the denomination of existing shares to be reduced and a draft supplemental charter was prepared and was available for inspection. The meeting would be required to approve the draft of the supplemental charter. Chairman Phillips certainly began as he intended to continue.

The South American services were, by now, clearly identified as a development and profit opportunity and a focus for significant investment. Six new cargo ships entered service by 1904: three large P-class vessels of over 4,000 tons were ordered within months of Philipps becoming chairman, destined for the Argentine refrigerated and general cargo trade, with advertised sailings out of London, Newport and Hull. Two of the four holds and the 'tween decks were refrigerated. Accommodation for migrants was described as 'comfortable'. Three smaller cargo vessels were available for West Indies and other services with some sailings out of Liverpool. Improvements in trade with South America were reported, with continuing depression in the West Indies.

The first of a series of 10,000-ton passenger/cargo liners, *Aragon*, ordered from Messrs Harland & Wolff, Belfast, in early 1904, was launched in February 1905 for the Brazil and River Plate route and the directors expressed the view that shareholders, in view of steadily increasing trade, would not regret the steps being taken to maintain and develop the Company's connections. They were reminded of the need for increased capital, with additional orders already placed with Harlands for two further mail steamers.[1]

The directors' minutes make it clear that Philipps was very much in charge. Many references, including directors' minutes, indicate that a submission by him to the board was, typically, swiftly approved 'after careful review of the circumstances'. He also appears to have been personally responsible for negotiations with government, the Post Office and other shipping companies. However, there were indications that shareholder support for him was not always 100 per cent: when, in December 1905, Deputy Chairman Ferguson and a Mr Curtis, a shareholder, proposed that Philipps be appointed managing director, Messrs Savory and Norton dissented, seeking postponement of the decision for a month. Regardless, when a vote was taken the proposal was approved, with one vote against and one abstention. The minority opposition may have been of the view that Philipps already exercised sufficient power and that change was too rapid. His developing reputation was endorsed by his appointment as a member of the Royal Commission on Shipping Rings, which sat from 1906 to 1909 and on which he proved to be a knowledgeable and diligent researcher.

Promotion of the Company increased very considerably: agencies in Buenos Aires and Rio de Janeiro were upgraded to Company offices, many new agencies were established across Europe, in South America and in home ports and industrial areas to secure cargo shipments. In 1904, and again in 1905, Phillips visited the West Indies and New York with the intention of extending services to that port and changes were made to the sailing schedules.

New Capital and Firm Direction

A further supplementary Royal Charter, considered by the Philipps brothers a priority, was very quickly sought and granted in July 1904. Its terms spoke volumes for their financial skills and ambitions. Three important changes were made. The first permitted an increase in capital of £600,000, for a total of £2,100,000. However, a public issue of preference shares did not attract support, unsurprising in light of the Company's financial situation, so that Philipps sought to call in the amounts outstanding on the existing ordinary shares. Shareholders were offered the opportunity to cancel progressively the £40 remaining due on the £100 shares

1 Nicol, *Scrapbook*, Report of Directors, 24 May 1905, p. 633.

with payments of £5 on eight dates through to October 1906 towards a preference share. They would then hold one ordinary share of £60 and a non-voting preference share of £40. The changes, while increasing available capital to only £1,500,000, strengthened the situation of ordinary shareholders, such as the Philipps-controlled trusts. The charter confirmed that debentures in issue, at various interest rates, totalled £350,000, due for repayment not later than January 1908.

Changes two and three ensured that the Company remain in British control and that it would be enabled to hold shares or stock in other companies, 'having objects altogether or in part similar to those of the Company'. The concern with overseas financial involvement was triggered by a spate of amalgamations and takeovers in the international shipping industry, the most worrying of which, to the Philipps brothers and to British interests in general, was the recent purchase of the White Star Line and other British companies by the American International Mercantile Marine Co. The charter amendments, drafted within a few months of Philipps's appointment as chairman, reflected the ambitions of the brothers: reorganisation of the Company finances, consolidation of Royal Mail's situation, with especial emphasis on the South America routes and, later, expansion through acquisition.

A significant development was an increasingly close business relationship with William, later Lord, Pirrie, chairman and major shareholder in the Belfast shipyard of Harland & Wolff. He was a man of repute and influence in shipping circles and a shareholder in several major companies. Pirrie, like the Philipps brothers, was something of a 'wheeler-dealer', an ambitious man for whom a key objective was to attract business to his Belfast yard through a series of financial deals. Already well connected with important figures in shipping, he had been instrumental in the creation, in 1902, together with the American J.P. Morgan, of the then controversial International Mercantile Marine (IMM) Co., which sought to create an international shipping conglomerate. Pirrie, a director, successfully encouraged his friend J. Bruce Ismay, chairman of the White Star Line, to join the group. Part of the arrangement with IMM companies was that Harland & Wolff would build new tonnage at cost price in return for all repair work and new orders.

At the same time Harlands acquired a 51 per cent stake in the Hamburg–Amerika Line.[2] Pirrie's experience, combined with the financial skills of the Philipps brothers, forged a formidable partnership that was quickly sealed by a cross-shareholding arrangement between Royal Mail and Harland & Wolff. Pirrie remained a close friend and business partner of Owen Philipps until his death in 1924.

Financial techniques not generally in use in Britain at the time but familiar to the Philipps brothers and to Pirrie were widely used by the threesome. By means of 'pyramiding', a company, say, an investment company, might gain control of an operating company by acquiring 51 per cent of the capital. Yet another investment company might then acquire 51 per cent of the holding company, giving it, for a relatively modest outlay, control of the operating company. Add to this 'leveraging', the use of capital that carried voting rights, against borrowed

---

[2] Green and Moss, *A Business of National Importance*, p. 270.

funds, which did not, and the way was clear for the Philipps brothers to establish a complicated arrangement of cross-shareholdings with associated companies. In time the Phillips controlled Royal Mail through a one-third shareholding while their associated companies held another third.[3]

In 1905 the Post Office withdrew the West Indies transatlantic mail subsidy, using, instead, whatever vessel suited its convenience with payment by weight, an arrangement that had applied to the South American mails for some years. Despite the loss of the mail contract in 1905, the Company maintained its regular services to and within the West Indies at a loss. In 1907 a new 10-year contract for the transatlantic service was agreed, payment by weight, as well as an inter-colonial service 10-year contract with subsidy of £25,000 per annum.

At the 1911 annual meeting the chairman advised shareholders, with a measure of satisfaction, that, following lengthy negotiations with the Post Office, a new six-year agreement had been reached for the transatlantic service with terminus at Trinidad and extensions to Colon, New York, Jamaica and Cuba. The agreement was jointly funded by the British and colonial governments, the subsidy being £63,000 per annum. This contract would prove to be the last subsidised transatlantic mail service to the West Indies. The directors continued to campaign for government support and subsidy towards the costs of the carriage of mail. As late as 1914 the chairman noted that the French government had agreed a £240,000 subsidy to a national company for a service to South America. He recognised that the Post Office was unlikely to follow suit but hoped that, when circumstances improved, the Brazilian and Argentine governments would make some contribution.

The annual report for 1904 spoke of an improved financial position, noting that trade on the South American routes had shown considerable development, with the three new P-ships proving attractive to cargo shippers and migrant passengers, although profit was by no means guaranteed due to port and other delays. Returns for the mail ships in 1903 were modest, most voyages, including those to the West Indies, recording a surplus of £1,000 to £2,000. *Nile* recorded deficits of £3,112 and £6,989 in successive voyages due to machine and crankshaft repairs. Most cargo ships trading to Brazil recorded appreciable losses.[4] The share price during 1903–04 reflected stock market uncertainty: in May 1903 ordinary shares were quoted at £30; in January 1904 they were £29, falling heavily to £18 in November before recovering to £22 in December.

The annual Weddell & Co.'s *Review* for 1904 identified for the first time Royal Mail ships, the three P-class vessels involved in the Argentine chilled/frozen meat trades. They were three of 43 ships listed, most capable of carrying frozen only. Even Royal Mail's older ships, which had been fitted with some refrigerated space, were not yet listed, suggesting that their cargo capacity was strictly limited. The following year a further five of the older ships, some of which had been

[3] Anthony Vice, *Financier at Sea. Lord Kylsant and the Royal Mail* (Braunton, 1985), pp. 16–17.

[4] Nicol, *Scrapbook*, Voyage Accounts, p. 1030.

equipped with additional machinery and insulated spaces, plus *Aragon* were listed as carrying chilled meat.[5]

Chairman Philipps had negotiated a highly competitive, possibly loss-making in the early stages, six-year contract to supply cement and other materials for Brazil's expanding railway network and the new Rio de Janeiro port works.[6] That arrangement was, no doubt, viewed as an investment in the future. In the years through to 1914 cargo ships were frequently chartered. Between 1909 and 1912, 70 voyages were made, mostly southbound to Brazil in its boom period, carrying manufactured goods and coal. Infrequently, refrigerated ships were chartered to carry Argentine meat exports.[7]

Improved revenues were anticipated when *Aragon* entered service with capacity for over 1,000 passengers and substantial cargo space. The reports to shareholders continued positive, with new tonnage, *Araguaya* and *Amazon*, coming on stream, although dock congestion in Buenos Aires and harbour building delays in Rio were proving costly. By 1910, 16 of the 68 ships listed in the *Weddell Review* were owned by Royal Mail. Seventeen of the ships listed were owned by the Liverpool-based Nelson Line.

In early 1906 the directors reported some significant developments. The service from the West Indies to New York was showing encouraging results and refrigeration equipment had been installed in five of the transatlantic steamers for the carriage of fruit. In addition, three vessels had been purchased for West Indies trading.

Rapid Expansion

The Company's first acquisition, in 1906, under the new regime was a 50 per cent holding of the Pacific Steam Navigation Company in the Orient-Pacific Line's Australian mail service, together with its fleet of four ships. No indication was given of the method of funding the purchase – no further shares or debentures were issued – or of the price paid. The service continued to be managed by the Orient Steam Navigation Company, the joint mail contractors, a not entirely satisfactory arrangement. It was acknowledged that the mail contract would expire in 1908 and it was proposed to tender jointly with the Orient Company.

But Phillips's attempt to break into the Australian trade was not a success. There was disagreement between the parties regarding management of the service, and when the contract renewal became due no solution was reached and Royal Mail withdrew, indicating that the requirement to supply new tonnage at considerable cost was unacceptable unless it managed its own segment of the service, with, no doubt, the intention of extending its influence in the sphere. Two of the ships

---

5 Weddell & Co., Review *of the Frozen Meat Trade*, 1904 and 1905.

6 *Fairplay*, various issues, 1903 to 1906.

7 Nicol, *Scrapbook*, Chartered Tonnage, pp. 1034–5.

bought from Pacific Steam were expensively refurbished and new tonnage was planned. It may be said that Philipps met his match in Messrs Anderson and Green of Orient Line. They clearly intended to make the contract their own, something of which Pacific Steam may have been aware when they sold out, and applied for, and got, the mail contract in their own right. The four ex-Pacific Steam ships were retained and allocated to other services, the 1906-built *Asturias* making the final Royal Mail voyage in early 1909.

It was not Philipps's style to take time to assess the success or otherwise of an investment before entering the market again. The acquisition of a complete or a controlling shareholding in a company was frequently the least expensive way to enter a new trade. In 1907 Royal Mail acquired a 50 per cent stake in the Shire Line, which traded from London to the Far East. Four of the Shire ships were bought and a new company formed, in which Royal Mail had a one-third share, to manage the Company's ships and those of the partners. By 1911 the two partners, Jenkins and Company and Thos. & Jno. Brocklebank, had withdrawn, leaving Royal Mail with 100 per cent ownership and with the company's five ships. In 1908 the Forwood Line, which employed two small vessels trading from London to Moroccan ports, was acquired.

In 1910, shortly after the death of Sir Alfred Jones, chairman of Elder Dempster & Co., Phillips advised his fellow directors that Lord Pirrie, already chairman and a shareholder of one of the Elder Dempster companies, had acquired from the executors all the considerable shipping and commercial interests of Elder Dempster. He added that a new company, Elder Dempster and Company Ltd, had been formed that would be entirely owned and managed by them, Pirrie and Phillips, during their lifetimes. A few weeks later, the directors, agreed the purchase of 200,000 £1 ordinary shares. This was a classic example of Philipps's operating style and his massive self-interest.

Green and Moss note that the price paid to the executor was £500,000, with £200,000 in cash, subscribed jointly by Royal Mail and Pirrie, plus £200,000 in debenture stock and £100,000 in preference shares in the new company.[8] The new company then issued ordinary, preference and £10,000 of management shares to a total of £910,000, which, with an additional £1m of debenture stock, gave it capital of £1,910,000 and control of many assets, including six shipping companies with 109 ships, mainly active in West African services.

The Pacific Steam Navigation Company was purchased early in 1910 with its fleet of 37 steamers. Only two years previously agreement had been reached for joint promotion of the interests of the two parties. The directors' minutes record that PSNC had only recently made approaches to Royal Mail to try to agree sailing dates for its new direct service to the River Plate and the west coast of South America, a matter seemingly deferred by the Royal Mail board. Meantime, the chairman negotiated purchase of the PSNC shares at par. Speaking to shareholders some months later, he noted that the imminent completion of the Panama Canal

[8] Green and Moss, *A Business of National Importance*, p. 29.

and the trans-Andean tunnel giving railway connection between Buenos Aires and Valparaiso presented opportunities for greater cooperation between the two companies, with economies including the amalgamation of agencies and other services.

In 1911 Glen Line and Lamport & Holt were acquired and in 1912 the Union-Castle Mail Steamship Company with 44 ships was bought jointly with Elder Dempster & Co. Ltd. In 1913 the whole of the ordinary shares of Nelson Steam Navigation Company and H. & W. Nelson Ltd. were purchased, securing Royal Mail's position in the Brazil and River Plate trades. Nelson Lines, Liverpool based, continued to operate its 17 refrigerated ships of 113,389 tons independently.

The very positive moves to consolidate and develop the South American services from 1905 with the building of five new A-ships in the 1905–07 period were underscored by a determination to secure the lucrative passenger trade, based, in some measure, on the significant numbers of British residents in the Argentine and Brazil employed by banks, railway and other companies. Passenger accommodation and facilities were vastly improved, luxury suites being introduced. The report for 1908 referred to 'high class accommodation ... similar to that of the best modern hotels'. At the same time strenuous efforts were made, through conference agreements, to retain a share of the increasing migrant trade from Iberia, which was clearly profitable, if only marginally so.

In this period, 1906, Chairman Philipps, by now an MP, was indefatigable: in February he negotiated with Harland & Wolff's Pirrie for a further mail ship for the South American service on very favourable terms, with the option of payment over three years rather than two. In June he was authorised by the board to negotiate personally the purchase of two or three ships (two were bought) from the Union-Castle Line for a new Southampton–Cuba–Mexico service and in early August he negotiated with the chairman of the Shire Line the share acquisition. In September he visited Brazil and the River Plate, commenting later, at a shareholders' meeting, that a major difficulty shipowners had to contend with, in both Brazil and Argentina, was inadequate port facilities, which led to congestion and delay at a number of ports, including Rio and Buenos Aires.

Increased Services

In early 1906 the first of the new A-ships, *Aragon*, was regularly scheduled for the fortnightly liner services out of Southampton via Cherbourg. By 1908 five of the A-ships were in service on the route, as well as some of the older vessels; the service advertised out of Southampton via Cherbourg was weekly, although the frequency was subject to change. The cargo services of the three new P-ships were advertised separately in the UK, but their migrant passengers boarded in north Spanish and Portuguese ports (see Table 7.1).

Table 7.1 Sailings Advertised from Southampton, May 1908

Date	Ports of call
15 May	*Asturias*, Vigo, Lisbon, Madeira, Pernambuco, Bahia, Rio de Janeiro, Santos, Montevideo, Buenos Aires
22 May	*Danube*, Coruna, Vigo, Oporto, Lisbon, St Vincent, Pernambuco, Bahia, Rio de Janeiro, Santos, Montevideo, Buenos Aires
29 May	*Amazon*, Vigo, Lisbon, Madeira, Pernambuco, Bahia, Rio de Janeiro, Santos, Montevideo and Buenos Aires

The directors' minutes shed some light on the Company's activities in the South American trades in the period and appear to support the decision to expensively build the new A-ships that consistently returned voyage surpluses less modest repair charges while the older mail ships were less successful and were burdened with higher repair and maintenance costs. The days of the older ships (*Clyde* was built in 1890) were numbered but they were retained pending the completion of further new tonnage in order to maintain the sailing schedules. Examples of their limited per-voyage profitability when compared with new tonnage are shown in Table 7.2. Four of them were offered for sale in early 1910, *Nile* and *Danube* priced at £50,000 each and *Thames* and *Clyde*, £30,000: £150,000 for the lot.

Table 7.2 Brazil/River Plate mail ships voyage profitability

Date	Ship	Profitability (£)
1908	*Aragon*	Surplus 6,641 Less repairs 540
1909	*Asturias*	Surplus 12,824 Less repairs 731
1909	*Clyde*	Surplus 1,224 Less repairs 1,344
1910	*Danube*	Surplus 2,460 Less repairs 1,468

The South American mail steamers returned a trading loss of £9,369 in 1902, a profit of £21,901 in 1903, £49,640 in 1904, £107,345 in 1906 and, in 1907, £115,296 – a solid endorsement of Philipps's strategy.[9]

Increased numbers of cargo services continued to operate from British east and west coast and continental ports to Brazil and Argentina. Company vessels were supplemented by chartered tonnage, some refrigerated. Of six voyages from home ports to Brazil in 1908, only one made a surplus, of £134; the others averaged losses of £500. The services were not regularly scheduled, sailings were made as and when freight offered, or when homeward cargo was discharged and the

9 RMSP, Directors' Minutes, 20 April 1910.

loading of outward cargo was completed. In time the Company's own cargo ships replaced the chartered tonnage, carrying general cargo outwards and returning with cargoes of bagged and bulk grains and other produce. In 1907 direct sailings began to Bahia Blanca in the south of the Argentine. Even the meat ships with their high-freight homeward cargoes were not guaranteed a profit. In mid-1909 *Pardo* showed a voyage surplus of £319 on an exceedingly long, but unexplained, voyage of 124 days. *Parana* returned a modest £1,428 in a slightly shorter time. These figures suggest inordinate port delays and, perhaps, less than satisfactory outward cargoes.

Other Company routes fared equally poorly: the new West Indies to New York service operated by older tonnage, including the four O-ships recently acquired from Pacific Steam, showed deficits in four of six voyages recorded in 1908–09. The Shire Line services to the Far East suffered losses consistently: typically, in 1911 *Pembrokeshire* recorded a deficit of £6,576, with additional repair costs of £718.

Voyage returns certainly indicate that the new ships were profitable. By 1909 five were in service in a fleet totalling 43 vessels of more than 1,000 tons, the majority of which were barely breaking even or were making significant voyage losses. The directors' reports of the period refer to the development of some services and the efficient operation of others, but the likelihood of profit in the period must be remote. The persistent voyage deficits of a large number of the cargo vessels, many of them chartered, employed through a period of difficult trading, are inconsistent with sound operation of the fleet. Yet comments at the annual meetings express no concern and modest dividend payments were made.

Increasingly the competitive demands of the South American service, in addition to passenger comfort and profitable cargo capacity, called for speed. The A-ships were usually designed for service speeds of around 16 knots, whereas French and German companies were building ships capable of 17–18 knots. (Hamburg-Süd's 14,000-ton *Cap Finisterre* made her maiden voyage to Buenos Aires in 1911. She had a service speed of 17 knots.)

Satisfactory Returns

Although there was depression in international shipping from 1904 until 1911, the reports to shareholders were generally upbeat. In 1906 Chairman Philipps advised them that receipts had increased in the year by £250,000 and that the business was steadily expanding, with mail and cargo services to Brazil and the Argentine bringing encouraging results.[10] Working costs, however, were greater due to the increased number of voyages made, some of them unprofitable. A serious and costly problem was delays at Buenos Aires, where trade had expanded well beyond the capacity of the dock facilities. Later in the year Philipps planned to

[10] *The Times* (London), 31 May 1906, Report of Annual Meeting.

visit the Argentine to see for himself how the business was being conducted and what improvements might be appropriate.

Referring to the support foreign governments gave to their steamship lines, he questioned whether the British government should not do more to support British companies in 'the commercial battles they were waging', invoking the name of the king as he did so. This was a theme to which he would return frequently, noting in 1911 that, as a result of German government policies favourable to shipping, two of the three largest shipping companies in the world were German.

Addressing shareholders in 1908, Philipps was able to announce that a dividend of 2.5 per cent would be paid (for 1907), the first for several years, before referring to continuing acute depression and labour unrest. Freight rates remained low. Competition continued fierce from British companies and from German companies in particular. His style when conveying information to shareholders and, as he reminded them, to competitors was invariably confident, if understated, a luxury he enjoyed on the basis of his knowledge of the Company's, and the Group's, true situation. Homeward freight volumes certainly rose in the difficult trading period to 1913, including, meat apart, wool, hides and, from Brazil, cotton, coffee and sugar.

His success in resurrecting Royal Mail was such that by 1912 he was greeted at the annual meeting with cheers. He was by then solidly reputed in the shipping business and a former MP (1906–10). He was appointed vice-chairman of the newly formed Port of London Authority in 1909 and knighted (KCMG) in 1910. He reminded shareholders that just nine years previously he presided over a Company that paid no dividend, set aside insufficient for depreciation and with one shareholder suggesting that the Company should be wound up and the ships sold. Now, he said, the Company was restored to the front rank of shipping companies, financially strong with substantial reserves that now totalled £420,000.

In early 1913 an article in *The Times* addressed rather more fully than usual the Company's remarkable progress in the 1910–12 period as the depression years passed. It noted a recent share price weakness and expressed the view that the report and accounts for 1912 gave no cause for concern, the weakness probably owing more to a reaction to the high share prices then prevailing. The rapid expansion was, it said, amply vindicated by very substantially increased profits, up 73 per cent in the year, from £273,000 to £473,000, only £163,000 in 1910, and a wise moderation in dividend policy: 6 per cent was paid. The value of the fleet increased by more than £2m in the year, to £6,904,553, as the tonnage of companies acquired was taken into account. The newspaper was not entirely uncritical, hinting that the results for the year might well have been better than stated and noting changes in the accounts presentation, resulting in less information for shareholders. Arnold notes that progressively Company accounts provided less information to shareholders about asset investments and obscured the development and use of secret reserves.[11]

In 1914 the chairman advised shareholders that, following two boom years, the shipping trade was in depression, with profits sharply down. Prospects in South America were adverse, both Argentina and Brazil being in crisis. Better news was the strength of the Company's financial situation: the total value of fully paid shares owned by Royal Mail was £4,543,000, which included fully paid holdings in five subsidiaries, the largest an investment valued at £1.5m in the Pacific Steam Navigation Company.[12]

Securing the Refrigerated Trade

A priority for Philipps was the security of the Argentine refrigerated meat trade and the potentially lucrative passenger services. The trade expanded dramatically as the quality of animal stocks improved and the refrigeration equipment became more reliable. Older liner tonnage with small cargo capacity was sold and, to supplement the five A-ships and three P-class cargo ships, five 11,500-ton D-class vessels were added to the fleet in 1911–12.

A formidable force in the trade was the Nelson Line, running out of Liverpool and London with a weekly service. It expanded dramatically in 1910, building seven new *Highland* vessels each with refrigerated capacity for more than 2,000 tons, three times greater than the A-ships and appreciably more than that of the P-ships, as well as space for 2,000 tons of general cargo. Its addition to the Royal Mail portfolio (in 1913) greatly strengthened the Company's situation in the trade. In late 1914 a subsidiary, RMSP Meat Transports Ltd, was formed and five 8,000-ton N-class vessels were ordered, the first two from Swan, Hunter in Newcastle. Building was delayed and it was 1918 before the *Navasota* entered service. These vessels were managed and officered by Royal Mail.

In 1905 British companies controlled two-thirds of Argentine killing and freezing capacity and were making large profits, paying good dividends and expanding the businesses. Two Chicago meat packers were attracted: in 1907 Swift bought a plant at La Plata and two years later the National Packing Company acquired the Argentine-owned La Blanca plant. Competition for the supply of cattle and sheep was fierce, and profitable to the producers of good-quality animals. A directors' minute in 1911 referred to the possibility of a further American company; Armour was mentioned, establishing a plant at La Plata.[13]

---

[11] *The Times* (London), 29 April 1913. A.J. Arnold, 'Privacy or Concealment? The Accounting Practices of Liner Shipping Companies, 1914–1924', *International Journal of Maritime History*, VIII, No. 1 (June 1996), pp. 50–51.

[12] *Shipping World*, 20 May 1914, Report of Annual Meeting.

[13] RMSP, Directors' Minutes, 26 June 1911.

A direct service was established to Bahia Blanca, in the south of the country, a further source of refrigerated produce.

In 1911 a market-sharing agreement was reached whereby the North American companies controlled 41 per cent of the trade, the British accounted for 40 per cent, leaving the Argentine quota at 19 per cent.[14] The agreement, hardly likely to be pleasing to the Argentines, was revised in 1913 and, again, in 1914.

Royal Mail's contract with the River Plate Fresh Meat Company was renewed in 1909, securing employment for the P-boats and then, in 1910, contracts with two other companies, La Blanca and Swift, became available. These required the availability of 10 steamers capable of 12.5 knots in order to maintain a weekly service. In the course of negotiations an agreement was reached with Furness, Withy & Co., which undertook to supply five vessels and maintain a fortnightly service to supplement Royal Mail's fortnightly service. The contract was signed in October and orders were placed with Harland & Wolff for five vessels, the D-class already mentioned, of 11,500 tons, capable of 15 knots, each with refrigerated space for 40,000 frozen carcasses as well as accommodation for nearly 1,000 passengers, mostly migrants.[15]

A further 10-year contract was agreed with Armour & Co. in January of 1914 for weekly shipments of 2,200 tons of meat, which included the 900 tons already contracted with Nelson Line. Loading was to take place at the La Blanca *frigorifico* at La Plata. At that time Royal Mail was operating three refrigerated lighters that loaded meat up river and brought it down to the ship's side in Buenos Aires and La Plata.

Argentine Economy Expands

The Company's passenger ships continued to call at Montevideo north- and southbound with small numbers of passengers and limited mail and cargo. Trade with Uruguay was never greatly significant through the long history of the service and details have not been included in this work. The value of imports from and exports to the east coast of South America increased dramatically in the early years of the 1900s, although, in the case of Brazil, there was a measure of correction after 1910.

A British consular report in 1903 stated that prospects for Argentina had never been more favourable: 'Undisturbed by any serious internal dissensions, freed from all dangers of war with the neighbouring States.' The report then noted that much needed to be done to enable the country to benefit from the improved situation. Given strict financial controls, lower taxation and judicial reforms, 'capital and

---

[14] R. Miller, *Britain and Latin America in the Nineteenth and Twentieth Centuries* (London, 1993), p. 152.

[15] RMSP, Directors' Minutes, 20 July and 10 August 1910; Nicol, *MacQueen's Legacy*, p. 229.

labour will flow into the country and add strength and vitality to the healthy and rapid growth of a rich and flourishing republic'.[16]

And those requirements were largely met as Argentina continued the dramatic expansion of its economy, with exports growing rapidly and the country's finances sound. Immigration increased throughout the early years of the century, up from 112,671 in 1903 to a peak of 379,117 in 1913, balanced by migrants returning home totalling 172,996. At a dinner in London in 1910 celebrating the Argentine centenary, a speaker, commenting on the close political and commercial links between the two countries, noted that the total import–export trade between Britain and Argentina in 1909 was estimated to be £52,000,000 sterling, up from £7,000,000 in 1885.

The continuing vital ingredient for the Argentine economy was heavy foreign investment capital, of which, just before 1914, Britain accounted for 60 per cent, with the French and Germans also involved, the former mainly in railway construction, the latter in the electricity industry.[17] Platt quotes a 1910 estimate of Britain's financial exposure in the country, public issues only, at near to £270m, £187m of that invested in railways, £19m in tramways and the rest in government loans and a wide range of public works. Sixty-seven British joint-stock companies operating in the country were listed on the London Stock Exchange.[18]

In this period four British companies came to dominate the financing and operation of the Argentine railways, having, over the years, acquired lines from local entrepreneurs eager to sell at a profit, and from the Argentine government. The businesses were usually backed by government guarantees, with modest taxation and considerable freedoms regarding the setting of freight and passenger rates, and concessions in terms of the imports of materials required for operations. The influence of the four companies was considerable but that did not protect them from public and political criticism. An attempt was made in 1907, through the Mitre Law, to regularise the situation, but the concessions were still considerable. The ability of the Argentine government to influence necessary investment, improved services and tariffs was strictly limited by the need for foreign investment capital. Nevertheless, total railway mileage increased from 10,281 in 1900 to 20,934 in 1915, nearly 72 per cent of which was British owned, and just over 14 per cent Argentine owned.[19]

The Golden Years, as one commentator described them, of the Anglo-Argentine connection just before 1914 obscured potential longer-term problems. Argentine exports depended increasingly on the UK and its free trade commitment to food imports, although preferences for empire food production sources were emerging. Other markets in Europe and North America were protected. The country's

---

16 Mr Clarke, Chargé d'Affaires at Buenos Aires, reported in *The Times*, 15 April 1903.

17 Rock, *Argentina, 1516–1987*, p. 169.

18 Platt, *Latin America*, pp. 291–2.

19 Lewis, 'British Railway Companies', in Platt, *Business Imperialism*, table p. 415.

balance of payments continued to be dependent on the support of foreign, mainly European, investments.

In the years immediately before the First World War, chilled and frozen meats and other animal products were by far the country's largest export to Britain as the vast pastoral lands were developed and exploited. From 1907, when the American meat-packing companies aggressively entered the South American market, a price war developed that was damaging to British interests and beneficial, in the short term, to the cattle producers. The market expanded: the output of higher-quality chilled beef improved prices to the cattlemen, encouraged continuing product improvement and promoted the growth of mixed farming.[20] Argentine meat came to dominate the British import market, progressively excluding the USA, previously the largest supplier, as that country's export surplus fell. By 1913 Argentina was supplying almost all British imports of chilled beef: of all meats imported, Argentina supplied 82 per cent of beef, frozen and chilled, nearly 30 per cent of total consumption, and 26 per cent of mutton and lamb.[21]

Total imports from Argentina rose from £19.1m in 1903 to a remarkable £42.5m in 1913, of which £14.7m was meat products (see Table 7.3). The country's share of the British grain markets continued to increase, although British Empire sources still dominated, with maize and wheat next in value, at £17.0m.

Imports from Britain also increased substantially over the 10 years from 1903, up from £8.0m to £22.6m in 1913. A consular report in 1908 noted that clothing, agricultural implements, coal and building and railway materials constituted 60 per cent of Britain's total exports to the Argentine, although that share had been reduced by German and other continental imports and those from the USA.

Royal Mail's new management readily identified the potential for expansion and developed a significant market share in the period through to 1914, although, in general, British tonnage entered and cleared in Argentine ports was declining, down from 42 per cent in 1890, 39 per cent in 1900 and 34 per cent in 1910.[22]

The limited depth of water in the River Plate and the approaches to the still inadequate dock facilities in Buenos Aires were a constant source of concern to shipowners, with costly delays commonplace due to congestion and inadequate lighterage facilities. Recognising the potential for continued increases in trade and the need to accommodate larger tonnage, in 1910 the Argentine government contracted a British firm to build a new dock system with greater depth of water alongside berths and in the approaches.

Argentine interests, not surprisingly, sought to share in the lucrative shipping trade. The London-based Argentine Navigation Company (Nicholas Mihanovich) operated in the coastal and river trades, and within a few years would become a subject of interest to Royal Mail.

---

20 Rock, *Argentina, 1516–1987*, p. 171.

21 Platt, *Latin America*, pp. 263–4.

22 S.G. Sturmey, *British Shipping and World Competition* (London, 1962), table 1, p. 23.

Table 7.3 British exports to/imports from Brazil and Argentina, 1903–13 (in £m declared value)

	1903	1906	1910	1913
Brazil				
Exports to Britain	6.7	9.1	17.5	10.0
Imports from Britain	5.6	7.6	16.4	12.5
Argentina				
Exports to Britain	19.1	23.8	29.0	42.5
Imports from Britain	8.0	19.0	19.01	22.6

Source: Platt, *Latin America*, pp. 319 and 323.

Crises in Brazil

Brazil, like Argentina, enjoyed a favourable balance of trade and continued to be largely reliant on foreign capital. It was expanding its railway network and docks and harbours as well as tramways, light and power and manufacturing capability. Much of the capital for these developments, especially railways and public utilities, was British. Investment in British-owned railways, which were generally profitable in the period, more than doubled between 1905 and 1913, to £51.9m, and in public works the 1905 figure of £6.6m increased to £55m in 1913.[23]

In the early years of the decade Britain continued to be the main exporter to Brazil, well ahead of both the USA and Germany combined. Products included cotton yarns, coal, iron and steel and machinery, jute and manufactured goods. New shipping tonnage, and old, from British yards was an increasing export as Brazil developed its own merchant service. However, by 1912 British imports were only about three-quarters of the total of the USA and Germany combined.

Conditions were periodically depressed, with recession in 1907–08, in a difficult period for importers generally due to reduced purchasing power of the country so that import volumes might increase in a period while the value would decrease. Protection afforded to the developing home industries further affected import volumes and values as Brazil's manufacturing capability increased greatly in the years up to 1914. An additional negative factor was that British goods were inclined to be expensive, especially in comparison with German manufactures, which benefited progressively from much-increased migration from that country. As the numbers of German importers increased, so the total of British import–export houses declined.

In 1913 Brazil experienced a second financial crisis and, following intervention by Rothschilds, was again bailed out, this time with a loan of £20m from

---

[23] I. Stone, *The Composition and Distribution of British Investment in Latin America, 1865 to 1913* (New York, 1987).

international sources. Severe conditions were attached with pressure applied by the British government, but, fortunately for the Brazilians, the outbreak of the First World War relieved them of much of the required regulation.[24]

The country's main exports into the early part of the twentieth century continued to be coffee and rubber, the former destined predominantly for the USA, a major consumer, most of it shipped in British vessels. Britain and Germany imported approximately half by value of that country's produce.[25] Although Britain was not a major consumer of coffee, a *Times* survey of British trade with Brazil noted that, of the total of just over 16m bags exported in 1907, British ships carried nearly 7m bags, most of it destined for trans-shipment to continental ports, with 6m bags shipped to Germany.[26] Miller states that Brazil accounted for over 70 per cent of the world's coffee exports just before 1914. Large quantities of rubber, mainly from the Amazon ports where British firms such as Booth Line dominated, were imported into Britain to satisfy the demands of tyre manufacturers, though most of it was re-exported.[27]

Fleet Expansion

At the beginning of 1903 the Company's fleet numbered 23 ships of above 1,000 tons, for a total of 89,160 tons, nine of them 15 or more years old, of which three were built in 1870–72. By April of the following year, *Avon* (1880) and *Para* (1875) had been disposed of, as well as the 1896-built *Ebro* and *Minho*, which were sold for further trading; the fleet consisted of 19 ships of 76,344 tons with seven vessels of approximately 29,278 tons building. Quite apart from the speed with which replacement tonnage was ordered, the fact that six of the seven new vessels were cargo ships was significant. Philipps identified the opportunity to dramatically expand and improve cargo services, and he seized the opportunity, no doubt aware that competitors, in particular the German Hamburg–South America Line, were building larger and faster vessels.

At the annual meeting in 1903 (his first), Chairman Philipps commented, in the context of a query regarding efficient ship operation, that, of the nine passenger steamers built in the past 16 years, only two, unnamed but built in 1900, were fitted with water ballast tanks, a development dated some 30 years previously and in common use since. Some of the mail steamers, he explained, had carried 200 tons of pig iron ballast outwards and homewards, with consequent appreciable loss of freight earnings. Reassuring his audience that he meant no criticism of the Company directors, he made the point that, as a result, revenues would continue to suffer for some time from the fact that the late manager, Admiral Chatfield,

---

24 Cain and Hopkins, *British Imperialism*, p. 267.

25 Consular Report, Rio de Janeiro, reported in *The Times* (London), 31 August 1903.

26 *The Times* (London), 3 December 1909.

27 Miller, *Britain and Latin America*, p. 159.

'with his brilliant naval record, had, unfortunately, not much practical knowledge of the economic working of a modern steamer'.[28] No doubt future vessels were suitably equipped.

The Philipps–Pirrie association was consolidated by the latter's offer to build new tonnage for the Company at cost price in return for all repair work and subsequent contracts. The twin-screw, 16-knot *Aragon* (9,588 tons), built at the Harland & Wolff yard in Belfast, entered service in July 1905 and was followed in 1906–08 by four similar ships of increasing tonnage, the last, *Asturias*, of just over 12,000 tons. She carried 300 passengers in first class, 140 in second and 1,200 in third. These vessels were the forerunners of Royal Mail's fleet of A-ships, which operated the service for many years and enjoyed a deserved reputation for reliability and luxury. Additionally, and importantly, most cargo spaces were refrigerated for the carriage of chilled and frozen meat homewards, as well as being available for general cargo outwards.

In 1909 *Avon* was the first of five A-ships to be equipped with 'wireless telegraphic apparatus' by the Marconi Company. Negotiations took place with Mr Marconi himself: he was able to reassure the directors that wireless stations were planned by the Brazilian government on the island of Fernando Norhona, to the north, and in the vicinity of Rio de Janeiro as well as at Punta del'Este, Uruguay. A complete set of equipment was purchased and installed for £525 per ship, with an additional charge of £200 per annum. Further, Royal Mail was to share monies earned and 'to supply suitable cabin for the apparatus and telegraphist, lodge and feed the operator'.[29]

An important factor in the continuing development of the A-ships was the progressive, if slow, improvement in the harbour facilities and the depth of water in the port of Buenos Aires and its approaches. These changes permitted access to larger vessels: the four new A-class ships built between 1911 and 1914 were of increased tonnage, around 15,000 tons. The first, *Arlanza*, was a triple-screw steamer equipped with the most up-to-date machinery and with superior passenger and cargo facilities.

In 1911–12 a series of five twin-screw, refrigerated D-ships entered service. The ships operated an intermediate, essentially migrant, passenger and cargo service out of Liverpool, a direct challenge to the activities of the Nelson Line, although that company was acquired in 1913. They had accommodation for 98 first-class passengers, 38 in second and 800 in steerage. The first, *Deseado* (11,475 tons), made her maiden voyage in 1912, as did her sister ships, *Demerara* and *Desna.* Within months *Darro* and *Drina* entered service: they were built to the order of Elder Dempster & Co., a subsidiary, although they were intended to be operated exclusively by Royal Mail.

---

[28] *The Financial Times*, 30 April 1903.

[29] Nicol, *Scrapbook*, Internal Memoranda dated 18 November 1908 and 16 June 1909, p. 169.

The financial arrangements whereby vessels were built by subsidiary companies were typical of Philipps, and it is clear that the initial costs were borne by the subsidiary. Directors' minutes dated August and October 1910 confirm that when the decision was made to build the five vessels, two were to be provided by Elder Dempster on the understanding that Royal Mail would take them over at any time, with due notice. Elder Dempster initially sought tenders from Messrs Furness, Withy (ship builders) for the two ships, although Bushell indicates that all five were built by Harland & Wolff. There is no clear indication in the Royal Mail accounts of the financial arrangements between the Company and Elder Dempster, but it does seem likely that the two D-ships were owned by the latter and, most probably, chartered to the Company. (No more than four D-ships were listed in Company accounts through the 1920s.) Elder Dempster, controlled by Phillips and Pirrie, was, no doubt, profitably reimbursed in due course.

A measure of the Company's priorities by 1914 was that all 14 of the largest units of the fleet, nine A-ships and five D-ships, all meat carriers, were built for and employed almost exclusively in the South American services. The annual report dated May 1914 listed a fleet increased to a remarkable 56 ships of over 1,000 tons, including five ships building, two of them, *Alcantara* and *Almanzora*, the largest in the fleet at 15,700 tons. Still operating were several of the older vessels, including *Thames* and *Magdalena* of 1889, by now relegated to West Indies and New York services. *Danube*, 1893, continued in service until 1917, when she made her 107th voyage to South America. A further 27 smaller craft were in service: harbour and cruising tenders, tugs, lighters and so on. Three additional large ships, including *Andes* and *Drina*, were not listed as belonging to Royal Mail at that date as they were nominally owned by subsidiary companies, although operating for Royal Mail. *Andes* was included in the Company fleet list from 1915, moving from the Pacific Steam Navigation Company. The fleet totalled 334,973 tons. When the tonnage of companies affiliated to Royal Mail is added, the total gross was 1.7m tons.

In 1908 *Amazon* began a series of summer cruises to Norway and the Baltic, extended to the Mediterranean when the market was firmly established. A further A-ship, *Arcadian* (8,939 tons, built 1899), formerly PSNC's *Ortona*, was refitted for cruising in 1910 and proved to be very successful. In 1913 Union-Castle's elderly *Dunnotar Castle* (5,824 tons, 1890) was purchased, renamed *Caribbean*, and operated successfully cruising between New York and Bermuda.

Of the remaining ships in the fleet, nine, the largest *Cardiganshire* (9,426 tons, 1913) maintained the Shire Line services to the Far East. She had accommodation for over 1,000 steerage passengers. Other vessels continued the transatlantic and local West Indies services, as well as the connections to Canada and New York and the London–Morocco–Canaries service established in 1908 when the Forwood Line was acquired.

Figure 7.1 *Alcantara* (1914). J & M Clarkson Collection

Further Capital Increases

The presentation of the accounts altered progressively, year on year, so that it became difficult to make comparisons or, indeed, to understand the changes. The voyage profit figure was no longer identified, reverting to the credit side of the balance sheet along with dividend payments, depreciation and, in time, with dividends from other companies. At the annual meeting in 1907 a major shareholder expressed dissatisfaction on the grounds that shareholders had as great a right to full information as the directors. The chairman regretted that 'he [the shareholder] thought it advisable to make the speech he had as the new form of presentation was in the best interests of shareholders', underlining his view that too much detail might be beneficial to competitors. Shareholders and competitors were, no doubt, confused by the stated profit for the year (1910) of £176,823, after depreciation: the figure included dividends on shares in other steamship companies. (The equivalent figure in 1908 was £136,206.)

Clearly, the accounts were baffling to some or most shareholders, although the majority, still hopeful of an improvement in the value of their shares, complied with the directors. The only real indicator of the progress of the Company was now the share price and the dividend payments.

The planned increase in the size of the fleet and the greater usage of chartered tonnage demanded much-increased capital and the issue of substantial debentures. In 1903 the Company's authorised capital remained at £1.5m, of which £900,000 was paid up. The uncalled sum, £600,000, was converted to 5 per cent preference shares so that, by 1906, the total paid-up capital was £1.5n of the authorised £2.1m. Debentures to the value of £350,000 were in issue and they were redeemed in 1907, as required. An issue of £700,000 of 4.5 per cent debenture stock was made in 1907 and a further £300,000 in the following year. A press notice announcing the second issue indicated that the debentures were redeemable after nine years, January 1918, and were made against the Company's property, valued at £3.78m.[30]

Authorised capital remained unchanged until March 1912, when a further supplemental charter increased the limit to £5m, at which time issued capital was £3,000,000, comprising £2,100,000 in ordinary shares and £900,000 in preference shares. In May 1913 ordinary £1 shares were issued in the value of £1.2m, for a total of £3.3m so that by 1914 the value of ordinary shares was £3.3m with additional additional £900,000 prefercnce sharcs for a total issucd capital of £4.2m.

The Company's increasingly strong financial position had enabled it to issue debenture stock totalling, by 1914, £4.2m, so that interest-bearing preference stock and loan capital at £5.1m well exceeded the ordinary share capital of £3.3m, implying, to some influential business people, an unhealthy dependence on loan capital, not an uncommon situation in large companies of the period. Certainly Philipps had his critics: a senior figure in Clan Line, a company that had rejected an approach from him, stressed that his company (Clan Line) would be run on sound business lines: 'it was not like the Owen Philipps' show'. *Fairplay* commented that the method of accounts presentation failed to show the progress made by the company in the previous year: 'it is impossible to see what the directors have set aside for depreciation'.[31]

For 1905, a 5 per cent dividend was paid in respect of the part-payments made on the £40 preference stock and by October 1906 the conversion of all the old ordinary shares to a combination of ordinary and preference was complete. The due 5 per cent was paid from 1906 on the preference shares and, more significantly, a dividend of 2.5 per cent was paid on the ordinary shares for 1907, the first such payment since 1902 and a small measure of the improving situation of the Company. The ordinary dividend payment was maintained, rising steadily to 6 per cent by 1912 and 1913. At that time the directors acknowledged that there had been some criticism of the level of dividend payments but argued that payments had been 'safe' in a rapidly changing financial situation.

Following the 1907 shareholders' meeting, a special meeting was held to discus the remuneration to be paid to the chairman in respect of his additional duties as managing director. After a lengthy discussion it was agreed that he

30 *The Times* (London), 22 October 1908.

31 *Fairplay*, 7 May 1914.

should receive 0.5 per cent on gross receipts in any year when 5 per cent dividend was paid on the ordinary shares and £3,000 in any other year.[32] While it would be 1911 before the 5 per cent dividend payment would be made, it is notable that the accounts for 1907 do not give a figure for gross receipts, reinforcing, in some measure, the concerns of a number of shareholders.

The progress of the ordinary share price from 1904 to 1914 is difficult to track. *The Financial Times* notes the market value of £60 ordinary shares, £60 paid, at £26 in January 1904, £24 the following year and in January 1906 '£85 ordinary paid-up', £48.[33] By January 1907 a £100 ordinary share, fully paid, is quoted at £54 despite the fact that the additional £40 contributed by shareholders was to be towards a 5 per cent preference share. In early 2011 the shares were quoted at £75, and the following year, by which time £300,000 of ordinary shares had been issued, the price quoted was £105, rising to £136 in 1913, before falling dramatically to nearer £100 by the end of the year as trade prospects declined.

Solid Progress

The advent of the Philipps brothers dramatically altered the fortunes of Royal Mail. From a company that appeared to be losing direction and at risk of being taken over, it became, within a very few years, a major player in worldwide shipping. This was a creditable outcome for Owen Philipps, who completed his first 10 years as chairman of Royal Mail in 1913. In that time the fleet had increased from 32 ships of average 3,164 tons for a total 101,257 gross tons to 57 ships of average 5,210 tons for a total of 334,973 gross tons. Ten vessels exceeded 10,000 tons. All were employed in the expanding South American services: seven were A-class passenger liners and five were D-class vessels that operated the important migrant trade from Europe and the homeward refrigerated meat trade from the River Plate.[34]

Transatlantic services to the West Indies continued with vital inter-island connections maintained, some contractual, as well as services to New York. In 1913 a five-year contract for fortnightly services from several ports in the West Indies to the east coast of Canada was agreed with the Canadian government with annual payment of £70,000. The terminal ports were Halifax and St John. Four small passenger/cargo ships with limited refrigerated space were allocated to the service. New to Royal Mail were routes from London to the Far East and to Morocco and the Canary Islands. Northern capitals and Mediterranean cruises were regularly advertised, and winter cruises between New York and Bermuda were popular.

---

[32] *The Times* (London), 16 May 1907.

[33] The figures are taken from film records of the *Financial Times* at the Guildhall Library.

[34] Two additional D-class vessels were in service but, still owned by Elder Dempster, were not included in the Company's list of ships.

By 1913 the Company had controlling interests or holdings in Forwood Bros, Pacific Steam Navigation Co., Shire Line, the Elder Dempster Group, Lamport & Holt, Union-Castle Mail Steamship Co. and Nelson Line. These companies, with the exception of Forwood Bros and Shire Line, operated independently. The acquisitions of H & W Nelson and Lamport & Holt were of special interest as they were considerable competitors on the Brazil/River Plate route. Nelson, in 1910, embarked on a programme to build 10 7,500-ton passenger/refrigerated cargo ships and, in addition to its Liverpool service, to begin sailings from London. No fewer than seven ships entered that service in 1910, three more the following year. Whether or not to counter a perceived threat, Royal Mail ordered its five rather larger D-class vessels before acquiring control of the company in 1913.

Lamport was also active in the Liverpool to River Plate and Brazil trades. Concurrent with acquisition by Royal Mail, it had on order three large passenger/refrigerated cargo vessels. The first of these, *Vandyck*, was briefly chartered to Royal Mail in 1912–13, as was her sister, *Vauban*, before they reverted to Lamport's New York to River Plate service, leaving the homeward meat trade to the new D-ships. Directors' minutes in February 1914 refer to Lamport & Holt building five refrigerated steamers for River Plate service. These were not, in fact, built, presumably due to wartime considerations. In anticipation of the costs, Lamport's capital was increased from £1m to £2m by issue of 500,000 of each of £1 ordinary and preference shares. An example of the Group's developing cross-shareholding practices was the transfer to Royal Mail of 200,000 of the ordinary shares for only 2s paid.[35]

Philipps was an extraordinary man, one of several such in the shipping business in the period. His objective was, quite simply, fame and fortune, perhaps in reverse order. By virtue of energy, nerve, determination and the cooperation of his close associate, William Pirrie, he achieved both, despite concerns by some shareholders who found his methods somewhat risky, if increasingly profitable. No evidence has been found of dissension within the board of directors, whether or not it existed. Despite a dramatic and hugely expensive ship-building and acquisition programme, Phillips's colleagues appear to have been compliant, yielding to his direction, in some cases appearing to give him carte blanche in major negotiations. Vital to the development of the Company was his appreciation of the potential of passenger and cargo services to South America. This move altered the focus of Royal Mail, a trend that was sustained over the next 60 years.

Green describes Phillips as the most prominent exponent of non-voting external finance in shipping of the period. By the end of 1912, paid-up capital was £2.1m, with a further £900,000 of preference shares in issue. Yet debenture stocks totalled £3.5m. One of the Group's bankers is said to have complained that the Company's expansion relied 'too much on borrowed capital and too little on their own capital'.[36]

---

35 RMSP, Directors' Minutes, 25 February 1914 and 15 July 1914.

36 E. Green, 'Ownership and Finance in British Shipping', in *Business History of Shipping. Strategy and Structure* (Tokyo, 1985).

Chapter 8
The First World War and its Aftermath

Most directors remained with the Company through the years of recovery. Chairman Philipps, knighted in 1909, was now Sir Owen Philipps, KCMG. Captain Jellicoe died in September 1914, aged 89, after 73 years in the Company's service. William Kenny retired in 1918 and Deputy Chairman Alfred Williams died in the same year. He was replaced as deputy to the chairman by Sir Joseph Savory. New to the board by 1919 were the Duke of Abercorn and Herbert Wright.

In early 1914 Royal Mail, in addition to its South American services, continued to operate transatlantic steamers on its mail routes to the West Indies. Two new 8,489-ton liners were on order, *Essequibo* and *Ebro*, each capable of carrying 250 passengers in both first and third class. The former made her maiden voyage to South America later in the year, *Ebro* following a few months later. Within months both were in government service. Smaller vessels still operated between the islands. A five-year contract with an annual payment of £70,000 for a fortnightly service from the West Indies to Canada, Halifax and St John was inaugurated in 1913: four steamers with passenger accommodation for nearly 200 and cargo capacity, some refrigerated, of roughly 5,000 tons. The West Indies–New York service was maintained, as were those services to the Far East and Morocco/Canary Islands.

Conflict with Germany had been anticipated for some time and limited plans were in place to deal with an emergency. The government had made it clear to shipping companies that at the outbreak of war it was of great importance to maintain regular services, especially those bringing foodstuffs into the country.[1] The immediate disruption to all forms of business and the danger of enemy warships at sea inevitably caused problems for British and allied shipping. Ports were congested, outward sailings were suspended for some weeks and several Royal Mail ships were held in foreign ports for long periods, awaiting permission to sail. A further blow to the Company was the closure for naval purposes, for the period of the war, of the port of Southampton, its main terminus and base for stores and ship repairs and the takeover by the War Office of its offices and premises.

The government determined to requisition ships required for naval and military service, rather than charter them, and a proclamation on 3 August 1914 enforced that decision. The ships were paid for at rates recommended by the Admiralty Transport Arbitration Board, which included leading shipowners, the so-called Blue Book rates, which were based on freight rates prevailing in the years immediately before 1914, most of them depressed, 1913 apart. These rates,

---

[1] RMSP, Directors' Minutes, 5 August 1914.

usually paid monthly and based on the vessel's gross tonnage, varied according to the type and size of vessel. They might be paid for a short period or, in the case of naval/military usage, for longer.[2] The payments appeared at the time to be generous and vessels were readily made available to the Admiralty. The rates were significantly improved only in May 1918, but they remained low in comparison with free market rates through the period of the war.

The shipowner was required to ensure that his requisitioned vessels were available in sea-worthy condition, to pay crew wages and costs, and arrange insurance cover. The government was responsible for fuel, wage increases for crew and additional insurance through the War Risks Assurance scheme, which guaranteed 100 per cent coverage for losses by the shipowner. By 1916 no fewer than 22 Royal Mail ships were in government service, with an additional nine under requisition to the Board of Trade. These included, not surprisingly, four of the five refrigerated D-ships.[3]

War Service and Losses

The outbreak of the war had an immediate effect on Royal Mail's services. Ten vessels were requisitioned during the first month. These were, in the main, the larger liners, which were used as hospital ships and troop carriers. A considerable number of officers and crew were men of the Royal Naval Reserve and they were immediately mobilised for naval service, some ships losing their entire complement of officers. Within days *Asturias* and *Drina* were fitted out in Southampton as hospital ships, although *Drina* soon reverted to her equally important role as a refrigerated cargo carrier. Two smaller cargo vessels were retained as store ships. Two passenger ships, *Arcadian* and *Caribbean*, were chartered briefly to the Canadian government as troop transports.

Seven ships, including *Arlanza* and the nearly new or just-built *Alcantara*, *Andes*, *Almanzora* and *Ebro*, were, over the next few months, fitted out as armed merchant cruisers, with eight 4-inch, later 6-inch guns, and depth charges. Five of them joined the Tenth Cruiser Squadron, which consisted of 24 merchant ships, which maintained patrols in the area between the Shetlands and the Norwegian coast to intercept neutral vessels suspected of carrying contraband into Europe.

---

[2] J.A. Salter, *Allied Shipping Control. An Experiment in International Administration* (Oxford, 1923). The monthly rates, which varied as the speed of the vessel were, initially:

Armed Merchant Cruisers – 25s (22 knots and over) to 20s (under 18 knots) per gross ton

Troopships – 13s 6d (under 12 knots) to 17s 6d (15–17knots) per gross ton

Cargo liners – 12s 3d to 15s 3d per gross ton less 6d after two months' service

Tramps – 9s 6d for over 5,000 tons dwt to 12s for smaller vessels less, 1s after two months' service.

[3] RMSP, Directors' Minutes, separate sheet attached dated February 1915.

The elderly *Oratova* and *Caribbean*, both built in 1889, also joined the Squadron, although they were soon found to be unsuited to the severe weather conditions frequently found in the area. *Caribbean* suffered persistent steering breakdowns. Nearing the end of their useful service, both were withdrawn and sold in 1915, *Caribbean* to the government for further trooping duties. The Squadron was disbanded in 1917 and the remaining ships were employed as convoy escorts. Further vessels were requisitioned as transports and for the carriage of vital supplies. Three of the Company's oldest vessels, *Magdalena* (1889) and *Tagus* and *Trent* (both built in 1899), gave sterling service, *Tagus* as a hospital ship. *Trent* was outfitted as a monitor depot ship and was involved in the 1915 sinking of the German commerce raider *Königsberg* on the East African coast.

In May 1915 all the refrigerated space in Company ships was requisitioned so that practically the whole of the insulated space of British ships was under government control. For Royal Mail this meant that a very significant proportion of the Company's tonnage was under requisition and, as a result, it was unable to take advantage of the high freight rates available at the time, caused, in part, by that very requisition policy.

Regular services from Liverpool were still, surprisingly, being advertised in August 1916. A notice in *The Times* listed weekly sailing dates from Liverpool for South America of *Amazon*, *Deseado* and *Darro*. By the following year, as the danger from submarines increased, publication ceased. *Amazon* was, nevertheless, torpedoed and sunk by a submarine off the coast of Northern Ireland in March 1918 when outward bound from Liverpool.

Thirteen Company vessels were sunk during the war in various forms of action, including eight ships torpedoed between March 1917 and May 1918 as the unrestricted U-boat campaign got under way. Notable was the sinking of *Alcantara* in February 1916, in a close-fought gun action against the German raider *Grief* while on blockade patrol off the Norwegian coast. Both ships sank: loss of life in *Alcantara* was 68 officers and crew. Other A-ships lost were *Asturias*, torpedoed while a hospital ship, and *Aragon*. *Asturias* was refloated and, as a constructive total loss, ownership devolved on the government. She was repurchased in 1919 and extensively refitted, returning to service in 1923 as the cruise liner *Arcadian*. *Aragon* was torpedoed and sunk outside Alexandria harbour in 1917 with the loss of more than 600 of the 2,700 on board.

A particularly unfortunate incident was the sinking in 1917 by *Darro* of Elder Dempster's small troopship *Mendi* (4,230 tons gross), when the latter was off the Isle of Wight en route from Plymouth to Le Havre with units of the South African Native Labour Contingent on board. In thick fog the two collided and *Mendi* sank in 20 minutes with the loss of 29 crewmen and 607 officers and men of the Labour Battalion.[4]

Forty-two ships of over 1,000 tons were listed in the annual report for 1918, dated 4 June 1919, including five A-ships and four D-ships. (*Drina*, though

---

[4] *Isle of Wight County Press*, 21 February 1992.

operating for Royal Mail, did not appear in the list of ships that accompanied the accounts through to the end of the 1920s.) The 1918 report noted that a number of Company vessels were in the process of being released by the government, mainly cargo ships. The majority of the large passenger vessels remained under requisition, so that the mail and passenger services to South America were not yet re-established. Nevertheless, every attempt was made to resume regular sailings where possible: *The Times* of 1 January 1919 carried an advertisement for weekly sailings from Liverpool to Brazil and the Plate by four D-ships and most other companies advertised resumed, if limited, services.

Several of the Shire boats, built for the Far Eastern service, traded to South America in the war years, mainly to Brazil, occasionally to Buenos Aires. *Brecknockshire*, en route to Brazil on her maiden voyage in 1917 with a cargo of coal, was captured when approaching Rio de Janeiro by the German raider *Moewe* and sunk.

Replacement of lost tonnage was dealt with in the short term in an unusual fashion. Chairman Philipps, in association with Lord Inchcape, chairman of the Peninsular & Oriental Company, made an offer in early 1919 to take over the 137 standard-built, war-loss replacement vessels (totalling 1.4m tons) being built for the government and now superfluous to requirements, at cost of £20m. The intention was to sell them to British owners to ensure that they would not be sold cheaply to foreign competitors. Most owners proved to be reluctant to buy, and Chairman Philipps, with what Bushell described as 'great magnanimity' (so far as the national interest was concerned), agreed to take over 77 of the vessels at total cost of £15,248,141 and disperse them throughout the Group.[5] The price of £39 per gross ton was well below the currently quoted price of £50 per ton for new vessels of similar design and they were economic to operate. Fourteen entered service with Royal Mail, others passing to associated companies; Elder Dempster acquired 24 vessels.[6] Peter Davies, commenting on what he describes as 'Phillips' blind faith in the future', acknowledges that had he, Philipps, not been prepared to acquire capacity at the earliest possible moment, his companies would have been unable to fulfil all their obligations and this could have opened many trades to foreign competition.[7]

The cargo ships *Segura* and *Severn* (each of 5,260 gross tons), built respectively as *War Swift* and *War Pansy*, were handed over by the builders in early 1920. A total of eight of these standard-B design ships entered service with Royal Mail in that year, all with S-names. They served the Company well: seven of them were still in service at the outbreak of the Second World War and all were lost to enemy action by 1943. Seven further standard-built refrigerated N-class ships of more than 8,000 tons were acquired by RMSP Meat Transports between 1918

5 Bushell, *Royal Mail*, p. 222.

6 Green and Moss, *A Business of National Importance*, pp. 45–6.

7 Peter N. Davies, *The Trade Makers: Elder Dempster in West Africa, 1852–1972, 1973–1989* (London, 1973), p. 180.

and 1920. *Navasota* began trading to South America in 1918. Five were still in service in 1939, two having been previously sold. All were sunk by enemy action between 1939 and 1944. Two additional large cargo ships were given 'Shire' names. One, *Glamorganshire*, was a C-type vessel capable of carrying over 11,000 tons of cargo. She was built in Japan as *War Armour*. Both made their maiden voyages to Brazil in 1919 and subsequently operated on a variety of routes, sometimes on charter. Simultaneously Chairman Philipps, in conjunction with Harland & Wolff's Pirrie, planned a massive rebuilding programme for the Group companies, many of the ships being built in Group-owned yards, in order to ensure that their slips remained occupied and that prices were competitive.

The first indication of Royal Mail's resumption of service out of Southampton is a note in Company records of the sailing of Pacific Steam's newly built *Orbita* in late September 1919 for Brazil and the River Plate. She appears to have made one or two voyages to the Plate pending the refitting of the Company's A-ships. The annual report for 1920 listed 51 ships of over 1,000 gross tons for a total of 326,246 tons. The total for fleets affiliated with Royal Mail was in excess of 2,000,000 gross tons.

A Profitable Period

Freight rates continued depressed through 1914, due, at least in part, to the overbuilding of tonnage in the years immediately prior. Royal Mail's profits plummeted and the directors were obliged to advise shareholders that profits were not sufficient to pay a dividend on the ordinary shares for the year, the preference share dividend being met by a transfer from the reserve fund.

From 1915 things changed: freight markets reflected a demand for tonnage in excess of that available, so that rates rose, due, at least in part, to the government's requisition policy and to ship losses due to enemy action. Shipowners whose vessels were requisitioned were less than happy to be tied to the Blue Book: in general, the rates available on the open market were by now well in excess of those. An article in *The Economist* in May 1915 stated that the shipowner who suffered requisition on a disproportionate part of his fleet was deserving of some sympathy, although the Admiralty was endeavouring to spread the load evenly.

The Company's business was severely affected, as were all others, by the wartime circumstances. Exports virtually ceased in the first year or two of the war, although freight rates improved from 1915. Chairman Philipps grumbled in his reports that the Company was unable to benefit 'beyond a very limited extent' because its considerable refrigerated cargo space was under requisition by the Board of Trade at fixed rates. He did concede, however, that the loss of passenger revenues was made good by improved freight earnings, in part due to improved rates paid by the government, a fact confirmed by the increase of declared profit from £98,232 in 1914 to a staggering £808,731 in 1915, a figure nearly twice that of 1913, and the resumption of ordinary dividend payments (see Table 8.1).

His comments during the period tended to be of a negative nature, giving to shareholders only the barest of information, consistent, perhaps, with his prior stated intention to give nothing away to the opposition – in the best interests of shareholders. In 1915, following the poor results in 1914, the financial press and shareholders continued to press for a fuller account of the Company's income, which included dividends from shares held in steamship and other companies.

Reports dwelt on the downside, the higher operational and War Risks Insurance costs, with little reference to the substantially increased freight rates, and charter income and ship loss insurance payments. The Company's cargo ships were, without doubt, benefiting from the dramatically improved freight rates. An article in *The Shipping World* in early 1916 noted that 'It [1915] has no parallel in the history of shipping. Freights reached a level undreamt of by the most sanguine, and values rose to an enormous height, which puts all previous booms entirely in the shade.' This was at a time when criticism of the excessive profits made by shipowners was commonplace, resulting in the introduction in 1916 of an Excess Profits Duty, a 40 per cent charge on profits, settlement to be made after the war or, in some circumstances, deferred or waived entirely. (The rate was increased to 60 per cent in March 1920 as freight rates continued to rise.)

From 1916 revenues rose from £335,840 to over £1m by 1920, while profits increased in the same period from £791,097 to £837,653. Large reserves were accumulated by Royal Mail and other Group companies by virtue of transfers from profit, made easier by the complicated cross-shareholding arrangements. A function of the reserves was to meet any post-war charges made by government through its 1916 Excess Profits Duty. The Treasury and Revenue had powers to waive the duty if funds set aside were used to finance capital projects, and it seems likely that Group companies transferred considerable sums to Harland & Wolff's major extension work and to new acquisitions.[8] By 1920 the reserves shown in Royal Mail's published accounts totalled £1.6m.

Another potential source of profit was the great increase in the value of tonnage, so that the value of assets was way in excess of the balance sheet entry, if still appreciably less than the cost of new tonnage, a very considerable concern for the shipowner. Profit was also to be made on ships sunk: Ronald Hope cites compensation received by the British India Company of over £100,000 for two 5,000-ton 27-year-old vessels that were sunk in 1916, although they had been written off in the company's books.[9]

---

[8] Green and Moss, *A Business of National Importance*, p. 37.

[9] Hope, *A New History*, p. 351.

Table 8.1 Revenues, profits and capital, 1914–20

	Revenue. freight/mail (£)	Profit on year (£)*	Ordinary dividend (%)	Capital auth'd and issued (£000)**	Value of fleet and investments (£)
1914	358,945	98,232	Nil	5,000 4,200	10,269,153
1915	827,652	808,731	6	5,000 4,200	10,161,116
1916	335,840	791,097	7	5,000 5,000	10,364,950
1917	475,949	764,446	7	6,500 5,000	10,437,902
1918	579,400	706,472	7	6,500 5,000	8,914,812
1919	842,462	953,600	8	6,500 5,000	11,214,793
1920	1,053,591	837,653	7	25,000 6,800	15,966,960

Source: Reports and Accounts.

* Profit figures quoted were published in a share offer document in June 1920. They differ from the figures quoted in the Annual Reports in that they are somewhat larger.

** Issued capital figure shown does not include items such as insurance and reserve funds, which were added in the accounts of the period.

Share/debenture offers: 21 February 1914, £700,000, 5% debentures; 14 November 1914, £750,000, 5% debentures; 11 March 1916, £800,000 ordinary stock, in proportion to holdings of ordinary and preference shareholders; 3 June 1920, £4,100,000 ordinary and £900,000 preference stock.

The directors' minutes for the period give some indication of earnings in the early war years. They show a surplus/deficit figure on a small number of commercial voyages with repair charges, where appropriate. The figures give only a crude indication of profit/loss per voyage, although whether charter/requisition charges were included is uncertain, if likely. They tell us no more than that only some voyages were profitable; deficits were more usual in the cases of the older vessels. For example, *Asturias*, May 1914: Surplus £8,017 less repairs, £972: + £7,045; *Demerara*, June 1914: Deficit £2,271 less repairs, £1,843: –£4,114.

By 1916 there was a general improvement in the figures. Two Brazil/River Plate cargo voyages yielded remarkable surpluses: *Denbighshire*: Surplus £33,015, no recorded charge for repairs; *Carmarthenshire*: Surplus £54,905 (a 102-day voyage). In the same year figures were given for some of the armed merchant cruisers: *Almanzora:* Surplus £19,270; *Ebro:* Surplus £10,320.

The level of authorised capital rose dramatically in the wartime period and immediately afterwards, from £5m to £6.5m in 1917, with £5m paid up, to £25m in 1920, the report for that year recording that shares to the value of £6.8m were in issue. A document dated just a few days after the annual meeting indicated the intention to increase paid-up capital to £11m with the immediate offer of £900,000 in ordinary shares at £110 and £900,000 of cumulative preference stock. In the same period debentures increased from £4.2m to £4.5m, £450,000 of 5 per cent stock having been cancelled in 1916. In 1916, £800,000 of ordinary stock was offered to existing ordinary and preference shareholders to fund the building of the four refrigerated steamers for the newly established subsidiary RMSP Meat Transports Ltd, it being considered preferable to fund the vessels in this way, rather than to issue debentures, 'in view of present conditions'.[10]

It is likely that the dramatic capital increases were defensive: shipping companies found that the value of tonnage, especially from 1917 when very high losses were incurred, greatly increased, as did the earning power of the assets. This heightened the risk of takeover; hence the increase in the level of authorised and issued capital by Royal Mail between 1917 and 1920. Most of the shares thus distributed were sold to Group companies usually in exchange for new shares in other Group companies. The 1920 offer of £900,000 ordinary shares was priced above par, at £110, the balance of £10 then being credited to the reserve account.[11]

Further acquisitions were made: in 1916 Royal Mail acquired an interest in Moss Steamship Company Ltd and Robert MacAndrew and Co. Ltd, both with interests in routes to the Mediterranean. In 1917 Coast Lines Ltd was formed following the purchase of most of the capital of Powell, Bacon and Hough Lines, Ltd for £800,000. Coast Lines developed into a mini-conglomerate, adding to its fleet, by 1919, a number of other small coastal companies that supplied connections with the Continent and between the country's smaller ports and the main overseas shipping outlets. The following year, along with French and Italian companies, a substantial holding was purchased in the Argentine Navigation Company, which had a large number of small vessels, including tugs operating on the Rivers Plate and Parana. In 1919 the whole of the shares in David McIver, Sons & Co., a long-established cargo line serving Buenos Aires and Rosario out of London, were acquired.

[10] Offer Notice dated 11 March 1916 attached to the Report to Shareholders held in the Guildhall Library. Other notices have referred to mortgages, Government Trade Facilities loans and so on. The method of funding may well have been adjusted at some stage.

[11] Green and Moss, *A Business of National Importance*, p. 37.

Trade with South America

Argentina and Brazil suffered severely in the early war years. Rory Miller notes that 'The outbreak of war in August of 1914 brought a temporary but almost total collapse of the financial and commercial infrastructures of Latin America.' Trade was brought to a virtual standstill for some weeks as shipping was reallocated under British government control to a wartime footing. Imports to both countries from Britain and other European countries were, for a time, prohibited and, although matters improved by 1915, the shortages were only partly remedied by supplies from the USA. Exports were restricted by the uncertain availability of tonnage due to European government requirements. Direct investment from Europe ceased as new capital issues were suspended and banks sought to call in outstanding loans, causing crises in both Argentina and Brazil.

British policies during the war caused a measure of resentment in some South American countries, not least Argentina: among them was the imposition of the so-called Black List of well-established German firms with which trading was prohibited. This was seen by some, quite reasonably, as infringing the sovereignty of those countries. A secondary intention of the Black List appears to have been an attempt to make it difficult or impossible for Germany to resume its considerable trade with South America after the war.

As the war progressed, British influence in the commerce of Brazil and Argentina increased as government agencies began to purchase large quantities of supplies for its allies by contract, thereby controlling supply and price. By 1916, 80 per cent of Argentine frozen meat exports were subject to contract. Producers of goods not considered essential, such as coffee, suffered due to the shortage of shipping.[12]

The USA, neutral until 1917, benefited greatly from the severe wartime limitations on trade with Europe, expanding into South America its already considerable involvements with the Caribbean and Central America. It became the most important import–export partner for many South American countries and increasingly the source of investment capital. US banks, prevented by law from investing in foreign subsidiaries before 1914, began to set up branches throughout South America.[13]

Argentina remained neutral throughout the conflict, a status somewhat at odds with its huge reliance on British capital (still 60 per cent of the total foreign investments in 1914) and Britain's share in the country's vital export and import markets. The country's political situation remained unstable, in part due to the effects of wartime conditions: national elections in 1916 brought narrow victory for the Radical Party of Hipolite Yrigoyen, who became president. Strikes,

---

[12] Miller, *Britain and Latin America*, pp. 180–83.

[13] V. Bulmer-Thomas, 'The Latin American Economies, 1929–1929', in L. Bethell (ed.), *The Cambridge History of Latin America, Vol. VI, Part I, 1930 to the Present* (Cambridge University Press, 1994).

including one in the port of Buenos Aires for improved wages and working conditions from late 1916, resulted in military intervention in 1918 and charges were made by influential British business interests of pro-German government sympathies.[14] Those British interests were themselves under pressure: there was increasing public resentment of, in particular, the dominant position of the four railway companies, whose fares, services and freight rates were considered to be unsatisfactory.

There may have been grounds for the charge of pro-German sympathies, although there is little concrete evidence. In 1916 *The Times*, commenting on the remarkable expansion of Argentina's export trade in 1915, noted the large shipments destined for Scandinavian ports and suspected of being traded to Germany: in a single month 20 steamers left Argentine ports destined for Scandinavia with nearly 100,000 tons of maize.[15] Roger Gravil comments that Holland, Denmark and Sweden, previously insignificant markets, shipped nearly 860,000 tons of maize in the first 10 months of 1915, most of it almost certainly destined for Germany. (Two German firms, Bunge & Born and Hardy & Muhlencamp, handled 30 per cent of grain exports from Argentina.)[16] In the same year German businesses, determined to retain their considerable interests in the Argentine, were active in Buenos Aires, establishing a German–Austrian Chamber of Commerce and actively promoting it.

The Argentine grain harvests of 1913–14 failed just as world cereal and meat prices collapsed. The economy was in depression by 1915, due, in part, to an increase in interest rates by the Bank of England, which prompted an outflow of capital from the country. There was concern to ensure that interest payments on British capital were maintained and a loan from the USA, in early 1915, of $3m at 7 per cent, described as 'somewhat onerous', was followed within months by a further loan of $2.5m.[17] Soon, however, demand for vital food supplies for Europe ensured that shipping tonnage was made available for the carriage of, especially, frozen and tinned meats, and export volumes and prices rose.

Imports from Britain, especially coal, and other European countries were severely affected in 1914–15, resulting in a steep decline in Customs revenues, a vital financial source for government in the absence of income taxation. Imports from Germany, the most important peacetime source after Britain, ceased entirely. The USA, already a significant supplier, was able to take advantage of the situation and seized the opportunity. Trade improved during 1915 when requisitioned tonnage was allocated to the South American trades, enabling limited import shipments to resume.

---

14 David Rock, 'Argentina from the First World War to the Revolution of 1930', in L. Bethell (ed.), *The Cambridge History of Latin America, Vol. V, c.1870–1930*, pp. 433–44.

15 *The Times* (London) *Annual Review*, 21 January 1916, p. 22.

16 R. Gravil, 'The Anglo-Argentine Connection and the War of 1914–1918', *Journal of Latin American Studies*, Vol. 9, No. 1 (May 1977), p. 63.

17 *The Times* (London), 21 January 1916.

The economy remained depressed until 1917, unemployment in that year reaching nearly 20 per cent. Export prices then surged, some of the meat-packing plants returning 50 per cent on capital invested, and, from 1918, recovery was well under way, although inflation forced the cost of living beyond the means of the majority and unemployment led to labour unrest and strikes and an increase in trade union activity.

A case has been made that Argentina and Brazil, and other South American countries, benefited from their isolation during the two world wars, and there is some evidence to support the theory. In the case of the former, gross national production increased from 19,896m pesos in the period 1910–14 to 25,491m pesos in 1920–24, while the value of exports increased by 12 per cent. Another important factor was the requirement to develop manufacturing capabilities to replace supply sources of a wide range of products.[18]

Brazil, too, suffered economic difficulties during the wartime period, with resulting labour problems, strikes and other forms of agitation from 1917 to 1920. Its main export commodity, coffee, was not considered vital to the war effort and allied shipping tonnage was not made available, although 1m tons of sugar was purchased by the British government in late 1914, as well as some less important products. Exports fell by 16 per cent in 1914–18, imports by 24 per cent by value.[19]

At the time of the outbreak of war in 1914 Brazil had for some time favoured closer ties with the USA, having, in 1910, renewed trade agreements with that country, the largest importer of its main export products, coffee and rubber, and an increasing source of imports. Influential voices favoured Germany. When the USA joined the war in April 1917, others, more favourably inclined towards Britain, asserted their influence and Brazil joined the Allies in October 1917, the stated reason being that the Germans had, in effect, initiated a state of war against Brazil by virtue of sinking three of its merchant ships. The immediate effect of this, apart from terminating German competition for some years, was to further increase the influence of the USA while reducing that of Britain. Fifty-three German merchant vessels in Brazilian ports were seized and the Brazilian Navy, most of its ships built in British shipyards, assisted the Allies with naval patrol duties.

Imports to Brazil from Britain inevitably decreased greatly in the early years of the war, down from £16.4m value in 1913 to £6.6m in 1915, dictated largely by the lack of shipping. There was progressive recovery to £10.8m in 1918, by which time the value of imports from the USA was £19m. Britain never recovered its primary situation as Brazil's main source of imports. The flow of British investment capital was similarly affected by the war, replaced by increasing funds from the USA.[20]

---

18 Gravil, 'The Anglo-Argentine Connection', p. 59 and table 83.

19 W. Dean, 'The Brazilian economy, 1870–1930', in Bethell (ed.), *The Cambridge History of Latin America, Vol. V*, p. 700.

20 Graham, *Britain and the Onset of Modernization*, pp. 316–17.

Planning for Peacetime

During the wartime period and immediately afterwards, control of Company ships was almost entirely in the hands of government in terms of routes maintained and cargoes carried. It was fortunate that the shipping requirements to meet the demands for vital food supplies permitted the maintenance of services to South America, so that Royal Mail's important contribution to British commercial involvement with Argentina and Brazil persisted.

Management continued its programme of capital expansion, and the development of the Company was maintained with small but tactical additions to the fleets in 1916 and 1917. Group companies similarly progressed. Rumours during 1916 of a possible amalgamation with P&O proved to be unfounded. (P&O added very substantially to its fleet in the wartime period, including the acquisition of the New Zealand Shipping Company and the Orient Steam Navigation Company.)

Phillips's acquisition of 77 standard-built ships for the Group in 1919 (14 were allocated to Royal Mail), at what appeared to be a very competitive price, was sound business in light of his need to replace lost tonnage and the great increase in shipbuilding costs immediately after the war. The ships served the Company well, if they were not all entirely suited to its trades. However, it was hardly a gesture of 'magnanimity', as Bushell described it: apart from the potential cost saving Phillips, and Inchcape, were concerned to ensure that government was not inclined, or obliged, to operate the ships to its own account as other countries did with wartime-built tonnage and ships confiscated from enemy countries. In the event the ships were no bargain: although values increased greatly after 1918 they slumped by the end of 1922. Hope gives an example of a ship that cost £45,000 in 1914, rose to £232,500 and at the end of 1922 was available at £70,000.[21]

Anthony Vice suggests that Philipps and his colleagues and other British shipowners were slow to appreciate that the fundamentals of the shipping business were transformed by the war. Most British businessmen anticipated a trade boom, with continuing prosperity following victory in 1918. Few were prepared for the realities of the situation.[22] The world's financial machinery was in turmoil; countries that had, of necessity, developed industrially in the wartime period were no longer importers of some goods and demand was reduced for others. Long-established trading patterns were cast aside. Owen Philipps warned shareholders of Lamport & Holt in 1919 of the problems that lay ahead: 'We may find it by no means easy to re-establish ourselves in our ordinary sphere of operations.'[23]

The reference was, among other things, to the difficulties to be anticipated in rebuilding existing services and market shares in the face of increasing competition from countries less severely affected by wartime conditions: the USA, European

---

21 Hope, *A New History*, p. 357.

22 Vice, *Financier at Sea*, p. 24.

23 Green and Moss, *A Business of National Importance*, p. 42.

countries such as France and Holland, and countries further afield, Japan among them. The opportunity for the USA to extend its trades and its merchant fleet after 1914 was seized, as Royal Mail's management was only too aware. By 1918 the country's fleet increased nearly five-fold, to 14.5m tons. A shipping board was established to operate this giant state-owned fleet.

The Dutch benefited from their neutral status, their shipping and shipbuilding industries making substantial profits. The Rotterdam South American Line, previously a small Baltic timber-trading company, expanded and introduced no fewer than nine cargo ships running from Rotterdam, Hamburg and Antwerp direct to Argentina in the 1920–22 period. These continental ports were, at least in part, serviced until 1914 by, among others, Royal Mail's services to the Continent and its trans-shipment service from Southampton.

The Germans were expected to recover and become, again, highly competitive. German industry was not on its knees at war's end: many companies, shipbuilders, steel producers and so on had profited from heightened demand, and capital was available for investment. Some ships seized after the war by allied countries were in time sold back to Germany and quickly entered service. In the South American trades the first new-building for the Hamburg South American Line, *Argentina* (5,668 tons), made her maiden voyage to the River Plate in late 1920 and the larger *Espana* and her sister ship *La Coruna* followed in January/February 1922. The 20,576-ton *Cap Polonio* was built by Blohm & Voss in Hamburg in 1914. She was surrendered to the British in 1919 and sold to Hamburg South America Line in 1922. She carried over 1,500 passengers. All North German Lloyd's vessels were confiscated in 1918. By 1920 two new cargo steamers were in service to Brazil and the River Plate. Between May 1922 and June 1924 three new 11,500-ton vessels were built for the service.[24]

A Measure of Success

Britain's dominance in world shipping would end as other countries developed industrial capacity and large merchant fleets from wartime profits, and, in the case of the victorious allies, from a share of the confiscated German merchant fleet. Its position as a major supplier of coal, which was progressively replaced by oil, steel, iron and engineering and other heavy goods, and the importer and re-exporter of cotton and other materials from India and elsewhere, was ended. There was certainly cause for concern in all spheres of business following the unparalleled domestic and commercial upheavals nationally and internationally. Nevertheless, after 1918 British shipowners spent £55m purchasing captured German ships.

However, Philipps was already planning the hugely expensive post-war investment in replacement tonnage in order to maintain the Group's competitive situation in an even more demanding post-war market, as indicated, in the case of

[24] Bonsor, *South Atlantic Seaway*, pp. 213 and 247.

Royal Mail, by the considerable increases in authorised capital. Few references have been found to one of his boldest and most far-reaching arrangements made in 1917 with Lord Pirrie. It was certainly not a matter that was discussed with Royal Mail's shareholders. An agreement was made with Harland & Wolff whereby that company was given 'first right of building on group new-buildings for a ten year period', with a five-year termination requirement. The agreement was clearly extended and was only terminated in 1930 when Philipps, by then Lord Kylsant, chairman of Harland & Wolff since 1924, under some considerable pressure, probably from a voting trustee assigned to investigate the Group's affairs, gave notice and the contract was ended on three months' notice.[25] Green and Moss note that in the period 1919–22, of the 28 ships built by Harland & Wolff in Belfast, 24 were for Group companies.[26] It is appropriate to consider whether or not this arrangement worked to the benefit of Group companies during the late 1920s, a period of depression, when other shipyards were scrambling to obtain orders and building prices were highly competitive.

An offer in 1920 of £1.87m for the General Steam Navigation Company was countered successfully by the P&O Group. Had it been accepted, Royal Mail, with the continuing expansion of its Coast Lines company, would have gained monopoly control of a very large share of Britain's coastal and short-sea services. In 1919 the acquisition of government-built tonnage not only replaced lost vessels but extended the fleet's cargo-carrying capacity. Despite the uncertainties of wartime operation, revenues and profits steadily increased, as did the value of assets, and dividends of average 7 per cent ensured that shareholders remained at least moderately happy.

The immediate post-war services to South America were maintained by the D-ships out of Liverpool. The liner requisition scheme was terminated in early 1919, Royal Mail's A-ships being progressively released from government service. Three had been sunk and a fourth was effectively a hulk lying in Plymouth and owned by the Admiralty. The remaining five vessels were returned to service in 1919–20 following substantial refits. The cost of the refurbishment of existing tonnage and the purchase and/or building of replacements was high, perhaps too high at a time of inflated prices in the immediate post-war boom.

The annual report for 1919 noted a revival of the passenger and migrant traffic that was countered by increased costs of fuel and other working expenses, port congestion and labour strikes. Outward cargoes were erratic: many Company ships were obliged to leave port with considerable empty space, in some cases, in ballast. Freight rates were low and they continued depressed until 1921. A more optimistic sign was the allocation of *Avon* to temporary cruising duties. Dividends recovered from the nil paid in 1914 to 7 per cent through to 1920, with an exceptional 8 per cent in 1919.

---

[25] Nicol, *Scrapbook*, Miscellaneous Matters, p. 811.

[26] Green and Moss, *A Business of National Importance*, p. 49.

Even through the period 1914–20 Philipps, in conjunction with Pirrie, added to the Group's huge and complex empire of shipping companies, shipbuilders and related ancillary businesses, from steelmaking and coaling companies to laundries. Most of the companies held cross-shareholdings in others and loans between them were not uncommon. Royal Mail was merely a unit in this conglomerate, albeit a substantial one. Pirrie was greatly influential in the wartime period and was largely responsible for the introduction of standard ship designs in 1918, with resultant increases in output. Phillips was no less highly regarded, his services being rewarded with a GCMG in 1918.

Chapter 9
Post-war Downturn and Collapse

The board report for 1920 listed seven directors: Sir Owen Philipps in the chair; Sir Joseph Savory his deputy. Others were the Duke of Abercorn, James Cameron-Head, A. Neville Lubbock, Edward Norton and H.E. Wright. Sir Joseph Savory died in 1921 and Messrs Wright and Cameron-Head in 1922. Edward Norton retired in 1922. They were replaced by J.W. Clark, formerly a manager of the Company, and Sir Leslie Scott, so that by 1923 there were only five directors on the board, Lord Suffield, Philipps's son-in-law, being added in 1925. In 1923 Philipps was created Baron Kylsant of Carmarthen and was styled The Lord Kylsant thereafter. During 1928 J.W. Clark left the board; he died in the following year, and was replaced by P.G. Mylne Mitchell, with, still, six directors in total. Mylne Mitchell became chairman in 1931 and two additional directors, Messrs A.B. Cauty and W. Lewis, were added to the board in that year.

From shortly after the end of the First World War Britain experienced exceptional difficulties. Debts built up during the war, the liquidation of foreign assets, general price increases of manufactured goods, including those of export goods, and industrial unrest hindered recovery to its dominant pre-war role. Freight rates after 1920 collapsed. Overseas market shares were under threat. Periods of recession persisted during the decade. For shipowners there was the added problem of 4m tons of wartime-built and German tonnage seized after the war that flooded the market and added to the prospect of increased competition. Between 1914 and 1921 world tonnage increased by 20 per cent to nearly 59m registered tons, while British tonnage, taking account of losses and ships acquired, remained unchanged at just over 19m tons, 32 per cent of the total. Britain's share of total world tonnage declined progressively thereafter. By 1932 world tonnage was approximately 69m tons, the British total under 20m tons.[1]

Nevertheless, in his June 1921 report to shareholders, for the year of 1920, the chairman displayed a measure of, perhaps misplaced, cautious optimism despite the fact that the boom conditions that prevailed immediately after the war had ended and there were clear indications of a trade slump, with freight rates under constant pressure. Even so, he described the results as favourable, with outward and homeward cargoes and passenger traffic to and from South America improving, though still far from pre-war levels. Fare reductions to stimulate the passenger traffic were, he said, impractical in light of high fuel and working costs. Foreign competition for reduced levels of trade, labour troubles and congestion in home ports and overseas all added to increasing costs.

---

[1] Hope, *A New History*, table, p. 359.

Further acquisitions were made after the war in a wide range of shipping-associated companies. By now the Group's cross-shareholding arrangements were complex and, no doubt, entirely bewildering to shareholders. Royal Mail owned shares in RMSP Meat Transports, Nelson Line, Union-Castle, African Steamship Co., among others, and over half of the Company's £5m ordinary shares were held within the Group.

Countries with long-established merchant fleets struggled to replace lost tonnage and regain traditional trade connections. Those with newly developed and, in some cases subsidised, fleets, especially Scandinavian countries and the USA, were determined to expand their services. Royal Mail, with benefit of the 14 standard-built ships, was relatively well positioned, although management was determined to build new tonnage suited to its liner services. The fleet in 1914 consisted of 56 vessels of over 1,000 tons for a total of 334,973 tons: in 1920 the figures were 51 ships for a total of 326,246 tons.

Resumed Services

The passenger service to South America from Southampton was resumed with the benefit of some of the refitted A-ships, one of which was withdrawn to resume a cruising programme. Some meat was now loaded in La Plata, some 30 miles down river from Buenos Aires, in the refrigerated D-ships that continued to sail out of Liverpool. On occasion a call was made in Montevideo to load cargo. The service to Brazil using mainly the S- and N-class ships was advertised, with two or three monthly sailings from London, Swansea and the continent. As cargo offered, these ships would proceed to Argentine ports, loading, for instance, grain in Rosario. A directors' minute in 1923 indicated that not all voyages were profitable in the early 1920s.

Emigrant sailings between Spain and Cuba were resumed. The Canada–West Indies contract had expired but was being maintained with agreed payments on a per-voyage basis and the long-established passenger service to the West Indies was suspended due to continuing heavy losses. The New York to Bermuda service was resumed in 1922. The Brazil and River Plate advertisement in *The Times* of 4 April 1922 covered all of the above and PSNC's service from Liverpool to the west coast of South America.[2] Three sailings were advertised from Liverpool and three A-ships were scheduled to sail from Southampton via France, Spain and Portugal (see Table 9.1).

[2] *The Times* (London), 4 April 1922.

Table 9.1 Sailings advertised from Southampton, April 19221

Date	Ship	Tonnage
7 April	*Avon*	11,073
21 April	*Arlanza*	15,044
5 May	*Almanzora*	16,034

This was the minimum two sailings per month service by ships, in the case of *Avon* certainly, most likely incapable of more than 15 knots. Two of PSNC's O-ships sailing out of Liverpool were scheduled to call at the River Plate, probably at Montevideo, proceeding to the west coast via the Straits of Magellan.

An interesting development was the termination of the long-standing Southampton–West Indies–New York service and its replacement with a direct Hamburg–Southampton–Cherbourg–New York service inaugurated by the sailing of Pacific Steam's *Orbita* in May. This was, in the circumstances, a risky development: competition on the New York route from British and continental companies was strong and long established. An intention was to capture the transatlantic services previously operated by German lines; hence the terminal port of Hamburg. The trading conditions were less than ideal and additional tonnage was essential to properly maintain the service. Bushell notes that three more of Pacific Steam's O-ships were used.

A further service to the west coast of the USA via the Panama Canal was inaugurated by the new motor vessel *Lochkatrine* (9,409 tons) in 1921. Clyde-built, she was the first of three oil-burning motorships built for the Company and allocated to the joint cargo service with the Holland America Line. *Lochgoil* and *Lochmonar* followed in 1922–23. Their cargo capacity was 11,000 tons and they were fitted with refrigerated space suited to the seasonal homeward fruit trade as well as very large general cargo spaces. Intermediate calls were made en route to Los Angeles and many other ports with terminus at Vancouver.

Philipps was determined to expand the fleet, confident of forthcoming improvements in trade. In a widespread atmosphere of economic revenge he determined to exclude any revival of the German merchant fleet and limit the expansion of the shipping activities of other European nations that had profited during the wartime period. He negotiated a government loan under the Trade Facilities Act of 1922 and raised further funds through new market issues. Hope notes that by 1922 Royal Mail had substantially increased its reliance on borrowed money, raising £25m since war's end requiring interest payments in the region of £1m per annum.[3] The annual reports for the period reflect difficult trading conditions, 'owing to adverse factors due to the world depression in trade'. By 1924 passenger traffic on the River Plate services had shown an appreciable increase and the service had been accelerated and was efficiently maintained:

3 Hope, *A New History*, p. 364.

special note was made of working-cost economies. Even in the difficult times the Company's cruise programme to the northern capitals and the Mediterranean as well as New York–West Indies continued to be popular.

A measure of some confidence was the order placed in 1923 with Harland & Wolff, Belfast, for two 22,000-ton, 18-knot motor-ships for the South American service. The first, *Asturias*, made her maiden voyage, Southampton to the River Plate, in early 1926. Her sister, *Alcantara*, followed a year later. An important factor in the switch to motor-ships was cost reduction: oil fuel was cheaper than coal, the tonnage used was appreciably less and fewer engine-room staff were required. With Asturias's entry into service, the intention was to make the A-ship sailings every 10 days rather than every 14 to combat ever-increasing competition. The schedule published in early April of 1926 reflected this move (see Table 9.2).

Table 9.2 Schedule of sailings, April 1926

Date	Ship	Tonnage
2 April	*Almanzora*	16,034
13 April	*Andes*	15,620
28 April	*Asturias*	22,048

In 1926, homeward general cargo traffic was described as 'practically stationery', with working costs continuing high. One piece of good news was that homeward meat and dairy freights were maintained and experimental shipments of fresh fruits were being well received in the trade. At the annual meeting in May 1926 Chairman Kylsant appeared confident, although there had been only a slight improvement in trade and commerce generally in the past year. The depression in the shipping industry was, if anything, more pronounced, due, in part, to the effects of the seamen's strike in August to October of the previous year. Despite difficulties, all the Company's scheduled sailings were made during that period. The general strike earlier in the year he dismissed as 'futile and unwise'. Passenger numbers improved in 1925 and there was a slight increase in outward cargo volumes, although there was no improvement in homeward volumes.[4]

The chairman reported to shareholders in May 1927 that prospects of a trade recovery in the past year had been blighted by the general strike of May 1926: revenues continued down and costs up. He then confirmed that an agreement had been reached in January to purchase the whole of the share capital of the Oceanic Steam Navigation Company, the White Star Line, which was owned by the International Mercantile Marine Company based in New Jersey, USA. He added that he had first attempted to purchase the company in 1919. The White Star acquisition brought not only increased involvement in the North Atlantic trade but also in Australian and New Zealand services via an interest in the Shaw, Savill &

4 *The Times* (London), 28 May 1926.

Albion Company. With a measure of confidence, a public offer of 2.5m cumulative preference £1 shares at 21s in White Star was made. A further acquisition was the Australian Commonwealth Line.

Kylsant, with no little pride, reported at the 1928 annual meeting that Royal Mail and its associated companies now owned 500 vessels aggregating over 2,700,000 gross tons. He reassured shareholders that a substantial payment due in respect of the White Star Line purchase had been made, with £2.5m remaining to be paid by the end of 1936. He confirmed that the splendid new head office in Leadenhall Street, London, was nearing completion and the new Royal Mail House in Manchester was now in use. But the hoped-for improvement in trading conditions was not evident.

On the South American route intense competition was being experienced from ships of increasing size and speed. The chairman attributed this, in part, to some foreign competitors receiving substantial government aid. He mentioned specifically the French and Brazilian governments: the former, he said, had made provision to give the Compagnie de Navigation Sud-Atlantique, which operated between Bordeaux and Buenos Aires, the sum of about £384,000 per annum over 25 years.[5]

In May 1920 the fleet numbered 51 vessels of over 1,000 tons, for a total of 326,426 gross tons. A total of 1.9m tons was attributed to ships of other companies closely associated with Royal Mail. Three of the A-ships, *Almanzora, Andes* and *Avon*, were refitted and operating on the South American service, with *Arlanza, Asturias* and *Araguaya* still undergoing conversion. These ships were essential for the maintenance of the service, although one or other was detailed for cruising dutics on occasion and *Araguaya* was allocated to the New York–Bermuda service for a time. *Asturias (I)* emerged from her post-war rebuild in 1923 as the cruise liner *Arcadian.*

Figure 9.1 *Alcantara* (1926). J & M Clarkson Collection

5 *The Times* (London), 23 May 1928.

The service to New York demanded additional passenger tonnage. *Orbita* (15,507 tons, completed in 1919) was chartered from Pacific Steam for the service in 1921 with her sister, *Orduna*. In 1923, along with *Orca*, of similar tonnage, also already in service, they were purchased. They were all built by Harland & Wolff and had triple-expansion engines and triple screws, although they would prove to be slower than their transatlantic rivals. *Orduna* carried 240 passengers in first class, 180 in second and 700 in third, and had cargo capacity of 9,324 tons. A fourth vessel was added in 1920: she was built for Norddeutscher Lloyd's North Atlantic service but she was surrendered to Royal Mail as reparation for wartime losses. She took three years to refit, sailing from Hamburg on her maiden voyage in April 1923 as *Ohio*, at 18,490 tons Royal Mail's largest ship. Capable of 17 knots, she completed the Hamburg to New York crossing in eight days, two days fewer than her consorts. The service was, no doubt, prestigious, though hardly profitable: a directors' minute of late 1923 recorded regular large voyage deficits in the region £15,000 to £20,000. Three smaller Royal Mail vessels, *Essequibo*, *Ebro* and the 1903-built *Orcana* (6,793 tons), acquired in 1920, were transferred to Pacific Steam in 1922 and used on its New York to Valparaiso service.

The first of the new twin-screw motorships, *Asturias*, made her maiden voyage in 1926, *Alcantara* following in 1927. Royal Mail's largest ships to date, they were exceptionally well fitted to carry 432 passengers in first class, 223 in second and 453 in third. They were at the time the largest motor vessels afloat: Bushell describes the public rooms as 'of a magnificence undreamt of by travellers in earlier days'.[6] They were also well equipped as cargo carriers, with refrigerated space and six cargo hatches equipped with cranes.

The number of ship sales exceeded that of new purchases and buildings: the elderly *Danube* (1893) and *Tagus* (1899) were sold in 1920; *Magdalena* (1889) and *Trent* (1899) followed in 1921–22. In the same period no fewer than ten cargo ships were sold as no longer required. In 1930 the venerable *Avon* was sold and broken up, and *Araguaya* was sold to Yugoslavian Lloyd for further trading. (She survived until 1942 when, aged 36 years, she was sunk during the North African landings when under French ownership.) Two *Shire* ships, *Cardiganshire* and Carmarthenshire, were sold in 1929 for conversion to whale product factories.

A Painful Recovery

The First World War shattered not only the international balance of power but also the established global trade and payments patterns. The hope of many was that the equilibrium would be restored after the war, but it was not to be. The long period of relatively unrestricted world trade was ended. The gold standard, the well-established mechanism for balance-of-payment adjustments, was abandoned and Britain's position as the major source of capital for nations around the world

[6] Bushell, *Royal Mail*, p. 238.

came to an end. Protection of trade and shipping interests by way of subsidies and other means would become all too common.

A matter of concern to Brazil and Argentina was the slow growth of Britain's economy through the 1920s as the USA increased both imports and exports. Between 1913 and 1929, US imports from Latin America rose by 110 per cent as compared with British imports, up only 45 per cent. American exports to the area increased by 161 per cent, thus reversing trade surpluses previously enjoyed by most Latin American countries.[7]

British government and private (company) loans, important to South American governments and to British companies operating in the area, were much reduced in the 1920s. There was a general reluctance by the Bank of England to invest in foreign issues after the war, and borrowing in the City of London became more difficult, with interest rates often exceeding those available elsewhere. Capital issues in the City between 1924 and 1930, at £132m, were less than one-third in value of those issued in New York. British influence in the area diminished 'progressively in the 1920s while US firms took full advantage of the changed financial situation. Funds were, however, available from Anglo South American banks: the Argentine railways raised funds locally in the late 1920s.'[8]

The stock market crash of 1929 and the resulting period of worldwide depression that extended through the 1930s inevitably had a damaging effect on the countries of South America. Their export-led economies were especially vulnerable to the difficulties caused to the economic and financial systems in the USA and Europe. In general there was reduced demand for their export products and a fall in prices. British exports to Argentina fell from near £43m in value in 1920 to £25.2m in 1930.[9] The causes were numerous: the loss of investment finance and credit, and altered import requirements in both Brazil and Argentina countries. Also, in the wartime period both countries had, of necessity, expanded their own manufacturing capacities.

The USA and Germany were especially aggressive in seeking contracts for public works and introducing new products to what were still expanding markets, while British sales and promotion techniques were subject to serious criticism. The growth of nationalism in Argentina led to increasing concerns regarding the excessive influence of British companies: the powerful railway and tramway companies were a particular cause of public and political concern, as were the American and British meat-packing companies.

The demand for meat slumped immediately after the war: the number of cattle slaughtered for export in 1921 was less than half the number killed in 1918. Prices fell by half.[10] The effect on the meat packers, whose numbers had increased during the profitable wartime years, and their suppliers and grain producers was

---

7 Bulmer-Thomas, 'The Latin American economies, 1929–1939', pp. 66–7.

8 Miller, *Britain and Latin America*, pp. 186–9.

9 'Annual Statements of Trade and Navigation', in ibid., p. 190.

10 Rock, *Argentina, 1516–1987*, p. 204.

ruinous. Depression resulted. Nevertheless, Argentine exports to Britain increased appreciably between 1920 and 1930. Meat, chilled and frozen, still the main export to Britain, continued to be dominated by American and British packing companies, which controlled the share of export shipments allocated to each member, a situation not always satisfactory to the smaller companies or to the cattle producers, who accused the companies of price fixing, to their disadvantage.

In 1922 the well-established British shipping and cold-store company, Vestey, bought the British and Argentine Meat Company, a thriving packer and exporter, and sought to consolidate and extend its share of the highly competitive, not to say cut-throat market, dominated by the American companies, Swift and Armour.[11] In 1923 the politically influential Rural Society, stimulated by a group of cattle breeders seeking higher prices for their cattle, threatened to halt deliveries to the *frigorificos*, demanding the establishment of a national packing house and a shipping line to exert some control over the packers. The packing companies prevailed, although one small government packing plant was established.

A measure of intention was the purchase by Vestey in 1924 of the Leibig plant at Fray Bentos, Uruguay, up river from Buenos Aires, the producer of meat extract, tinned corned beef and, later, chilled and frozen meat. From 1925, Vestey, the Americans and the smaller companies fought a fierce 'meat war' for market share. Shipments to Britain were greatly increased, while freight, wholesale and retail prices were slashed, sometimes to loss-making levels and at great cost to the participants.

The only beneficiaries were the cattle breeders, who were able to increase prices as demand escalated. In 1927, by which time there was widespread concern regarding the damage being done to British producers and the nation's economy and to smaller companies involved in the trade, a settlement was reached: the three large companies agreed to revise export quotas for themselves and for the smaller companies. In 1927 Vestey built the Frigorifico Anglo in South Dock in Buenos Aires, shipping many thousands of tons of beef, mutton and canned products with the benefit of its own fleet of ships, the Blue Star Line.[12]

Argentina remained heavily dependent on trade with Europe and, especially, with Britain. This became a matter of concern for the government, which feared that Britain, with a substantial trade deficit, would take discriminatory action to relieve the deficit, cutting purchases from Argentina in favour of empire producers. The USA had already, in 1930, raised protective tariffs on Argentine meat, corn and wool, causing exports to that country to reduce by half during the 1930s.

As the effects of the Great Depression worsened, the British government came under pressure from companies whose export earnings had fallen and from dominion countries that sought to increase their share of the British market. A 1932 conference in Ottawa resulted in the application of imperial preferences

---

[11] Sturmey, *British Shipping*, p. 374. In 1920 Vestey established its Blue Star Line of refrigerated steamers when Royal Mail refused to supply meat for its outlets in Britain at acceptable freight rates.

[12] P. Knightly, *The Rise and Fall of the House of Vestey* (London, 1981), pp. 70–72;

under which Britain removed a ban on the taxation of food imports and agreed to import as much as it could from empire countries and enjoy preferential access to the markets of the empire. Trade with South America was not a priority.[13]

Brazil in this period experienced continued political uncertainty, with inter-state disagreements and elements within the army becoming increasingly influential. In 1930 revolution brought about a shift of power away from control by the elite, including the São Paulo coffee interests. The expansion and centralisation of the state was an important feature of change in the years immediately afterwards.[14]

London, as opposed to New York, continued to be an important source of finance for Brazil. The federal government operated a valorisation scheme, which placed a value on retained coffee stocks, an attempt to effect some control on the vital market, and, in 1921–22, borrowed £9m from a consortium of London banks. In Brazil the continuing dependence on overseas banks imposed constraints on policy-making and was a source of concern. These factors, allied to the seeming failure of the British government and export companies to re-establish strong business connections, led, inevitably, to a continuing reduction in the still substantial influence in both Brazil and Argentina, which accelerated during the 1930s.

The economy remained depressed throughout the decade. Imports from Britain fell drastically from £24.3m to only £8m in the period. Manufacturing extended beyond cotton goods, food processing and so on to include a developing iron and steel industry, although all were, in some measure, affected by reduced imports of raw materials. The USA and Germany, as in Argentina, monopolised the supply of new products. Exports to Britain dipped during the 1920s, recovering by 1930.

The Kylsant Collapse

Public concern had been raised about the presentation of the Company's accounts in June 1929 (for the year 1928) with qualifications by the auditors, Price Waterhouse & Co., in respect of a reduced level of depreciation allowance and the valuation placed on Royal Mail investments in group companies. Three weeks after the annual meeting, Kylsant's brother, Lord St David, strongly criticised the accounts and the issue of £2m 5 per cent debenture stock. Speculation concerning the Company's financial stability obliged it to issue a statement, meant to be reassuring, at the end of the year. This was against the background of worsening

---

[13] S. Perry, *The Vestey Group. History of a Global Family Business* (London, 2008), pp. 65–9. Seven companies were involved in the Argentine chilled/frozen meat business at that time: three were British, Vestey the largest; three were American, Swift and Armour dominating; and the Argentine company, Sansinena, which accounted for about 10 per cent of shipments.

Rock, *Argentina, 1516–1987*, pp. 224 and 242.

[14] B. Fausto, 'Brazil: the social and political structure of the First Republic, 1889–1930', in Bethell (ed.), *The Cambridge History*, pp. 828–9.

trade conditions and generally falling share prices. Price Waterhouse was briefed to provide a full report on the position of Group companies.

In March 1930 the publication of the accounts of Lamport & Holt, a subsidiary, disclosed alarming discrepancies between the book and market values of its reserve investments, causing shock in shipping and financial circles and raising further doubts about the financial status of Royal Mail. The Company was put in the hands of the Official Receiver in September.[15]

The *Financial Times* reported on the presentation of the accounts for 1929 at the 18 June 1930 annual meeting. Chairman Kylsant in his statement underscored the successes of the Group, by now the world's largest shipping conglomerate, listing the companies wholly or partially owned, Royal Mail's shareholdings in each and noting that reserve funds totalled £8,950,000. He reminded shareholders of his good connections with government departments dating back to the arming of merchant ships before the war and the disposal of the government-owned fleet of war-surplus shipping in 1918 in conjunction with Lord Inchcape. But all was not well: reference was made to outstanding government loans to the Group under the Trade Facility and Loans Guarantee Act totalling £4.5m.[16] Royal Mail's high level of debt, made worse by the 1927–28 additions to the fleet of Oceanic Steam Navigation Co., £7m and the Commonwealth Government Line for £1.7m, and the complex cross-shareholding arrangements would prove to be its undoing.[17] No dividend was paid for the year.[18]

Control was already shifting away from Kylsant. Some weeks before the AGM the directors and auditors met with government representatives and bankers and fully disclosed Royal Mail's financial predicament. Resulting from this meeting, a three-man committee was formed to advise the directors on possible courses of action. It consisted of senior directors of the Midland Bank and Glyn, Mills and Company and Sir William McLintock, an accountant, who represented the Treasury and the government of Northern Ireland. The Rt Hon. Walter Runciman MP, a shipowner and banker, was invited to become deputy chairman of Royal Mail and to join the boards of all Group companies.

Importantly, the various parties to the outstanding loans agreed continued support. Voting rights related to the Company's investments were vested in a small committee: its task was the reorganisation of the Group, an immensely

[15] Davies, *The Trade Makers*, pp. 218 and 221.

[16] RMSP, Annual Report to Shareholders for 1929.

[17] Davies, *The Trade Makers*, p. 214, Kylsant personally, with associates, held £1,673,500 Royal Mail shares. With shares held by subsidiaries the total was £3,062,502. The total of ordinary stock was £5,000,000.

[18] Nicol, *Scrapbook*, p. 715. Dividends from 1920 were 7 per cent; from 1921–24, 6 per cent; from 1925, 5 per cent; from 1926, 4 per cent; and from 1927–28, 5 per cent. A list, probably prepared by T.A. Bushell, who, in 1939, wrote the Company's centenary history, indicates that the trading loss in 1921 would have been in excess of £900,000 had proper depreciation costs been applied. Losses averaged approx. £500,000 in the period 1922–29.

difficult task in view of the many companies involved and the complex cross-shareholdings, as well as the interests of debenture-holders and shareholders. As he addressed shareholders at that June 1930 meeting, effectively defending his record, Kylsant was already aware that he had been sidetracked. Two months later he resigned as chairman of Harland & Wolff, a position he had held since 1924. Then in September he resigned from his chairmanship of Royal Mail and from all his directorships.

There was widespread press and public anger as it became clear that shares in the many Royal Mail companies were valueless; debentures and loans would only be partly repaid and the process might take years. The *Economist* summarised in some detail the crisis situation in February 1931: 'A great organisation with a paid-up share and loan capital of £80m, controlling the largest merchant fleet in the world, has been reduced to a condition on the verge of bankruptcy.' The article considered the effects of worldwide trading conditions that were outside the control of Royal Mail and the extent of mismanagement and unwise financial policy, offering broad criticism as far back as the post-war period, the purchase of the 77 government vessels and Kylsant's overly optimistic view of business prospects at that time. Acknowledging the damage caused by the world slump, the newspaper added that only three subsidiary companies were thought to be operating profitably, Union-Castle, Shaw, Savill and Coast Lines.[19] *Fairplay* later detailed the 'deficits' after depreciation for the period 1921–29 that were not shown in the Company balance sheet. They ranged from £904,153 in 1921 to £115,328 in 1928, and they were made good only by transfers from sales of steamers and recovered tax payments, which were not shown in the accounts.[20]

On 13 May 1931 summonses were served on Kylsant and Harold Morland, a senior partner of Company accountants, Price Waterhouse, in respect of three charges relating to the issuing of false balance sheets and prospectuses with intent to mislead shareholders. Following preliminary hearings in June, the trial began on 20 July at the Central Criminal Court, both defendants pleading not guilty. Morland was cleared on both counts. Kylsant was found guilty on the charge of issuing a false prospectus and sentenced to 12 months in goal. An appeal was lodged and he was released from Wormwood Scrubs, after only 24 hours, on 31 July. The appeal hearing in early November was dismissed and Kylsant was returned to Wormwood Scrubs to serve his sentence. He was released from gaol in August 1932, retiring from public life shortly thereafter. He died in his sleep in 1937.[21]

---

19 *The Economist*, 7 February 1931.

20 *Fairplay*, 27 June 1940.

21 For fuller details of events from mid-1929 to 1932, see Nicol's *Scrapbook*, pp. 724–50; Green and Moss, *A Business of National Importance* and Vice, *Financier at Sea*. Nicol notes that T.A. Bushell later disputed a list of Kylsant's personal investments valued at £5.4m published in Fairplay's *Annual Review of Shipping* for 1929. Most were in Group companies, some were joint holdings.

In the meantime a number of Royal Mail's directors had resigned: the Duke of Abercorn, Lord Suffield, Sir Leslie Scott and A.N. Lubbock. Kylsant, at pre-trial hearings, was obliged to defend himself against the implied criticism that, due to his dominating personality, he would vigorously pursue personal projects and that directors were not always fully informed on financial matters, especially before the finalisation of the annual accounts. Certainly directors' minutes and reports over a period of years do not give the impression that his colleagues, with few exceptions, were inclined to question or counter his wishes. This may explain why no board members accompanied him into the dock.

At the annual meeting in December 1931, newly appointed Chairman P.G. Mylne Mitchell spoke of a further downturn in world trade, with shipping especially affected, and ever-increasing numbers of ships being laid up worldwide. Shareholders hardly needed further bad news. Sir William McLintock, one of the voting trustees whose function it was to pursue the restructuring of the Company, added to the gloom: he advised that the Company's main assets, its ships and its investments, had a combined book value of £17,493,000. However, it was now estimated that the real value of the assets was only £8,500,000! A major explanation for the loss was the fact that shares in White Star Line Ltd, Lamport & Holt Ltd and Elder Dempster & Co. Ltd were regarded as having no value.

The complicated reorganisation plan, the Scheme of Arrangement proposed by the trustees, was effective on 1 January 1932, although it was not finally approved until June. Two new companies were formed to continue existing services, Royal Mail Lines Company with 52 ships and West African Lines Company with 55. In 1935 the Royal Mail Realization Co. was incorporated and took over the remaining properties and assets of RMSP in order to discharge the Company's liabilities to debenture-holders and other creditors. The winding-up order was made in February 1936. The total loss amounted to £22,481,535. Creditors were expected to receive no more than a shilling in the pound; shareholders nothing at all.[22] The trustees spent years resolving this massively complex affair: it was not until 1936 that the Royal Mail Steam Packet Company was finally liquidated.

From the confusion of the collapse of Royal Mail (RMSP), in August 1932 a new company, Royal Mail Lines, Ltd, was incorporated, with Lord Essenden as chairman and P.G. Mylne Mitchell and C.C. Barber as directors.

A number of writers have researched in detail the background and the circumstances that contributed to Royal Mail's collapse. They generally agree that the turmoil of the immediate circumstances after the First World War contributed to depressed conditions of commerce and industry through the 1920s. These resulted in, rather than a measure of hoped-for recovery, the calamitous events of 1929 and the years of the Great Depression in the 1930s. However, the Company's situation – it owned a conglomeration of 140 companies associated with shipping, shipbuilders, brokers, steel makers, coaling and other services – was unwieldy. The complicated cross-shareholdings and over-indebtedness were most certainly

---

[22] Nicol, *McQueen's Legacy*, Vol. 1, p. 165.

contributory factors – all against a background of totally changed post-war trading patterns and severe competition in shipping.

Kylsant, with his close associate Pirrie, chose to commit to a programme of expansion through new building and acquisition funded by loans, including some from government under the Trade Facilities Act. In the circumstances it was the wrong course of action. Disaster followed.

Moss and Green attribute some of the longer-term problems of the shipping industry to the effects of the Kylsant case and the losses suffered by investors. Despite moves to tighten accounting and audit procedures, investors remained cautious of shipping stock. In time, shipowners' reluctance to borrow funds affected fleet replacement programmes, which allowed foreign companies the opportunity to gain control of much of the British shipping industry.[23]

---

[23] Green and Moss, *A Business of National Importance*, pp. 213–14.

Chapter 10
Royal Mail Lines Ltd

The RMSP Scheme of Arrangement, which sought to satisfy, in due course, the claims of the Company's many creditors by selling and otherwise disposing of assets, established two operating companies. The first of these, Royal Mail Lines Ltd, included the fleets of the Royal Mail Steam Packet Company, RMSP Meat Transports Ltd, Nelson Steam Navigation Co. Ltd and David McIver and Co., all operating services to South America. Sir Frederick Lewis, chairman of Furness, Withy & Co. Ltd, was chosen as chairman by the voting trustees responsible to the realisation companies. He was described as a practical shipping man who would be able to rationalise the new company's South American services and those of Furness, Withy. Other directors represented the principal creditors of the former RMSP companies.[1]

Lord Essenden, formerly Sir Frederick Lewis, was in the chair at the first annual meeting of the new Company in May 1933. Other directors were P.G. Mylne Mitchell, general manager, and C.C. Barber, manager, with Frank Charlton, previously secretary of White Star Line and of the voting trustees, J.M. Eddy, William Lewis and Walter C. Warwick. Lewis retired during 1933 and Eddy was replaced, in 1938, by Malcolm Baird, a partner in Linklaters & Paines, legal advisers to the trustees during the reorganisation. Frank Charlton was appointed, in 1937, as representative on the Company board of the Ministry of Finance for Northern Ireland, a shareholder. He held the position for many years.[2]

The nature of the board had changed significantly. No more than six directors served in this period. All had considerable shipping or financial interests. In addition to Essenden, Charlton and Warwick were closely associated with Furness, Withy, the latter being managing director of Houlders & Co. in which Furness held a substantial interest. This balance, which persisted through to the final days of Royal Mail Lines, was clearly beneficial to the Company at the outset but it gave Furness very considerable, perhaps inappropriate, influence in Company matters.

Ships and Services

The Company's £4m capital consisted of 4,000,000 fully paid £1 shares that were distributed to creditors including the Northern Ireland government as fully paid

---

1 Green and Moss, *A Business of National Importance*, pp. 153–4.

2 RML 81/13, Letter dated 12 March 1937 from the Ministry of Finance for Northern Ireland to the secretary to the board of Royal Mail Lines.

up, although a premium of 16s 3d per share gave the new Company working capital of £3,250,000. Altogether 880,000 shares were allocated to the Royal Mail Steam Packet Company in care of the realisation company as payment for the vessels sold to the new Company.[3] In October 1934 the shares were valued in RMSP's accounts at £1,144,000.

The fleet of the new Company consisted of 50 vessels, a number of them elderly, and included tugs and tenders, totalling 429,328 tons, according to the annual report dated 31 December 1932. Five of these were A-ships and five were 14,000-ton intermediate passenger/cargo *Highland* ships built in 1928–32 and previously operated by the Nelson Line. (A sixth Nelson Line vessel, *Highland Rover*, was sold in 1932.) The *Highland* ships had substantial refrigerated cargo space and carried 150 passengers in first class, 70 in intermediate class and 500 in third/migrant class.

The routes to be serviced reflected the continuing importance of the Brazil/Argentina trade. Indeed, Royal Mail's main function was now to maintain that service. All ten of the largest vessels were allocated to it, the A-ships sailing out of Southampton, the *Highland* ships out of London. The seven post-war-built N-ships also had refrigerated space, so that the Company's involvement in the Argentine meat trade was strongly maintained.

Five of McIver's six cargo ships maintained their several services from Liverpool to Brazil ports and to Montevideo, Buenos Aires and Rosario; one, the 1913-built *Sicily*, was quickly sold. The North Pacific route to Vancouver via the Panama Canal, in conjunction with Holland America Line, was maintained with the three 1921–23-built *Loch* ships. Other cargo vessels operated services to the West Indies and ports in Venezuela, and to Brazil and Argentine ports. The service to Brazil, with calls at southern ports, continued. An outward general cargo from London and Antwerp might include whisky, biscuits, machinery and pianos, with steel plates and rods, coils of wire and other products from Swansea. Coffee was loaded in most ports for the homeward run and, in Rio Grande, which was in the cattle country, obnoxious items were loaded for discharge in Le Havre, Antwerp and London.[4]

A 1939 sailing schedule for *Sarthe* on the Brazil service included loading outwards in London and Swansea, with calls at Pernambuco, Bahia, Rio de Janeiro, Santos and the southern ports of Rio Grande and Porto Alegre. Company ships, in particular those on regular liner services, continued to carry mails to South American ports and would continue to do so in the years ahead.

From the very earliest days of the new Company the directors were faced with difficult and potentially expensive decisions, which they took briskly. The minutes of their first meeting in August 1932 record lengthy discussion of the need for new and faster tonnage for the South American trade to combat strong competition from German, French and Italian vessels, some of which were able to make the

---

[3] *Shipbuilding and Shipping Record*, 11 October 1934. Annual Report to Shareholders.

[4] J. Robson, 'Royal Mail in the 1930s', in *Royal Mail News*, No. 65, June 2006. The writer served as a Cadet in *Araby* in the mid-1930s.

passages to Rio as much as five days more quickly than Company ships but which were thought to be operating at an appreciable loss, although they benefited from government subsidies.

It was suggested that a conference be arranged with the French and German lines indicating that Royal Mail planned to build speedier tonnage and inviting them to reduce their speed to 19 knots in consideration of Royal Mail doing likewise. A meeting was arranged with the chairman of the Hamburg–South American Line. Some weeks later Chairman Essenden reported to his colleagues that the Hamburg Line and the principal Italian and French lines had agreed a limitation of speed, although no indication was given of that speed. (The Hamburg Line's largest vessel at the time was *Cap Arcona*, 27,561 tons, built in 1927. She was capable of 20 knots). The prospect of an agreed limit on speed will have been attractive to all parties on the basis of cost reductions and, certainly, it was a shrewd move by Essenden, bearing in mind the relative weakness of the Company's position.

A first consideration was increasing the speed of *Asturias* and *Alcantara* to a guaranteed 18 knots by replacing their motor engines with geared turbines and extending and reshaping the bows. By June 1933, with a new Argentine trade agreement signed and loan facilities arranged, an order was placed with Harland & Wolff for the work to proceed at cost of £186,145 per vessel. *Asturias* resumed service to the Plate in 1934, *Alcantara* in May 1935. The remaining A-ships, vital to the maintenance of the services to Brazil and the Plate were elderly: *Arlanza* (built in 1911) and *Almanzora* (1915). *Atlantis* (1913) was involved mainly in cruising.

A problem for management was that not only were a number of vessels in the fleet 20 years old, or thereabouts, and no longer operating efficiently, but also several were large wartime-built cargo ships not entirely suited to the Company's trades, especially in a time of severe depression. Company vessels were laid up at times in the early 1930s and superfluous tonnage was sold, mainly for scrap. Two ships not in the 1932 list, the 1910-built *Highland Rover* and *Severn* (1919), were sold and within months ten further ships were disposed of, including the 26-year-old *Arcadian*, *Parana* of 1904 and two 1912-built refrigerated D-ships. By April 1934 (accounts for 1933) the fleet was further reduced by three vessels to 38 ships, totalling 345,440 tons with a value of £4,302,400. The disposal of vessels continued until early 1937, *Nictheroi* and *Nagoya* being sold for further trading, by which time the fleet numbered 34 ships.

The matter of new liner tonnage was addressed. In late 1936 tenders were sought from six companies against a specification for a new 21-knot steam-turbine passenger vessel. Harland & Wolff gave the lowest quotation, £1,360,000, plus significant additional costs for decoration of public rooms and refrigeration and insulation. A loan facility, £750,000 at 2.75 per cent over ten years, was arranged with the Northern Ireland government and the order was placed in March 1937. The name *Andes* was confirmed and her keel was laid on June 16th. The intention was that *Andes*, *Alcantara* and *Asturias* would maintain the South American service, the older A-ships being, in due course, retired.

In April 1938 it was announced that a second new ship was under construction at Harland's Belfast yard. *Lochavon* (9,205 tons) would make her maiden voyage to South America later in the year, although she was intended for the joint, with Holland–America Line, North Pacific service. *Andes* (26,689 gross tons), the Company's largest ever ship, was due to be launched the following year. Two further ships were sold and *Arlanza* (1912) was withdrawn from service and scrapped later in the year.[5]

A measure of the concentration of resources on the Brazil/Argentine service is gleaned from an advertisement in *The Times* of 4 April 1939 (see Table 10.1).

Table 10.1 Services to Brazil/Argentina

Southampton service		**London service**	
Dates	**Ship**	**Dates**	**Ship**
15 April, 10 June	*Asturias*	8 April, 17 June	*Highland Chieftain*
29 April, 24 June	*Alcantara*	22 April, 1 July	*Highland Princess*
27 May, 22 July	*Almanzora*	6 May, 15 July	*Highland Brigade*
		20 May, 29 July	*Highland Patriot*
		3 June, 12 August	*Highland Monarch*

On the same page in *The Times* is an advertisement for Vestey's Blue Star Line, which offered competition to Royal Mail with its small fleet of 13,000-ton, 16-knot, passenger/refrigerated cargo vessels sailing mainly out of London.

A major acquisition was reported in early 1939. The Liverpool-based Pacific Steam Navigation Company, for so many years closely associated with the Royal Mail Steam Packet Company and owned by it from 1910, was purchased from the still-active trustees of the Royal Mail Steam Packet Company for £600,000.[6] The combination with Pacific Steam restored the domination of trade from the UK to both the east and west coasts of South America. In fact, in most respects Pacific Steam operated over the years independently from Royal Mail, with virtually no cross-over of routes, administration or sea staff. Benefits, of course, quite apart from agreements concerning sailings, passengers and so on, were the continuation of the practice of each company representing the other in ports and cities within Europe and in South America.

With the recent past in mind and anticipating the purchase, a trade newspaper commented somewhat pointedly that all should be well (with the acquisition) 'as long as care is taken to ensure that tendencies towards amalgamations and large consolidations are not carried too far'.[7]

---

5 *The Times* (London), 6 April 1938.

6 Green and Moss, *A Business of National Importance*, p. 193.

7 *Shipping and Shipbuilding Record*, 13 October 1938.

Sound Financial Development

The accounts for the year 1932 showed a voyage profit of £524,326 after all deductions except depreciation, despite the continuing trade depression. However, profit until 4 August, the date of Royal Mail's incorporation was due to the transferor companies, leaving only £215,686 to the Company's account. From the £3.25m share premium the sum of £1,867,500 was applied to a reduction in the book value of the fleet. Within the complex financial situation of the fledgling Company, somehow, from 1933, investments were made in government securities.

Trading through the conditions of worldwide depression in the 1930s, with costs cut to the bone and millions unemployed as product demand collapsed, was extremely difficult. Many ships were laid up in ports around the world, sometimes for months. Company reports make few references to 'laid-up' tonnage, although the 1934 report neatly refers to 'eliminating uneconomic voyages without impairing the valuable goodwill'.

The 1933 annual report noted that 'shipping has become increasingly aggravated by restrictions and exchange difficulties', with strict quotas on meat and import duties on butter and fruit. The tone was no more cheerful the following year, underlining increased foreign competition fostered by subsidies, quotas and barter schemes that tended to depress freight rates. Annual voyage profits in 1933 were down to £409,813, falling further, to £390,327, in 1934. In that year a loan of £75,000 was repaid to the Royal Mail Steam Packet Company.

Thereafter there were some indications of trade recovery, with finances helped by significant cost reductions as tonnage was sold off and all-round economies were effected, including cuts in staff salaries. The year 1935 marked a breakthrough for the new Company: a first dividend of 3.5 per cent was paid. Annual voyage profit rose to £534,935 and £130,000 was set aside to a fleet replacement account in recognition of the need to replace tonnage in the near future.[8] These developments were a measure of sound management in still-difficult trading conditions.

Dividend was increased in the following year to 4.5 per cent. The chairman encouraged shareholders with talk of improved freight rates, which applied mainly to tramp ships but with some benefit to liner services. He welcomed the new Anglo-Argentine trade agreement, which gave promise of further trade opportunities between the two countries, although a modest improvement in freight on meat shipments was effectively cancelled out by tariffs still imposed.

Subsequent annual reports were somewhat more confident, although voyage profits, a record £743,055 in 1937, fell to £612,442 in 1939. Cargoes were said to be satisfactory, with a good share of the meat and fruit trades. Passenger numbers increased and, perhaps surprisingly in a time of acute depression, cruises, including one in 1936 to Honolulu, were described as well patronised and, presumably, at least marginally profitable. A measure of some confidence was the purchase in 1937 of RMSP's substantial Buenos Aires offices and the building of

---

[8] Nicol, *Scrapbook*, RMSP/RML Transition, p. 790; *Financial Times*, 1 April 1936.

new offices and stores at Victoria Dock in London, by then, and for many years to come, the Company's London terminus. Also purchased was a controlling interest in the Marconi Steamship Co., which operated a 7,402 gross ton refrigerated vessel, *Marconi*, in the River Plate meat trade.

From 1935 the accounts began to include sums such as 'cash on deposit and current accounts with bankers', £456,453. In 1936 this deposit amounted to £1,025,000. The reserves figure in Table 10.2 below does not include these figures. By 1937, with dividend payments increased to 5 per cent, substantial financial assets were being developed. Voyage profits were increased, at £743,055, and the fleet replacement and capital reserve funds totalled £1m, with an additional £100,000 in general reserve. Cash on deposit totalled £1,250,000. Addressing the annual meeting (for 1938) in April 1939, the chairman confirmed that reserves now totalled £1,310,000 and noted that the £3,484,700 fleet valuation included 'substantial payments on account of the mail and passenger liner *Andes* now under construction'. In 1939, government, corporation and industrial investments totalled nearly £1.5m, and Pacific Steam was acquired at cost of £600,000.

Table 10.2 Voyage profits, capital and investments, 1932–39

	Net profit on voyages after charges (£)	**Ordinary dividend share price**	**Capital auth'd/issued debs/loans (£)**	**Value of fleet* Reserves investments (£)****
1932	524,326	Nil Not quoted	4,000,000	4,811,450 243,214
1933	409,812	Nil Not quoted	4,000,000	4,302,400 610,614
1934	390,326	Nil Not quoted	4,000,000	3,573,000 602,877
1935	534,935	3.5% Not quoted	4,000,000	3,295,000 878,253
1936	631,086	4.5% Not quoted	4,000,000	2,957,100 1,726,942
1937	743,055	5% 32s	4,000,000	3,095,110 2,013,579
1938	617,993	5% 21s 9d	4,000,000	3,484,700 2,790,800
1939	612,442	5% 18s	4,000,000 957,000	4,259,500 1,875,000 1,493,282**

Source: Reports and Accounts.

* After deduction for depreciation.

***Figure* quoted is for major investments in government, company and trade securities only.

The Brazil and River Plate services showed good returns: meat shipments continued satisfactory, if still affected by tariff impositions, while shipments of fruit, butter and eggs were maintained. Fruit and general cargoes from the North Pacific were improved. Three special tourist voyages to Brazil and Argentina were made in January and February, and *Atlantis* cruises were well supported.

Royal Mail shares were quoted on the London Stock Exchange from March 1937. In August the £1 ordinary shares at 32s were overpriced and they fell steadily through the remainder of the year to 21s 9d by January 1938 and 18s at the beginning of the following year. The market adjustment does not appear to have been a matter of great concern, except, no doubt, to shareholders, as Company profits continued to be satisfactory.

A measure of some confidence in Royal Mail's progress was the announcement at the annual meeting of Furness, Withy in July 1937 by Chairman Lord Essenden (also of Royal Mail) that two blocks of Royal Mail shares, total unstated, had been acquired from the realisation companies, which were appointed by the voting trustees to dispose of RMSP properties. He noted the common interests of the two companies, the South American and the North Pacific trades, and commented that Royal Mail had made steady progress since its incorporation in respect of its earnings and in building up a strong balance-sheet position.[9] A block of 750,000 £1 ordinary shares, approximately 20 per cent of the total, was bought by Essenden on his own behalf at £1 7s 6d per share. The earlier purchases, total unspecified, gave Furness, Withy/Essenden 34 per cent of Royal Mail shares, a substantial, but not controlling, interest that it retained for many years.[10]

A few months previously, in late 1936, Essenden had exerted pressure on the Treasury and the realisation companies to permit him to purchase their Royal Mail shares. At that time the Treasury expressed itself unhappy with the sale of a large number of shares to him because it feared that Royal Mail would again become part of a considerable shipping group controlled by one man, Essenden, or his successor. (Furness had, in 1935, after lengthy negotiations, taken control of another former RMSP company, Shaw, Savill & Albion.) The concern was justified in light of the strong Furness, Withy presence on the board. A compromise was agreed: the stock held by the realisation companies would be sold to Essenden, the remaining shares, 1,142,069, held by the Treasury and the Northern Ireland government, being sold to the public. There can be little doubt that his real interest, and that of Furness, Withy, was to acquire control of the Company.[11]

Speculation persisted regarding Essenden's intentions: in early 1938, on a visit to Argentina, he was obliged to categorically deny at a press interview that Royal

---

[9] *Fairplay*, 29 July 1937.

[10] Green and Moss, *A Business of National Importance*, p. 192 and *The Times* (London), 21 June 1937.

[11] It seems clear that, with the sale of shares held by the realisation companies, the Treasury and the Northern Ireland government, all Royal Mail's shares were now available to the public.

Mail was to be merged, in due course, with Furness, Withy–Houlder interests.[12] Sturmey's view of where the power lay from the outset is clear; he noted: 'Two years after the acquisition of Shaw, Savill and Albion the Royal Mail Line and Pacific Steam Navigation passed into the Furness Group.'[13] With or without the shareholdings the already established structure of the board of directors would ensure that Furness, Withy effectively controlled Royal Mail over the next 30 years.

The year 1938 brought a return to depressed trade conditions and political uncertainty. Voyage profit was £617,933, with reserves totalling £1,310,000 and a dividend payment of 5 per cent. Cargo shipments continued to be no more than satisfactory, large quantities of fruit being shipped from the Argentine and from the Pacific coast. Freight rates declined from the improved 1937 levels.

A State of War

On 3 September 1939 Britain and France declared war on Germany, which had been pursuing an aggressive foreign policy and had invaded Poland two days previously. Despite Britain's naval strength, it was soon evident that the Germans had anticipated events rather more effectively than the British and their allies: 58 British merchant ships were sunk before the year end, half of them by mines laid in coastal waters, including the Thames estuary. *Araby* was the first Royal Mail vessel to enter active service: she sailed from London for France on 17 September laden with army stores and equipment.

Andes was due to begin her maiden voyage from Southampton to South America on 26 September 1939, the centenary of the Royal Mail Steam Packet Company's original charter. She would be the largest and fastest British liner on the South American route. In the event, following the outbreak of the Second World War, she moved from Belfast to Liverpool, where her expensive fittings were removed and stored, and she was refitted to carry over 4,000 troops. She sailed from there on 9 December 1939 for Halifax, Nova Scotia, returning to the Clyde with Canadian troops.

Three Company ships were lost in the first three months of the war, including *Lochgoil*, which, on 6 October, struck a mine in the Bristol Channel. She was beached but later declared a constructive total loss. *Loch Avon*, built only in 1938 for the North Pacific service, was torpedoed when approaching the Irish coast in a small, unescorted transatlantic convoy. No lives were lost in either sinking. In December *Navasota* was torpedoed and sunk 160 miles from Lands End; 37 of the 81 man crew were lost.

Publication of the accounts for 1939 was delayed while government ship hire rates for the period from September were negotiated with the Ministry of Shipping. When produced in June 1940, they confirmed that Ministry policy required the requisition of entire ocean liner fleets so that the whole of the Company's fleet was now hired by the government to its account. Agreed hire rates were: operating costs plus 5 per cent

12 *The Times of Argentina*, February 1938.

13 Sturmey, *British Shipping*, p. 370.

depreciation plus 5 per cent interest on the original cost per vessel with variations for certain conditions. War risk insurance would be paid for by the Ministry.

Referring to the ship losses, the chairman commented that replacement tonnage would cost considerably in excess of payments received under war risk insurance. He added that Company finances were strong, with voyage profits for the year of £612,442 and reserves of £1,875,000, and that an order had been placed for four cargo ships. Thirty-one ships were in Company service at the end of December. The dividend paid was 5 per cent.

Trade Uncertainties

South American countries were, inevitably, much affected by the Wall Street crash of 1929 and the subsequent depression. Export prices fell and there were difficulties in obtaining foreign loans as the financial crisis spread through Europe and around the world. Between 1929 and 1932 Argentina's exports fell by more than 60 per cent, with some recovery after 1932. The difficult conditions were the seed-bed for the rise of fascism: both Brazil and Argentina were affected and symptoms would persist for a number of years.

British export volumes to both Argentina and Brazil declined between 1930 and 1938. Most Latin American economies were still driven by the export of primary products, minerals, meat, cereals and coffee, although both Argentina and Brazil benefited from advances in their industrial sectors, reducing, in some measure, the dependence on imported goods. Nevertheless, as export prices fell dramatically, imports had to be cut back severely in order to try to achieve a trade balance, with foreign debt still to be serviced. Imports into Britain from Argentina were appreciably down, and those from Brazil largely unchanged through the 1930s. Account must be taken when viewing Table 10.3 of price adjustments and of the depreciation of the currencies of both countries in the period.

Table 10.3 Exports to/imports from Argentina and Brazil, 1930–1938.

	1930	**1935**	**1938**
Argentina			
Exports to	25,234,000	15,257,000	19,338,000
Imports from	54,714,000	42,282,000	37,004,000
Brazil			
Exports to	7,970,000	4,757,000	5,185,000
Imports from	7,514,000	6,758,000	7,421,000

Source: Annual Statements of Trade and Navigation.[14]

[14] Miller, *Britain and Latin America*, Tables pp. 190, 210 and 216–221.

Figure 10.1 *Highland Chieftain* (1929). J & M Clarkson Collection

Brazil's trade with Britain was affected by new preferences (import tariffs), although its volume of trade with Britain was appreciably less than that with the USA and Germany. In the early years of the decade Britain remained closely involved with loans relating to public debt finances. The currency tumbled in value and coffee prices fell from US$0.50 per kilo in late 1929 to US$0.29 within months. At the time huge stocks of coffee were held in an attempt to influence price.

Meat exports continued vital to Argentina, and Britain remained by far the major importer. There were, however, demands from home and empire countries for the application of import duties on the products and severe volume reductions to protect suppliers in Australia, New Zealand and South Africa in the early years of the Depression. An initial requirement was for monthly volume reductions of 5 per cent during the first year of the agreement and reduction or removal of a range of import duties, terms potentially devastating to the Argentine economy.

The proposals caused an outcry in Buenos Aires and put great pressure on the new Argentine government, which took power in an army-led coup in 1930. Vice-President Roca, with a team of negotiators, was sent to London. In time the Roca–Runciman Agreement of 1933 was signed.[15] (Sir Walter Runciman was the chief British negotiator.) Very much to Britain's advantage it controlled imports into Britain of beef and other meat products from Argentina. Shipments of chilled beef were limited to 90 per cent of the 390,000 tons shipped in a one-year period in 1931–32 for three years, and imports of frozen beef, mutton and lamb were restricted to 65 per cent of shipments in the same period. Britain agreed not to impose duties on meat imports for the time being. The Argentines agreed to

[15] Rock, *Argentina, 1516–1987*, p. 225. The agreement, which was for three years, was renewed in 1936 by the Eden–Malbran treaty.

reduce tariffs on almost 350 British goods to 1930 levels and agreed, among other concessions, to committing itself to favoured treatment for British companies. Argentine-owned *frigorificos* were permitted to supply no more than 15 per cent of meat exports in an effort to counter the criticism that foreign packers were controlling cattle prices and, effectively, the price of meat for home consumption. The arrangement was extended in 1936 for three years, at which time export meat quotas were further reduced, chilled beef by 5 per cent, and a small per-pound import duty applied.

Further concessions were made by Argentina over debt repayments, foreign exchange and investments, and a commitment to purchase only British coal. One beneficial effect of these measures, for British interests, was that levels of trade between the two countries remained steady through to the end of the decade.[16] Rock notes that, although the 1930s were years of declining British influence in Latin America, in trade negotiations with Argentina Britain still held the upper hand and emerged with most of the benefits.[17] In a very difficult period for both countries, Britain perhaps overplayed its hand, with political repercussions. Argentine historians still speak of the 1930s as the 'infamous decade', a time when foreigners, mainly British, ran Argentina's economy.

In this period of the application of quotas to meat imports from Argentina, the Vestey Group, while maintaining its meat-packing operation in Argentina, recognised the increasing limitations of the trade and reduced its weekly Blue Star Line sailings from Buenos Aires to fortnightly. It then invested heavily in developing its involvement in the Australia/New Zealand trade for which five new, fast, vessels were built specifically for shipments of chilled beef, the carriage of which over a 45-day voyage was still limited. Vestey's decision was, no doubt, influenced by limitations on its share of the market by the South American Conference arrangements, but it also reflected a cautious view of the prospects for the Argentine meat trade.

Royal Mail's management reports of the period did not reflect especial concern with quota arrangement on meat shipments, although the negotiations were closely observed. Its considerable refrigerated tonnage continued in the trade, most likely with benefit of a good share of the conference allocation, although details are not available.

Royal Mail survived and thrived. Bushell notes that, despite the difficult trading conditions in the 1930s, the new Royal Mail Line, free from the entanglements of Group policy and operated as a single Company, soon proved that its shipping

---

[16] A. Graham-Yooll, *The Forgotten Colony* (Buenos Aires, 1999) pp. 251–2. The agreement caused bitter dispute within Argentina, politicians being accused of a sell-out to British interests.

[17] Rock, *Argentina, 1516–1987*, pp. 224–5. Argentine imports from Britain remained at approximately 23 per cent of the total from 1933 to 1939. Exports to Britain were steady at about 36 per cent of the total.

business was sound.[18] The recovery of the Company in what was still a very difficult economic climate, its return to payment of dividends within three years and its ability to obtain sufficient credit and profit to fund the building of the Company's largest liner and to set aside substantial reserves was most creditable. The Royal Mail realisation company continued its work of distributing assets of the Steam Packet Company through the remainder of the decade. In 1941 a meeting was held in London at which it was intended to distribute £75,000 of the remaining funds of £79,357 to creditors.

[18] Bushell, *Royal Mail*, p. 247.

Chapter 11
The War Years, 1939–45

The directors in 1939 were unchanged since 1937: Lord Essenden continued in the chair, with Messrs Mitchell and Barbour, now respectively managing director and general manager. Frank Charlton and W.C. Warwick were both directors of Furness, Withy. In addition W. Lewis and S. Malcolm Baird. Lord Essenden died in June 1944, W.C. Warwick replacing him as chairman and Sydney J. Forster being appointed a director. The board of Pacific Steam included several Royal Mail directors.

Shipping movements were chaotic in the early years of the Second World War, due to, among other things, a shortage of loading and discharging berths in Britain as a result of the closure of some ports, including Southampton, to commercial activities. Sailings were invariably delayed as naval authorities organised escorted convoys to and from UK ports and in North and South Atlantic harbours for homeward-bound traffic.

Despite these limitations and disruptions, a healthy profit of £723,337 was declared for 1940 and the fleet replacement account totalled £3,298,000. An unusual item featured in the accounts: 'Profit on voyages and from Hire of Vessels required by H.M. Government and Rents of Properties and charging expenses, provision for deferred repairs, sundry payments to Superannuation to Widows' and Orphans' Association and Pensions, £1,041,812.' Quite where this sum fitted within the annual accounts is uncertain. It did not recur. The chairman in his report gave no information on ship movements and casualties for security reasons. Instead he launched into his usual, surely untimely, attack on the failure of government to support shipping interests in times of depression and in the face of state-supported foreign competition.

The following year he commented, evidently with some relief, on the decision of government not to nationalise and operate the large number of ships being built to its account but to make them available for sale to shipping companies. The nationalisation option he described as 'Poor reward for all the Shipping Industry has done for the Nation'. Royal Mail managed 19 government-owned ships during the war, some of which were later purchased.

Profits increased to £908,420 in 1941, remaining near to that level before increasing to £948,432 in 1944 and exceeding £1m in 1945. By then Royal Mail was awash with cash: reserves totalled £5,871,434, with £2m set aside for tonnage replacement. An undisclosed number of shares held in the new British South American Airways was acquired by BOAC on behalf of the government when it nationalised air transport.

Wartime Losses

Twenty Company vessels were lost in the wartime period, including two new ships. Thirty-four ships were owned in 1939 and 12 new ships were delivered. At the end of 1945 the fleet totalled 23 ships, including three smaller craft, for a total of 215,255 tons. The losses were devastating: most of the 20 vessels lost were torpedoed by submarines. Only one of the larger vessels, *Highland Patriot*, was sunk, at the cost of three lives. Three cargo ships, *Navasota*, *Somme* and *Culebra*, suffered heavy casualties. Thirty-seven men, including the captain, chief engineer and all the deck officers, died when *Navasota* was torpedoed and sank within eight minutes. *Culebra* (3,044 tons), running regularly from the West Indies with cargoes of sugar, was sunk in the Atlantic following a gun battle with a submarine and was lost with all hands in January 1942. The following month *Somme* disappeared without trace in the Atlantic, all crew lost.[1]

Two passenger liners were converted within months of the outbreak of war for use as armed merchant cruisers and fitted with 6-inch guns. HMS *Alcantara* initially patrolled the South Atlantic to afford protection against enemy raiders to the many Allied ships still trading to South America and the East via South Africa. She was involved in an inconclusive exchange of gunfire with a German raider, *Thor*, in July 1940, sustaining some damage. In 1943 she was refitted as a transport.

HMS *Asturias* was outfitted for similar duties, although she was less fortunate. She was torpedoed by an Italian submarine in the South Atlantic, about 400 miles from Freetown, on 24 July 1943, when escorting, along with five anti-submarine frigates, a floating dock that was being towed from Bahia to Dakar. The dock continued safely to Dakar. *Asturias*'s engine-room was badly damaged and flooded to a height of 30 feet. Towed to Freetown, she was anchored in the river: the crew effected limited repairs, shoring up bulkheads, pumping out flooded spaces and so on before being repatriated to the UK, leaving a skeleton Royal Mail Care and Maintenance crew on board. Such was the damage that she was declared a constructive total loss and passed into the ownership of the government.[2] In early 1945 she was towed to Gibraltar, where she was dry-docked and temporary repairs were effected before being towed to the Harland & Wolff yard in Belfast. On completion of repairs she was outfitted as a troopship and migrant carrier in the ownership of the Ministry of Transport and managed by Royal Mail.

Two vessels scheduled for disposal in 1939 gave excellent service in the war years. The 1915-built *Almanzora*, which had completed her final voyage to South America, was used mainly for trooping duties and the 1913-built *Atlantis*, which served as an armed cruiser in the First World War, travelled many thousands of miles in a variety of roles, being used mainly as a hospital ship from 1940. In

[1] Bushell, *Eight Bells*, passim.

[2] Geoffrey Penny, 'The Torpedoing of H.M.S Asturias. My Own Memories', in *Royal Mail News*, No. 43. The writer was Assistant Purser in the ship. He remained on board in Freetown until June 1944.

addition to *Andes*, the *Highland* ships were converted to carry troops and they were involved in operations worldwide.

Most Company cargo ships continued in their regular trades under government control, bringing in cargoes of essentials materials including foodstuffs, especially refrigerated meat. *Pampas* was one of four merchant ships that left Alexandria in March 1942 in a heavily supported convoy loaded with vital supplies for the beleaguered island of Malta. Threatened by Italian naval units and attacked by dive bombers, only three of the four reached Malta. All three were sunk by bombs at their berths, although some of the essential stores were saved.

Other cargo ships were converted for troop carrying a replacement: *Pampas*, built in 1944, was converted into a headquarters infantry landing ship capable of carrying 650 troops and saw service in the Normandy landings in 1944, one of a number of owned and managed ships involved. Later *Pampas* was refitted to carry up to 1,000 men and, as HMS *Persimmon*, saw service in the Far East.

During the wartime period 12 new ships were delivered to the Company, including eight of the P-class motor cargo vessels of 5,400 tons built in Belfast, of which two, *Pampas* and *Pardo*, were lost to enemy action. From the same yard, four large twin-screw refrigerated ships of nearly 10,000 tons, *Deseado, Darro, Drina and Durango* were delivered between 1942 and 1944.

Substantial Profits

Wartime tends to be profitable for shipping companies, in financial terms, with benefit of income from government charters and compensation for ships sunk. All British shipping was taken over on charter by government, freight rates being set to allow owners a profit of 5 per cent on the agreed value of each ship and depreciation of 5 per cent. The financial arrangements for tonnage replacement were complex: when a ship was lost, the agreed depreciated cost of the vessel in 1939 was paid to the owner. A further payment was made only when the ship was replaced. Figures produced by *Fairplay* showed that liner companies, between 1939 and 1946, increased their reserves from £30m to £113m and investments and cash holdings from £59m to £151m.[3]

Cargo shipments were controlled by government, which contracted with its counterparts and companies overseas for regular supplies, whether meat, which was shipped frozen,, grain, sugar or military equipment, so that revenues were generally consistent, ship losses apart. The downside was the ever-increasing cost of building replacement tonnage, although income, including insurance settlements in respect of vessels lost, generally allowed for substantial set-asides for that purpose.

Voyage profits, after deductions, in the years 1940–45 varied between £723,337 and £1,082,963, while reserves/investments/cash, the investments usually in government securities, rose from £6.3m in 1940 to £10.7m in 1945,

---

[3] Sturmey, '*Fairplay*' in *British Shipping*, p. 145 table.

with substantial additional ship replacement and other funds. Shareholders were kept satisfied with dividends of 5 per cent in 1940, 6 per cent subsequently, and an additional 2 per cent capital profit distribution in 1945 (see Table 11.1). Share prices strengthened as reserves and investments built up.

Table 11.1 Voyage profits, dividends and share prices, 1940–45

	Net profit on voyages after charges (£)	Dividend (%) and share price		Capital authorised and issued (£)*	Reserves/ investments/ cash (£)**
1940	723,337	5	18s 9d	4,000,000	6,312,964
1941	908,420	6	17s	4,000,000	8,389,283
1942	871,282	6	24s 3d	4,000,000	7,362,368
1943	882,617	6	24s	4,000,000	8,182,823
1944	948,432	6	22s 3d	4,000,000	10,317,302
1945	1,082,963	6 + 2	24s 3d	4,000,000	10,682,916

* No debentures were in issue in this period. Loans of just over £1m were shown in 1940 and 1941 accounts. They were identified as made by the Ministry of Finance for the N. Ireland government and were secured against ships building. The loans ceased to be identified from 1942 and were not commented upon in the Annual Reports. Four P-class cargo ships built by Harland & Wolff in Belfast entered service in 1940–41.

** The Investments/cash figure is used as an indicator of reserves, no specific figure being given in the accounts. By 1946, when figures for the previous year were included in the accounts, a specific 'Reserves' figure of £5,871,434 was given for 1945.

Wartime Pressures in Latin America

The outbreak of war in 1939 presented Latin American countries with severe economic problems in terms of access to import–export markets, shipping services and credit facilities. By mid-1940 most European markets, which had absorbed some 30 per cent of exports, were lost, as was the greater proportion of imports. British purchases, by now bulk-bought by government and shipped, usually in British tonnage, continued but they were increasingly confined to essential foodstuffs, frozen meat, grains, sugar and raw materials, payment for which was retained in 'special accounts' to which access was strictly limited, payments for British-sourced goods.

Exports from the Latin countries declined after 1941 and they built up huge surpluses with resultant price falls. Brazil, which by now was exporting meat, lost one-third of its exports and was obliged to cut back its coffee production. Argentina lost 40 per cent of its overseas markets. Plans were made to develop manufacturing output and to maintain employment through a public works programme. Both governments introduced policies of purchases of excess production and seeking alternative outlets within Latin America.[4]

When the USA declared war on Japan, Germany and Italy in December 1941, following the attack on Pearl Harbor, the prospect of greatly increased trade and economic aid arose for Latin American governments. But any benefits would come at a price: commitment to the Allied cause was demanded by the Americans. At a conference of Foreign Ministers in Rio de Janeiro in January 1942, most Latin American countries, with the exception of Argentina, Chile and Uruguay, agreed to sever diplomatic and economic ties with the Axis powers. Agreement followed on the purchases of large quantities of strategic materials by the USA from several Latin American countries. Later in the year Brazil declared war. The USA began to apply pressure on Argentina, a matter of concern to the British government as it sought to secure essential food supplies that could not have been sourced elsewhere at the time.[5]

Relations between the USA and Argentina deteriorated, stirred by increasingly active nationalist groups and political turmoil and with American accusations of pro-German sympathies. At the same time Argentina's relations with other Latin American countries came under pressure. Brazil, favoured by the USA, was seen as a threat to its neighbour and there was even consideration of military action by the Argentine. Revolution, army led, followed in June 1943, with Colonel Juan Peron prominent. (By June 1944 he was vice-president.)

In late 1943, in face of American threats to impose sanctions against Argentina, the British Foreign Office urged that no precipitate action be taken. It pointed out that military operations planned for 1944, the Second Front, might be prejudiced if vital supplies were curtailed. Argentina was expected to supply in that year 40 per cent of carcase meat, 29 per cent of tinned meat, 70 per cent of linseed, 14 per cent of wheat and 35 per cent of the hides imported into Britain.[6]

In June 1944 relations deteriorated still further: the American ambassador in Buenos Aires was withdrawn and Britain was persuaded to follow suit. Argentine government assets in the USA were frozen and further stringent cuts were applied to imports. The Argentine government was described as fascist and its members Nazi collaborators. The British, ever conscious of the need for continued food shipments, argued against a total trade ban, signing a new contract for meat and egg supplies in October 1944.

Only when Argentina finally declared war on Japan and Germany in March 1945 did the Americans ease trade restrictions in some measure, although the US government persisted with accusations that members of government and the military had been Axis supporters during the war. Peron, with support from trades unions and a strongly anti-American stance, was elected president in

[4] *Financial Times*, 10 May 1940 and 4 January 1941.

[5] Thorp, *The Cambridge History, 1930 to the Present*, pp. 118–24.

[6] Humphreys, 'Latin America and the Second World War', in Thorp, *Latin American Economics, 1939–1950*, p. 124.

February 1946. Rock, summarising the complex wartime breakdown of relations between the USA and Argentina, suggests that trade and financial pressures through the 1930s led to the collapse of the conservatives in 1940–43 and the rise of the anti-American nationalists.[7]

The limited information given in the annual reports and accounts sheds little light on the wartime activities of management, although they were under great pressure. The principal function, apart from safeguarding the interests of shareholders, was to manage the Company fleet and additional tonnage placed under its control as best it could and as required by government, which effectively controlled every aspect of the operation.

Political considerations, both at home and abroad, were never far from their minds, as were their concerns with the threat of nationalisation of shipping, the likely level of competition to be faced and how to ensure that suitable tonnage was available after the war to speedily renew services.

Of equal concern were the political and economic situations in the countries served by the Company. Overseas staff continued to be active: offices in Rio de Janeiro and Buenos Aires, among many others, continued their peacetime activities of liaison between ship and shore authorities and cargo agencies.

7 Rock, *Argentina, 1516–1987*, pp. 258–61.

Chapter 12

Post-war Recovery

Walter Warwick remained in the chair in 1946 with his five colleagues, Messrs Mitchell, Barber, Baird, Charlton and Forster. Sir E.H. Murrant, Chairman of Furness, Withy since 1944, was appointed to the board and became deputy chairman. Frank Charlton was also a director of Furness, Withy, since 1944; he would become deputy chairman of that company in 1948 and chairman in 1959 when Murrant retired from the role. They were charged with the considerable task of urgently restoring the Company to peacetime operation in what were, inevitably, very difficult conditions.

The Liner Requisition Scheme ended in March of 1946, by which time some Company ships were either refitting or had already resumed service prior to refitting. So great was the demand for passenger space to Brazil and Argentina and return cargo capacity that *Highland Monarch* reopened the service in wartime guise. New tonnage was urgently needed to supplement the fleet of 23 ships. The final two of four large refrigerated vessels, the D-class, entered service in 1944 and three more general cargo vessels were purchased under the Government Disposal Scheme. Additionally, four standard American-built Liberty-class ships were acquired in early 1947 at the knock-down price of £136,126 ($544,506) each and they were in service within months. An order was placed with Harland & Wolff for a new passenger/cargo liner.[1]

Addressing shareholders in early 1947, the chairman reported on the fleet reconstruction and on rebuilding work in hand on repair and store facilities in London and Southampton that were destroyed or seriously damaged by enemy action. Further considerable costs, he added, would accrue in the shape of government-imposed increased crew wages and improved accommodation and conditions. (These changes were long overdue: in the immediate post-war period most seamen and engine-room staff in older ships were still housed in open accommodation, 12 or more in a space, often with no running fresh water.) He was, nevertheless, able to reassure those present of the 'sound financial position of the Company', with investments in government and other bonds valued at in excess of £3m. The future, he thought, was 'uncertain', and he reminded his audience of experience after the First World War.

Royal Mail, like most of the pre-war vintage British liner shipping companies, was largely re-established in its pre-war trades and anticipated the future with some confidence. Short-term difficulties were inevitable as manufacturers and harbour facilities were restored and port congestion eased. Commenting on the

1 PSNC 23/5, Chairman's Report to Shareholders.

likely development of air traffic, already a matter of concern to shipowners, the chairman expressed the view that 'sea travel will retain its popularity with the travelling public'. Soon afterwards the directors were relieved to be assured by government that shipowners were free of the threat of nationalisation. This was at a time when government was considering taking control of a number of industries, for example coal, steel and railways.[2]

In 1949, disaster: the new turbine-powered intermediate-class liner, *Magdalena* (17,547 tons), a replacement for the lost *Highland Patriot*, was launched in May 1948 by Harland & Wolff, Belfast, and sailed on her maiden voyage from London to Buenos Aires in March 1949. Homeward bound with a good cargo, she ran aground on a reef outside the harbour of Rio de Janeiro, sustaining damage to nos 1 and 2 holds, with some flooding of the spaces. The following day, when under tow, she broke in two in the harbour entrance, the forward part sinking and the stern section drifting across the harbour and grounding. All passengers and crew were rescued. The insurance underwriters made a payment of £2,250,000.[3]

Resumption of Trade

Competition in the South American trade recovered quickly after 1945 and within a very few years it intensified. Houlder Bros. and Vestey's Blue Star Line resumed regular sailings to the Plate, the latter with four new 10,700-ton vessels ordered immediately after the end of the war. The first, *Argentina Star*, entered service in June 1947. She and her sisters had substantial refrigerated space and they carried over 50 passengers in first class on regular services from Liverpool and London. Lamport & Holt resumed its Brazil/Argentine service. (Blue Star purchased the company in 1944 and the Booth Line in 1946, the latter more involved with the North Brazil/Amazon trades.)

Of much concern to British interests was the post-war recovery of competitive European lines, especially those of Germany and Italy, with benefit of substantial financial assistance. In 1949 the USA gifted $42m to West German shipping companies to help with tonnage rebuilding, and the West German government, in 1951, extended a further £40m loan at low interest rates. The Hamburg–Süd Line was able to resume sailings to the Plate in 1951 with the new 7,000-ton *Santa Ursula*, five sister ships following by 1953. Italian companies were similarly supported.[4] The Italia Line resumed sailings from Genoa in January 1947 using elderly tonnage: the *San Giorgio*, built in 1923, carried several hundred passengers in third class. The French SGTM company built two 16,000-ton vessels after the war for its service. The first, *Provence*, sailed in 1951 from Marseille and another French group, Compagnie de Navigation Sud Atlantique, resumed services

2 RML, Chairman's Report for 1947.

3 Nicol, *MacQueen's Legacy*, Vol. 2, p. 191.

4 Hope, *A New History*, pp. 397–8.

in 1952 with two new 12,000-ton ships, *Laennec* and *Charles Tellier*, the latter with accommodation for over 400 passengers, most of them in third class.

Still more significant was the introduction in 1949 by the newly nationalised Argentine Dodero Line of the first of three 12,000-ton refrigerated and passenger-carrying vessels. *Presidente Peron* made her maiden sailing from London, having been built by Vickers-Armstrong at Barrow-in-Furness. This development is discussed later. Dodero, with further new tonnage, opened services to Amsterdam and Hamburg in 1951 and to Italian ports in 1952.[5]

Politics in Argentina

An important event in Argentina was the election to president in 1946 of Juan Peron, with powerful army and trade union backing and substantial majorities in both houses of congress. He won on a popular platform of higher wages, nationalisation of the central bank and foreign-owned enterprises, including public utilities, improved education for all and a social security programme. His 1946 five-year-plan was designed to achieve economic independence: it called for industrial growth to reduce the country's reliance on imports, the growth being funded by the country's huge wartime sterling balance. One result was, opponents argued, stagnation in the production of beef and grain, the country's main exports, inflation and slow economic growth.

Peron had made clear in his election campaign that he intended to nationalise all foreign-owned public services, achieve economic self-sufficiency and establish an independent line in foreign affairs. Obvious targets were the seven privately owned British railways and a number of other companies which had become increasingly unpopular with the public and with trades unions during the wartime period, due, in part, to services considered to be inadequate but mainly to nationalistic inclinations. Strikes resulted: management was criticised, though the Argentine government continued to be quietly supportive. (The railway companies had been negotiating for some years with the government with a view to a sale.) In early 1947, after months of negotiations, a settlement was agreed for the purchase of the railways and some smaller associated companies for payment of £150m, of which £126m was in blocked Argentine sterling balances in London. The amount agreed was somewhat below the initial British valuation of £250m but higher than the London Stock Market valuation of £130m. Argentina acquired control over a railway system of 30,000 km with half its rolling stock pre-dating 1914.[6]

In the chaotic international and political situation of 1945–46, a priority for Britain, and for Argentina, was the re-establishment of export trades with South American and other countries and, in particular, the restoration of the vital meat and grain imports from Argentina. In September 1946 agreement was reached on a

5 Bonsor, *South Atlantic Seaway*, pp. 482–3.

6 Graham-Yooll, *The Forgotten Colony*, p. 256.

four-year meat contract with a further extension in 1948. In 1949, a five-year meat-for-coal imports agreement was agreed, with some concessions on the import of manufactured goods. However, rather as the meat production of the USA available for export declined at the beginning of the twentieth century, so, with increasing population and improved wages, did the share of Argentine production available for export decline from the 1950s.

The meat packers also came under pressure. Immediately after Peron's election victory the management of Vestey's Anglo meat-packing plant in Buenos Aires was obliged to cooperate with the labour unions in establishing new working conditions and rates of pay. Perry notes that 'from this moment the Vestey organisation's days in Argentina were almost certainly numbered as Peron declared his determination to transform Argentina's semi-colonial economy'. Political interference and disagreement with cattle suppliers over prices persisted. By 1970, under threat of legal action related to monopoly activities, losses were such that the plant was closed in 1971 and, in the same year, the Fray Bentos plant was sold to the Uruguayan government.[7] The American packers, Swift and Armour, came under similar pressures, the former's assets being nationalised in 1971.

In the latter part of 1948 meat shipments from the Argentine became very uncertain due to a dispute between the British and Argentine governments that resulted, for Royal Mail and other meat shippers, in serious freight losses. At the time, with food rationing still imposed in Britain, the Ministry of Food remained responsible for meat imports. Three months of negotiations ended in early 1949 with an agreement that the Argentines considered to be 'a very hard bargain', with reduced prices compounding, for them, a shortage of sterling reserves.

The agreement was renegotiated in 1951, again a tedious process, with shipments reduced or halted for a time, with improved terms for the suppliers and reduced quantities of meat, still shipped frozen, for the British. From a total of 350,000 tons of frozen meat available in the year to June 1950, shipments were reduced to only 200,000 tons of meat and offal plus 30,000 tins of corned beef. Inevitably, the shortage of meat in Britain continued and, for the shipowner, the surplus of refrigerated tonnage remained. The owners were highly critical of the efforts of the government negotiators and attempted, without success, to obtain compensation from the Ministry of Food for the freight losses sustained.[8]

The Company's very real concern was that when refrigerated spaces were not used for the homeward passage, revenue, and on occasion profitability, was lost, even if general cargo or bagged grain or the like was carried at a lesser freight rate. Chairman Warwick made clear his wish that the British government should withdraw from the trade negotiations in favour of the shipping companies experienced in the trade. A five-year trade agreement was reached with Uruguay

---

[7] Rock, *Argentina, 1516–1987*, p. 279.
Perry, *Vestey Group*, pp. 150–51.

[8] *Shipping and Shipping Record*, 3 May 1951.

in 1949, mainly for meat shipments that, though relatively small, were important in what was increasingly an uncertain market.

By late 1950 meat supplies remained unreliable. No shipments were made between July 1950 and April 1951. (At that time Houlder Bros, part of the Furness, Withy Group, transferred some tonnage to other routes operated by its parent.) Other refrigerated products, poultry, butter and fruit offset, at least in part, freight losses, and general cargo volumes were satisfactory. Passenger revenues continued to be satisfactory, with still much movement between the Continent and South America, including migrants.

Trade prospects with Argentina in 1952 were dire: droughts caused harvest failures and severe cattle losses, greatly restricting export prospects. Quite apart from a persistent shortage of animals for slaughter, exports were restricted by an ever-increasing demand for meat for the home market. In 1928, 40 per cent of meat produced was exported: in 1950 the export figure was 21 per cent and, in 1951, 14 per cent.[9] As exports of meat and other products fell, so did total trade with Britain as Argentina was obliged to severely curtail imports: by the mid-1950s trade had fallen to about half of the immediate post-war level. These statistics appear to reflect accurately the very considerable difficulties in the period.

Meat shipments remained restricted through 1952, improving in 1953 with an anticipated 20,000 tons per month, although Company pronouncements continued gloomy. The new trade agreements with the Argentine and with Uruguay provided for the resumption of chilled beef shipments after 14 years, with improved freight rates and a superior product for the home market. Shipments improved significantly in 1955: the total rose to 250,000 tons, of which 45 per cent was chilled, up from 144,000 tons, 9 per cent chilled, in 1954. Also in 1955, government involvement in the Argentina meat trade ended, freeing Royal Mail and the other conference lines to negotiate directly with the meat packers with, most probably, input from the Argentine government. Shipments of refrigerated butter, poultry and fruit contributed to revenues.

American Influence after the War

The USA dominated the world economy at the end of the Second World War. It produced more than half of the world's manufactured goods in 1945 and it owned half of the total supply of shipping, up from only 14 per cent in 1939.[10] Its position enabled it to control post-war economic recovery: the Marshall Plan launched in 1947 was a four-year aid programme for Europe, greatly profitable to the USA, but with the almost total exclusion of South American countries, to their considerable unhappiness.

---

9 Rock, *Argentina, 1516–1987*, p. 297; Colin Lewis, 'Anglo-Argentine Trade, 1945–1965', in David Rock (ed.), Argentina in the Twentieth Century (London, 1975), p. 121.

10 Thorp, *The Cambridge History, 1930 to the Present*, p. 129.

Although the Latin countries retained some hope of support, none was forthcoming. This was due, in some measure, to the US intention that pressure by other Latin American countries would persuade Argentina, under the influence of Peron, to abandon its political and interventionist policies. On the American shopping list were political stability, the development of industrial capability, tariff reductions and a welcome for foreign capital. Further intense pressure was put on Peron in 1948 when the Americans determined that Marshall Plan dollars would not be used to purchase Argentine goods: instead, grains and other essentials would be supplied by rapidly expanding and subsidised American, Canadian and Commonwealth countries. Peron desperately tried to persuade the Americans of his good intentions, but without success: his plans were in tatters. The USA had put him firmly in his place. Denied access to markets in receipt of Marshall Aid, Argentina was obliged to revert to trade with lesser countries, such as Spain and Brazil, its share of wheat and corn sales collapsing.[11]

Exports to Europe by both Argentina and Brazil fell sharply between 1938 and 1950, by 20 per cent in both cases, while exports to the USA and Canada increased substantially. After 1945, Latin American countries in general were inclined to the pessimistic view that, with declining markets in Europe, their export-led economies were unlikely to be viable in the years immediately ahead, given the inevitable loss of foreign trade revenues. There was a general move towards import restrictions and tariffs: Brazil introduced several in 1947, greatly reducing the need for British services. Industrialisation, with the production of manufactured goods an important element, inevitably and only slowly reduced the need to import.[12]

Throughout the 1950s – Peron was ousted by a military coup in 1955, although his supporters continued to be a political force over many years – Argentina struggled, in difficult economic circumstances, to develop export markets in manufactured goods and to encourage foreign investment. Trade with Britain continued to decline: imports from Argentina fell by £8.5m in 1953–54, although exports recovered in the same period and the UK still accounted for about one-quarter of meat exports into the mid-1960s.[13]

The post-war political situation in Brazil, with the military and labour, including a considerable communist element, active remained persistently unsettled. Despite this, with a more soundly based economy, much of the country's foreign debt was cleared, prompting a return to budget deficits and inflation. Progress was made in improvements to the infrastructure, including the construction of oil

[11] Rock, *Argentina, 1516–1987*, p. 292. In protracted discussion with the American ambassador, James Bruce, he argued that his seemingly anti-American views were 'domestic rhetoric' and that he was active in seeking to combat communism.

[12] V. Bulmer-Thomas, *The Economic History of Latin America Since Independence*, 2nd edn

(Cambridge, 2003), p. 257.

[13] Rock, *Argentina, 1516–1987*, table 33, p. 323.

refineries, a tanker fleet and improved port installations. Reduced overseas credits adversely affected imports, although the situation eased by the 1950s. Trade, both imports and exports, increased in 1951–52, imports exceeding exports, with resultant payments difficulties. By 1954, trade declined dramatically following the settlement of outstanding commercial debt. UK exports to Brazil, at £55m in 1951, slumped to under £9m and imports declined by £30m in the same period. Labour unrest led to a series of strikes during 1953, the major demand being for substantial wage increases. The subsequent unrest led to the suicide of President Vargas in August 1954 under extreme pressure from the military.[14]

The Fleet

At the end of 1946 Royal Mail operated 23 sea-going ships of 225,859 tons, with a further four building. The cargo fleet was relatively up to date, 14 of the 17 ships having been built during the war years, with purchases of further recently built tonnage planned. Five of the six passenger/cargo liners on the Brazil/Argentina service were somewhat more dated. The four intermediate *Highland* ships were built between 1928 and 1930, and, still popular with passengers, had at least a few years of service ahead of them, though at 16 knots maximum speed they were slow. *Alcantara* was built in 1926. *Andes* (1939) was the exception.

By late 1947 the refitting of Company ships was near to completion and services had been restored on most routes. *Andes* made her maiden South American voyage in early 1948 and was well received in her ports of call, with a visit from President Peron in Buenos Aires. The number of her first-class passengers was reduced from 403 to 324 to allow space for improved crew accommodation. Tourist-class berths remained at 204, the cabins being suitable for first class when cruising by removing the upper berths. In company with *Alcantara* she maintained the Southampton service for the next 10 years, the *Highland* ships continuing to sail out of London. By 1954, clearly chasing the developing holiday trade, the A-ship services were advertised as 'Sunshine Voyages to South America', the ships being available as hotels in Buenos Aires and in Rio, awaiting the return sailing.

The three ships purchased from the Ministry of Transport entered service in 1946: *Loch Ryan* (9,904 gross tons), built as *Empire Chieftain* in 1943, was employed on the North Pacific route from 1946. The two others, renamed *Teviot* and *Tweed*, were rather smaller 7,000-ton cargo ships with limited refrigerated space that was used only infrequently. On one most unusual voyage in the 1950s, *Tweed* carried a cargo of frozen lamb from Puerto Deseado in Southern Argentina to one of the *frigorificos* in the Plate, 30 miles from Buenos Aires. There, after discharging the lamb and replacing it with frozen beef, she proceeded to Santos and Salvador, where she topped up her cargo space with rice and sugar for UK

---

[14] Boris Fausto, *A Concise History of Brazil* (Cambridge, 1999), pp. 311–21.

ports.[15] *Brittany*, one of a new class of cargo ships, made her maiden voyage in 1946, followed a year later by her sister ship, *Araby*. The four American-built Liberty ships also entered service in 1947, each renamed as B-ships, *Beresina* etc. They had large cargo capacity and were employed for the next 10 years mainly on the Brazil/Argentina services. Two Harland & Wolff ships with considerable refrigerated space, mainly for the carriage of fruit, were built for the North Pacific service, *Loch Garth* and *Loch Avon*. At the end of that year the fleet numbered 33 ships of 277,823 tons, an increase of 10 in a period of two years despite the sale of the 1914-built *Almanzora*.

Ship operating costs were many and varied: voyage repairs, especially on older tonnage, were expensive, as were fuel and crew costs, which tended to be fixed even in passenger ships carrying fewer passengers than capacity. Efficient turn-arounds in port when loading or discharging cargo were essential. Delays caused by inefficient working practices, the norm in the period, or labour disputes invariably upset sailing schedules, a cost factor out of the control of the shipping company. In 1938 Royal Mail's ships spent 48 per cent of their time in port. By 1954 the figure had risen to 56 per cent.[16] Two weeks discharging and loading cargo in terminal ports, London's Royal Victoria Dock and in Buenos Aires was not unusual.

The unfortunate *Magdalena* apart, most tonnage built in the 10-year post-war period was for the Caribbean and Pacific services. Shipowners were much concerned at the near-doubling of building and fitting-out costs compared with pre-war. A press report in 1948 illustrated this: an 8,000-gross-ton general cargo vessel ordered in April 1939 and delivered in August 1940 cost £369,000. A broadly similar 8,500-ton vessel ordered in October 1945 and delivered in May 1947 cost £638,000. A comparable ship ordered in March 1948 would cost in the region of £700,000 to £750,000, and prices were still increasing. A major shipbuilder noted that, quite apart from the difficulties of obtaining on-time delivery of manufactured items, reduced labour hours coupled with absenteeism resulted in output by some yards reduced to two-thirds of pre-war levels. The resultant delays inevitably affected costs of refitting and refurbishment work being carried out on most of the Company's ships.[17] Owners complained that the compensation paid for war losses fell far short of replacement costs and that taxation on profits should be urgently reconsidered.[18]

In 1950, two 12-passenger E-ships of just under 8,000 tons were ordered for the West Indies services. The first of these, *Ebro* and *Essequibo*, entered service

---

15 *Royal Mail News*, the newsletter of the Royal Mail Association, issue 25, June 1996. Copies available in the library of the National Maritime Museum, Greenwich.

16 RML, Chairman's Report for 1955.

17 *Shipbuilding and Shipping Record*, 4 March 1948, p. 296.

18 *Shipbuilding and Shipping Record*, 6 September 1951, pp. 308–9. Shipping and Taxation-1. The memorandum prepared by the General Council of British Shipping for submission to The Royal Commission on Taxation of Profits and Income.

Figure 12.1 *Andes* (1939). J & M Clarkson Collection

in 1952, two further vessels of the class following in 1955–56. *Loch Gowan* (9,718 tons, 12 passengers) was built for the North Pacific service. In 1954–55 four 7,300-ton cargo ships were ordered from Harland & Wolff's Govan yard, the first, *Tuscany*, delivered in 1956, costing £438,000. A sister ship for *Loch Gowan*, *Loch Loyal* entered service in 1957. The introduction of the eight new cargo ships, the E- and the Y-classes, enabled the company to re-establish itself strongly in the West Indies trade and the new *Loch* ships strengthened the service to the west coasts of the USA and Canada.

After 1947 the Company continued to manage ships for the Ministry of Transport, including *Asturias*, which was refitted to carry migrants, mainly to Australia and New Zealand. On one occasion her passengers numbered 1,340. She remained in this role until 1954, when she was employed as a troopship. *Almanzora*, on release from government service in 1945, was chartered to Elder Dempster to assist on the West Africa run while new tonnage was being built. She appears to have doubled as a government transport in the period, carrying servicemen home to the West Indies. When, in 1947, Elder Dempster took delivery of their second post-war liner, *Apapa*, she was laid up off Cowes before being broken up the following year.[19] *Atlantis*, bought by the Ministry of Transport in 1946, was refitted as an emigrant ship and continued in service until 1952,

[19] M. Mortimer, 'The last days of *Almanzora*', *Royal Mail News*, No. 14, September 1993. Mr Mortimer was a junior officer in the ship in 1947–48. There is some uncertainty about the last days of *Almanzora*. She is not listed in Royal Mail's accounts

when she was sold for scrap. A former German vessel, *Ubena,* was surrendered to Britain in 1945, renamed *Empire Ken,* and managed by the Company.

At the end of 1955 the Royal Mail fleet totalled 35 ships of 302,208 tons; this figure included two refrigerated lighters of over 1,000 tons. One vessel, the 26-year-old *Lochmonar*, was sold and broken up in 1949, having been declared a constructive total loss after grounding in the Cayman Islands. Pacific Steam's fleet totalled 14 ships of 128,243 tons, including the new *Reina del Mar* (20,225 tons), and her elderly consort, *Reina del Pacifico* (17,872 tons).

Confidence in the Future

From 1946 the consolidated accounts, with PSNC, reflect the developing financial situation over the next 10 years. Operating profit, used in Table 12.1, includes profit from all sources, including investments, although by far the greater proportion is derived from current activity. However, the annual trading profit, the only real guide to business conditions, was given in the directors' report published within the accounts and it could vary quite substantially from the operating figure, as indicated in the comments, below, relating to the 1955 accounts. The reserves and the undistributed profits figures cover all reserve accounts, that for fleet replacement being the largest. Among the current assets in 1946, and subsequently, was a substantial investment in government and other securities: £3.6m.

In early 1947 the liquid position of the Company was declared to be 'substantial and satisfactory', with over £8.4m of reserves and assets of over £17m. The profit for the year, as opposed to the operating profit, at £2.4m, was exceptional against a capital of £4m. Helpful in the build-up of reserves was the Income Tax Act of 1945, which permitted tax allowances on replacement tonnage; such allowances were, however, related to the original cost of the ships. In the early 1950s further government assistance was given to shipowners in the form of an investment allowance, although Royal Mail's directors would persistently complain, with some justification, that insufficient support was given to the industry, which was obliged to counter increasing foreign competition benefiting from more favourable tax regimes.

The following year, 1948, the chairman cautiously anticipated the future. He welcomed the handover by the Ministry of Transport of responsibility for the allocation of freight tonnage and passenger accommodation, a timely release from wartime restriction. He spoke of the establishment of a World Trade Charter, the object of which was the liberalisation of international commerce, but noted that individual countries were already manoeuvring to ensure that they retained the right to impose restrictions.

Despite the difficulties in the South American trades, 1951 was an exceptional year, with profit of £586,562 after transfer of £700,000 to fleet replacement.

---

for 1947, suggesting that she was already in government ownership though manned by the Company.

Operating profit was in excess of £4m, with reserves increased to just over £11m and assets of more than £26m. Within that figure were investments in government and other securities totalling over £10m and a deposit with bankers of £2.2m for new tonnage, although only three vessels were on order at that time. By 1953 the annual profit was a rather more modest £228,562 after tax and depreciation but with no stated transfer to fleet replacement. Even so, dividend paid was 10 per cent. The chairman's statement acknowledged that Group profit was 'considerably less than in the previous year'. Operating profit remained strong at £2.4m.

Chairman Warwick warned shareholders at the annual meeting in early 1954 of difficult trading conditions on South American routes. The value of exports to Argentina of British manufacture fell from £21m in 1952 to less than £15m in 1953. The fall in the value of exports to Brazil was steeper still: down from £52m to £18m. The very real concern was that these important markets would be lost, replaced by the USA, Germany and Japan, all of them determined to take a share of the market. He called for 'urgent official steps to be taken' to support the country's exports, although he refrained from elaborating. By 1955 exports to Brazil, vital to the Company's cargo trades, totalled only £6.7m.

On a slightly more positive note, he expressed appreciation for the government's proposed 20 per cent investment allowance. It was welcomed, he said, as a helpful step in dealing with the very difficult problem confronting the industry, namely the 'crippling burden of taxation' that made it impossible to set aside adequate additional reserves to cover the high cost of new ships.

Table 12.1 Profits, reserves and liabilities, 1946–55

Year	Capital (£m)	Operating profit (£)	Reserves/ undis. profit (£)	Liabilities (£)	Fixed/current assets (£)	Dividend (%)	Share price
1946	4	2,280,461	8,370,459	4,953,531	17,323,990	7.5	26s
1947	4	3,081,599	8,221,304	6,704,260	18,925,564	7.5	34s
1948	4	3,173,525	8,719,886	7,275,631	19,995,517	7.5	31s 6d
1949	4	3,231,907	9,580,579	7,684,150	21,429,729	7.5	26s 3d
1950	4	2,684,877	9,715,858	8,517,049	22,232,907	7.5+2	24s
1951	4	4,026,667	11,044,189	11,249,176	26,293,365	10	28s
1952	4	3,393,165	12,210,476	11,895,681	28,196,157	10+5	28s 6d
1953	4	2,440,723	12,471,250	9,807,407	26,278,657	10	27s
1954	4	2,044,625	13,140,767	9,479,553	26,620,320	10	33s 3d
1955	4	2,163,583	13,744,891	10,317,076	28,061,967	10+2	34s 6d

Notes:

Consolidated accounts include Pacific Steam Navigation Company and two/three other small agencies.

Reserves are identified in accounts as 'Reserves and Undistributed profits'.

Asset figures include fixed and current assets.

Operating profit includes voyage plus investment profits, as opposed to the annual profit given in the report of the directors.

In presenting the 1955 accounts, in May 1956, Chairman Warwick warned that short-term prospects must be viewed with caution. New administrations in both Brazil and Argentina faced problems of recovery that would be aided by stimulating overseas trade and the removal of import and export restrictions. He offered no comment on the likelihood of the Brazilian and Argentine governments acceding to his wish. In the absence of further political and industrial upheaval, he felt 'sober confidence' in the future.

A 'surplus' was reported, no longer referred to as a 'profit', of £232,867 after deduction of a whole range of charges, the amounts unspecified. After adding a dividend contribution from PSNC and deducting dividend payments to shareholders, a carry-forward of only £210,590 remained. Nevertheless, a maintained dividend of 10 per cent plus a bonus of 2 per cent, described as 'reasonable', was paid on the basis of what were declared to be good trading results. Also encouraging to investors was the share price performance: it picked up slowly after the war, 24s in 1945, peaking at 31s 6d in 1948. A dip followed, to 24s in 1950, and then a sound recovery, by 1955, to 34s 6d.

Pacific Steam, 100 per cent owned, returned good profits in the immediate post-war period. In 1947 the figure was £525,591, which was allocated to its own tonnage replacement funds, no dividend being paid, as yet, to Royal Mail. Its ship-building programme proceeded, as it always had, without financial help from its parent. Nevertheless, high building costs were a persistent complaint, with replacements costing two or three times the amount set aside by depreciation: the two newly built E-ships cost £1.75m.

Trade Restrictions and Discrimination

Restoration of South American services, passenger and cargo, was achieved by 1947 with a combination of refitted tonnage and purchased or newly built cargo vessels. Only one new ship was ordered immediately after the war, in part due to the more than doubling of building costs since 1938–39. There was a strong demand for passenger berths, especially southbound, as servicemen and other expatriates returned home after war service, and for outward and homeward cargo space to meet increasing British exports and the demand for imports. Passenger movements were adversely affected by currency restrictions and dock strikes in major home ports, including London and Liverpool, which led to congestion and delays. A further urgent priority was the exclusion of foreign shipping from the Company's long-established services and expansion where possible at a time when German and Italian vessels were unable to resume trading with Brazil and Argentina.

Although shareholders were reassured of the Company's financial situation and confidence was expressed in trade prospects, difficulties loomed. In 1948 the directors called for close and friendly international relations before commenting on the dangers of discriminatory trade restrictions operated by a number of nations. Their particular concern was the move by several countries to apply restrictions on the carriage of exports and imports with preference for ships sailing under the national flag. They followed the lead of the USA, which decreed that 50 per cent of all aid cargoes to Europe and elsewhere should be carried in American vessels. Later the Americans extended the 50 per cent rule to commercial, that is, non-aid, cargoes. The traditional trades of most British liner companies were severely affected by these flag and other restrictions, and within a decade proud names, P&O, British India, Clan Line and Bibby Line were struggling to continue profitably in business.[20]

Ironically, the USA reacted vigorously with Senate Committee hearings when similar cargo carriage limitations affected its own trade with South American countries, including Brazil and Argentina. Argentina required that all imports and exports for government purposes, the majority of the country's imports, were carried in its own-flagged ships, which were free from restrictions applied to the use of some of the more modern loading and discharging facilities in Buenos Aires.

Brazil also controlled the carriage of cargo and further placed foreign tonnage at commercial disadvantage, with decrees that all non-Brazilian shipping using its ports be classed as 'non-preferential', its own ships receiving berth priority in Rio and Santos and other ports, sometimes causing lengthy waits for loading or discharging facilities. National ships also benefited from lower costs for pilotage and lighthouse fees and reduced consular fees for shippers.[21]

An insight into the concerns of the Company board was contained in a letter dated October 1949 from Chairman Walter Warwick to the chairman of Harland & Wolff, Sir Frederick Rebbeck, following the loss *of Magdalena.* Confirming that the vessel would not be replaced, although substantial funds, including the insurance money, were available for the purpose, he noted the 1948 delivery to the newly established Argentine national shipping company, the Dodero Line, of *Presidente Peron* (12,627 tons), the first of three twin-screw intermediate liners built by Vickers-Armstrong Ltd of Barrow-in-Furness for a Buenos Aires to London service. She was capable of 19 knots, carried 74 first-class passengers and, most importantly, had 350,000 cubic feet of insulated space for refrigerated cargo, sufficient for approximately 3,500 tons of cargo as opposed to Royal Mail's *Highland* ships, which were able to lift nearer to 5,000 tons but were appreciably slower.[22] He added, 'these changed circumstances render it necessary that we should proceed cautiously and rather wait on events before deciding upon further very heavy capital expenditure'.

Chairman Warwick no doubt enjoyed a good business relationship with Rebbeck and he conveyed to him rather more information than was generally given to shareholders, expanding on the 'uncertainty' of the trade relationship with Argentina and the unrealistic range of exchange rates applied by that country following a sterling devaluation. He described the revised rates as a 'very serious

[20] Hope, *British Shipping*, pp. 396–7.

[21] *Shipbuilding and Shipping Record*, 10 February 1952.

[22] Bonsor, *South Atlantic Seaway*, pp. 482–3. The two further vessels, *Eva Peron* and *17 de Octobre*, each accommodated 96 passengers.

method of discrimination' designed to obtain large increases in payments for meat and other exports.[23] Certainly Royal Mail suffered as a result. Argentina, like Brazil, was persistently slow in settling debt, and with large payments due at the time of the peso adjustments, the losses caused by the new rates of exchange were substantial.[24]

The decision not to replace *Magdalena* was significant. At a time of political instability in the Argentine and uncertain trade prospects in that country and in Brazil, it was perhaps unsurprising. She was described as a replacement for *Highland Patriot*, sunk in 1940, although the likelihood must be that she was intended to be the first of a class of replacements for the *Highland* ships, now nearly 20 years old and becoming increasingly expensive to operate. However, no evidence has been found to substantiate that theory. Certainly the speedy post-war introduction of large passenger/refrigerated tonnage by the Argentine and former belligerent countries was something of a shock to Royal Mail's management and a firm statement of intent by President Peron. The concern of the directors in the latter stages of the war was to ensure that Royal Mail recovered its strong pre-war position in the South Atlantic trades at the end of hostilities, and their focus was on the inevitable recovery of the German and Italian lines, always powerful competitors.

The outcome was that the Company, with only two liners, the by-now venerable *Alcantara* and the 1939-built *Andes* on the South American mail service, was obliged to accept that its proud reputation on the route was much diminished. The mail and passenger service was in decline, the situation made worse by the uncertain supply of meat, readily handled by the *Highland* and the D-ships. In the immediate future the substantial available capital was diverted to the building of new cargo vessels for both the Company's West Indies and North Pacific services and for Pacific Steam's west coast routes.

By 1955 the mood in British shipping circles was gloomy. Although the country's shipyards were booming, with new orders from British and foreign owners, the press expressed concern that Britain's share of much-increased world tonnage continued to decline, down from 50 per cent in 1914 to a mere 20 per cent. The fleets of most European countries were greatly increased since 1939, Norway's by 50 per cent. Of special interest to Royal Mail, Brazilian tonnage was greatly increased; that of Argentina was 3.5 greater than its pre-war size. Most of the increases were of tramp-ship tonnage belonging to the newly emerging 'flag of convenience' fleets of Panama, Liberia and Honduras, which benefited from reduced costs, freedom from taxation and regulation, with resultant operating cost reductions.[25]

---

[23] Nicol, *MacQueen's Legacy*, p. 183. Letter dated 4 October 1949.

[24] *Shipbuilding and Shipping Record*, 24 May 1951.

[25] *Shipbuilding and Shipping Record*, 1 December 1955.

Chapter 13
The End of the Line

Walter Warwick continued in the chair until 1960, at which time he retired, aged 85. H. Leslie Bowes, who had been chairman of Pacific Steam and had moved to London as managing director of Royal Mail in 1958, became chairman. The report to shareholders for 1960, dated 24 April 1961, was presented by Bowes. Other directors at that time were Frank Charlton, newly appointed chairman of Furness, Withy, Sir Errington Keville, a Furness director, C.G. Mathews, R. Stancliff and C.W. Varney. J.J. Gawne and Sir Gilmour Jenkins joined the board in 1960 and 1961 respectively.[1]

The directors' report for the year of 1956 was bullish: operating profit, before adjustments, nearly doubled, up from £1,813,802 in 1955 to £3,479,907. This was attributed to abnormally high freight rates at the time of the Suez crisis. In that period Company cargo vessels regularly carried good outward general cargoes with homeward freights of bagged grain from Rosario and Buenos Aires plus, often, shipments from Brazil. Although conditions in Argentina continued unsettled, with frequent labour unrest, meat exports totalled 335,000 tons in 1956, compared with 225,000 tons the previous year.

The results were a windfall for shareholders. On top of a 15 per cent dividend, a one-for-one share issue was announced, raising capital from £4m to £8m, the first increase since the establishment of the Company in 1932. The intention was to capitalise a portion of reserves and undistributed profits, totalling £17,545,202, through the issue of 4m £1 ordinary shares. The stock market was clearly aware of the plan: the value of Company £1 shares rose on the announcement from an already high 42s to 45s 6d, having been 38s in early January. The wholly owned Pacific Steam Navigation Company likewise doubled its capital from £1.5m to £3m.[2]

The building of new tonnage for the South American service was confirmed, with the improvement of trade a factor in the decision. Three new 20,000-ton, 17.5-knot passenger/cargo vessels were ordered from Harland & Wolff in 1956 with cost anticipated at over £15m and delivery from 1959.

Trading conditions returned to normal during the early part of 1957 as the Suez Canal reopened after being blocked for several months. Soon, however, due to a world trade slowdown and an oversupply of tonnage, largely operated under flags of convenience, conditions became depressed and would remain so for the next

---

1 Sir Errington Keville was chairman of Furness, Withy from 1962 to 1968. J.J. Gawne was a director of Furness, Withy.

2 *The Times* (London), 14 May 1957, Chairman's Report.

few years.[3] Chairman Warwick described the fall in freight rates in late 1957 as 'drastic', and noted that these conditions persisted through 1958, though with only two or three Company ships unemployed for short periods.[4] (At the time a large amount of British and foreign tonnage was laid up rather than operating at a loss.) Port charges and other operating costs increased appreciably. Tramp-ship freight rates fell by up to 50 per cent, and the availability of bulk shipments declined dramatically, affecting homeward freights for the Company's cargo ships. The introduction of new cargo tonnage, the three Y-class ships, at such a time was unfortunate. Rates for refrigerated tonnage were less affected, controlled as they were by conference arrangements. The impact on earnings was very severe. An immediate result was the decision to sell two of the four wartime-built Liberty ships and to withdraw the 1926-built *Alcantara* from service, as it was no longer possible to operate her economically.

Warning Signs

Meat shipments were steady through 1957, all refrigerated units being fully employed. However, the circumstances of this trade, vital to the Argentine and to Royal Mail, were critical. An article in *The Times* of June 1958 noted that herds had declined from 66,900,000 in 1956 to an estimated 37,700,000, with slaughtering exceeding calving by 3,400,000. The situation, the article commented, was 'seriously pre-occupying the authorities'. Friday was now a meatless day in Buenos Aires, as it had been when drought last seriously diminished the herds, and as it would be frequently in the future. Dairy produce and fruit imports from Argentina and Brazil continued to be satisfactory. Passenger numbers on the South American service were down, although migrant traffic was increased.

Trade with Brazil and the Argentine was a developing problem: exports to Britain from Brazil in 1956 were a little more than a quarter in value of the figure in 1951. And British exports to Brazil fell sharply between 1955 and 1957. In 1956 British exports to Argentina were half, by value, of those from West Germany and a quarter of those from the USA.

A direct result of the situation was the freeing of *Andes* to make six Mediterranean cruises in the summer of 1958. In the previous two or three years it was not uncommon for *Andes* to make a small number of cruises each year,

---

[3] Sturmey, *British Shipping*, pp. 210–11, table p. 212. Flags of convenience: a term applied to vessels operated under the flags of Panama and Liberia, and others, but owned by foreign nationals. The benefits for owners included reduced running costs, regulation and taxation. Flags of convenience fleets increased from 4.4m tons in 1950 to 11.3 m tons in 1956. Source: *Annual Reports, Chamber of Shipping.*

[4] RML, Chairman's Report for 1958. A Chamber of Shipping report dated 22 May 2011 noted that in January 1958 288,000 tons of British shipping was laid up. By January of 1959 the figure was 1,048,000 tons, easing to 756,000 tons by October 1960.

as did *Alcantara.* The latter vessel was entirely unsuited to cruising: although her first- and second-class accommodation was admired by passengers, half of the berths, 462, were third/migrant class. A press article referred to her cruise programme for 1956: fares for an outward run to Ceuta and return from Gibraltar in July ranged from £20 to £25, five- to ten-year-olds half price.[5] It is unlikely that her cruises covered costs, although the alternative, a lay-up berth in Southampton for several weeks, would have been a considerable expense.

By 1959, although operating profit exceeded £2m, conditions generally were described as depressed, with no prospect of material improvement in trade with Argentina, Uruguay and Brazil for some time and with direct cash losses covered by transfers from reserves. Addressing shareholders in May 1960, Chairman Warwick cited a list of adverse circumstances: low freight rates, high costs, currency devaluations and the developing problem of flags of convenience and flag discrimination, in particular a decree by the Brazilian government that 70 per cent of imports must be shipped in vessels owned or chartered by Brazilian companies. This action was, at least in part, a retaliation against the Brazil–Europe conference, which had, in 1959, re-established the deferred rebate system, effectively shutting out the non-conference ships of Lloyd Brasileiro. (At that time Royal Mail's monthly Brazil cargo service was jointly operated with Lamport & Holt. The frequency was reduced to a loss-making fortnightly service.) The London-based Chamber of Shipping, concerned by this development, pressed the government to persuade the Brazilian government to change its policy. The chairman summarised: 'Until freer trade and increased cargoes materialise we cannot look for any substantial betterment in our trading results.'[6]

A serious blow in 1960 was a strike by tally clerks in London that paralysed the docks and caused serious losses to the Company. The chairman reported to the annual meeting in May 1961 that he was in no doubt that certain export cargoes had been permanently moved from the Port of London following the disastrous stoppage. In this period strikes by groups of workers were all too common in ports across the country.

With the new A-ships due to enter service in 1960 in the London to Buenos Aires trade, and freights uncertain, three of the four 30-year-old *Highland* ships were sold in 1959 for further trading.[7] The last of the class in Royal Mail service, *Highland Monarch*, was broken up at Dalmuir in early 1960. A measure of the uncertain homeward cargo situation was the chartering out or laying up temporarily, usually in Falmouth, of some of the Company's refrigerated D-ships: in late 1958

[5] *Shipbuilding and Shipping Record*, 8 December 1955.

[6] RML, Annual Report to Shareholders, May 1960.

[7] *Highland Brigade* and *Highland Princess* were sold to Greek owners, intended for a service from Genoa to Australia. *Highland Chieftain*, renamed *Calpean Star*, was sold to a company based in Gibraltar. She was converted for use in the whaling industry as a store, accommodation and refrigerated transport ship. In 1960, when inbound to Montevideo for repairs, following a boiler-room explosion, she sank off the main channel to the port.

Darro and *Tweed* were recorded as laid up, *Drina* and *Durango* having just re-entered service.[8]

In anticipation of the entry into service of new tonnage, the 20-year-old *Andes* was withdrawn from service in 1959 and extensively refitted as a first-class-only cruise ship, for which she was very well suited. She proved popular with passengers at a time when the cruise industry, as we now know it, was in its infancy. In light of all the circumstances only a supreme optimist would comment to shareholders in mid-1960 that he confidently anticipated that the new A-ships would be extremely popular with the travelling public.[9]

Up to this time returns from the cargo services had been reported as 'satisfactory', especially those to the Caribbean and the North Pacific. However, the services were in decline, with only modest outward cargoes and poor freight rates. Rates for homeward cargoes of sugar were very low due to the availability of laid-up tramp tonnage and the introduction of vessels converted or built for the carriage of bulk cargoes. Ships on the West Indies route frequently proceeded, after discharge, to the west coast, Pacific Steam territory, loading homeward cargoes of bagged fishmeal. Other homeward freights were grain, phosphates, coal or sulphur from Gulf ports for UK or continental ports. An attempt was made to establish a Central American service, jointly with Holland America, using three new PSNC Island-class vessels and chartered tonnage, but this was short-lived due to limitations imposed by several of the countries involved.

In 1959 Pacific Steam introduced three new cargo ships and the following year the first of two tankers, the *William Wheelwright* (46,400 tons), entered service. She was followed by the *George Peacock* (28,500 tons). Both were chartered on 'satisfactory' terms. (Simultaneously, Furness, Withy established, in conjunction with British Petroleum, the Warwick Tanker Company Ltd and, in 1960, two 23,000-ton tankers were built.) Royal Mail's move into tankers was a modest one and it is uncertain if further investment was planned. The annual report for 1959 anticipated that the two 'would prove to be a welcome source of regular income and the Company will reap the benefit of diversifying its activities'.

There was a general reluctance by liner and cargo shipowners to enter the tanker market in the 1950s, dominated as it was by the large oil companies' own fleets. Although the major tanker operators expanded their building programmes, demand exceeded supply and profitable charters were available, as with Pacific Steam, though most went to overseas companies. The approach of P&O was rather more dynamic: when, in 1955, still investing heavily in liner and cargo-liner tonnage, management determined to establish a fleet of tankers, Lord Geddes, an acknowledged expert, was recruited as tanker advisor.[10] The initial plan was for 25 ships of 20,000 tons dwt. This was amended to 14 ships of over 35,000 tons, most

---

8 RML, Board Minute, 17 October 1958.

9 RML, Chairman's Report to Shareholders, 27 May 1960.

10 Geddes was appointed to the P&O board in 1957 and became chairman of Trident Tankers on its foundation in 1962.

of which would benefit from long-term charters. Initially the ships were operated by a number of group companies until, in 1962, Trident Tankers was formed to manage all of them and, by 1964, P&O was the UK's largest independent tanker owner.[11]

The P&O chairman, Sir Donald Anderson, speaking to shareholders in early 1962, referred to the continuing shipping slump, which, he said, had taken place against a generally prosperous British and world trade background. He added: 'But for the group's tankers, the results would have been even worse. They now had 14 in service and they were making a useful contribution towards profits.'[12]

By 1960 the operation of *Reina del Mar*, scarcely five years old, had become increasingly difficult in face of 'rising costs, air competition and political upheavals such as that in Cuba'. Nevertheless, PSNC resolved to ensure that 'every effort will be made to ensure that this beautiful liner will continue to uphold British prestige on the west coast of South America, to which the Pacific Company has provided a passenger service from Liverpool since 1868'.[13]

The fortnightly cargo service to Brazil continued to be adversely affected by high and increasing costs, low freight rates and the harsh limitations on non-Brazilian tonnage. In 1960 a compromise was reached with Lloyd Brasileiro, a major national operator trading to UK ports, which agreed a two-year deal to charter space in Royal Mail/Lamport & Holt ships rather than outside tonnage at cost of 15 per cent of the freight received. The following year senior representatives of both companies flew to Brazil for further negotiations, and within months it was decided to discontinue the service, the five ships involved being switched to the PSNC west coast service.[14] The closure of the long-standing cargo-only service to southern Brazil ports was a considerable blow. The D- and the new A-class ships would adequately maintain the trade connections. A Portugal–Brazil trade agreement required that cargo between the two countries be first offered to Lloyd Brazileiro. In the same period Uruguay announced that all government cargo must be carried in national-flag ships.

A Message from the Chairman

A memorandum from Chairman H. Leslie Bowes was circulated to senior staff in May 1961. It laid out clearly the developing situation of the Company in rather more bleak terms than his public pronouncements. He noted that there had been no improvement in Company trades, some of which, he added, 'suffer from a great dearth of homeward cargo, while others are carried on at unremunerative rates of

---

[11] D. and S. Howarth, *The Story of P&O* (London, 1986), p. 157.

[12] *Shipbuilding and Shipping Record*, 5 April, 1962. RML, Chairman's Report for 1960.

[13] *The Times* (London), 24 May 1961, Chairman's Report, Royal Mail Lines.

[14] *Tuscany, Brittany* and *Pilcomayo* were redeployed and, later, *Paraguay* and *Pampas*.

freight which, for a variety of reasons, cannot be raised to world market levels'. He added that, although 'massive economies' effected in the four years past had been swallowed up by ever-increasing costs, further endeavours must be made. The three new A-ships, he said, were 'doing very well', yet the whole tone of the piece was mildly desperate. The causes of the Company's situation were largely out of his control: he spoke of flag discrimination, calling for a live-and-let-live approach by foreign governments, permitting the Company to 'carry on with the service we have operated for so long'.[15]

In the prevailing economic and political conditions the directors' options were few. Costs had already been cut by the laying up and selling of ships and the closing or reduction of Company offices and agencies. The Rio de Janeiro and Santos offices were reduced to agency status in 1962 and other offices were downsized. The long-established London Docks Works, which assisted with maintenance work while ships were in port, was sold in 1962, contributing some £200,000 to cash resources. There was little to be done in terms of cost reductions in ships still trading: these covered crew, repairs and stores and fuel economies. (By 1965 further cost savings were made by reducing the numbers of catering and engineering staff on most of the ships, and the loss-making carriage of passengers on D- and E-ships was ended.) A modest attempt was made to integrate duties duplicated within the London office and Pacific Steam's Liverpool headquarters, but progress was slow. The shipowner's traditional means of countering cost increases was to increase freight rates – an impossibility at that time.

Chairman Bowes, commenting on disappointing results for 1961, spoke of substantially reduced meat shipments and unavoidable increased costs, including seamen's wages. Income was so reduced that the sum of £350,000 was transferred from the fleet replacement and the depreciation funds to cover normal depreciation charges. He added that the Company's cash position was improving only very slowly and the time was not right to consider arranging long-term finance to cover the overdraft. He then advised shareholders that no dividend would be paid for 1961.[16] (The chairman of Houlder Line reported to shareholders that, although its two refrigerated ships on the Argentine route carried good cargoes during 1961, freight rates were so low that they had 'not even earned their depreciation'.[17]) The situation was, clearly, dire. Many of the Latin American countries were suffering severe problems, political, economic and financial. Some applied severe restrictions on imports; others introduced exchange controls and/or currency devaluations.

The year 1962 was critical for the Company: trading was described as 'largely unprofitable' and £497,000 was transferred from reserves to cover fleet depreciation with a dividend payment from reserves of 3 per cent. More significant and concerning were the financial arrangements made between Royal Mail and

---

[15] Typed sheet, 'Memorandum from the Chairman', dated 25 May 1961 and signed 'H. Leslie Bowes'.

[16] *The Times* (London), 30 May 1962.

[17] *Shipbuilding and Shipping Record*, 11 January 1962.

Pacific Steam. During the year Pacific Steam paid two dividends to Royal Mail totalling 300 per cent on its £3m share capital; this transaction enabled the parent company to make income-tax recoveries of nearly £3.5m. The funds were used to reduce bank indebtedness, resulting in a significant fall in interest charges. Pacific Steam was left with a debt that was liquidated by the formation of a new, jointly owned, company, Pacific Maritime Services Ltd, which operated the two new tankers.[18] These machinations were worthy of Owen Philipps in his prime and must certainly have caused some alarm and confusion among shareholders.

A Nation in Deadlock

'A Nation in Deadlock' was a description applied to Argentina following Peron's 1955 fall from power. Argentina had become a second-ranked nation in Latin America, unable to find a stable international position and largely isolated from the world community. Peron's successive replacements failed to establish political and economic stability. Argentina's share of world trade in agricultural goods declined from 1.92 per cent in 1950 to only 0.57 per cent in 1968, with prices largely unchanged in the period but with volumes increased as North America, Australia and Europe dominated the market. Prospects hardly improved with the establishment in 1960 of the European Economic Community, but Argentina was relegated to the secondary role of supplier in times of scarcity. The availability of meat for export was not consistent, although, much later, in the 1960s, Britain still purchased 25 per cent of exports. Italy, in second place, accounted for about 12 per cent.[19]

In 1956 Argentina held trade talks in Paris with representatives of nine European countries, including Britain. The objective was to resolve the country's debt problems, relics of the Peron era, which totalled $450m, comprising government debts, arrangements with central bank and liabilities to private concerns over long-term orders already placed. The debt to Britain totalled £20m. Agreement was reached for settlements over a ten-year period at an interest rate averaging 3.5 per cent. British hopes lay in an increased share of Argentine imports, mainly oil and raw materials and not especially helpful to Royal Mail.[20] After Peron's 1955 departure there was some relaxation in regulations related to imports/exports, although shipments of material for state-owned utilities continued to be carried in national vessels.

Attempts to control persistent inflation through devaluations, foreign loans and foreign investments were only partially successful. Government inducements encouraged major American and European companies to invest, for example Ford, Peugeot, Coca Cola, Olivetti, Unilever, ICI. Critics argued that the multinationals

---

[18] *The Times* (London), 30 May 1963, Chairman's Report.

[19] Rock, *Argentina, 1516–1987*, p. 320 and table p. 323.

[20] *The Times* (London), 31 May 1956.

grew at the expense of Argentine businesses, an echo of the attitudes to British companies just a few years earlier.

The state of the economy worsened in 1961 with labour unrest and strikes. The Minister of the Economy, Dr R. Aleman, resigned, having 'lost faith in his country's monetary and economic policy'. He had earlier led a mission to Europe that aimed, in light of the development of the Common Market, to secure Argentina's export markets. Recession followed the removal of President Frondizi in 1962, although recovery swiftly followed as record harvests coincided with export price levels not known for many years.

A press article in mid-1964 was headed 'Crisis grows in Argentine meat industry'. It noted the complete failure to deal with the crisis in the meat business and aired the gloomy view expressed in some quarters that by 1975 Argentina would be a meat importer. It reported that the government had recently authorised the province of Corrientes, which in 1961 was the fourth of 22 provinces in importance as a beef producer, to import meat from Uruguay. Soaring home demand from an increasing population, periods of drought and disorganisation between government, the meat producers and the packers were blamed. Argentina was no longer able to feed its own people and meet its commitments to Britain and to new customers such as Italy, Spain and West Germany. In light of the situation, the article added, several of the most modern beef-carrying vessels had been withdrawn from the River Plate run and sent elsewhere for trade, some to South Africa.[21]

Meat exports to Britain continued to be uncertain, due, in part, to a cap placed on import levels by the British government and a failure of Argentine suppliers to meet even the agreed quotas, due, as a rule, to drought or livestock disease. A question in the House of Commons in May 1963 concerned the cap of 203,000 tons applied by the government on imports in that year. The response was that the tonnage quoted was the same as for 1960: for the two immediately previous years the figures were 153,000 tons (1961) and 181,000 tons (1962).[22] Royal Mail and other shipowners were placed in the invidious position of being poised between the Argentine suppliers and the British government's protection of home and other, mainly Australian and New Zealand, supplies through the import caps. Chairman Bowes, speaking in May 1964, was predictably unhappy about the import curbs, describing them as the 'Government's panic action' at a time when there was some evidence of recovery in the trade, although he later acknowledged that Argentina did not even meet the permitted import figures in 1963 due to drought in 1962.

Juscelino Kubitschek de Oliveira replaced Vargas as president of Brazil in 1955, although his election was immediately followed by a bloodless revolution rapidly quelled with the support of the military. He promised economic growth with industrialisation and a higher standard of living for the rapidly increasing

[21] *The Times* (London), 21 May 1964, report from a correspondent in Buenos Aires.

[22] *The Times* (London), 7 May 1963, Report on Question Time in the House of Commons.

population. And, largely, he delivered. His five years in power were ones of dramatic development in, mainly, the industrial sector, aided by an influx of foreign companies lured by financial incentives and Brazil's huge market potential. Ford and General Motors were among those to establish themselves in the São Paulo area. Airline communications within the country were greatly improved and the merchant service revived by the purchase of 80 ships, making it the largest in Latin America. Work was begun on the building of a new capital city, Brasilia, in central Brazil, which became the seat of government in 1960.[23] From 1963 the economic situation was dire, with a soaring cost of living and a collapse of the cruzeiro. Once again, the government fell to a military-supported revolutionary movement, the president, Goulart, leaving the country for exile in April 1964.

The Fleet

Against this changing background Royal Mail's new, traditionally outfitted tonnage continued to occupy the slipways of Harland's yards in Belfast and Glasgow. Seven new ships were added to the fleet in the period 1955–57: two further 7,800-ton Harland & Wolff-built E-ships joined the West Indies services and *Loch Loyal* (11,035 tons) increased to five Royal Mail's representation on the joint Holland America service to North Pacific ports. Four of a new Y-class of 7,400-ton cargo ships (the first was *Tuscany*) entered service in 1956–57. At that stage the fleet totalled 40 vessels of approximately 342,000 gross tons. In addition, Pacific Steam operated 14 vessels of 128,243 tons, including two passenger/cargo liners and two new cargo ships. The 20,000-ton *Reina del Mar* entered service in 1956.

Commentators have noted the persistence, through the 1950s and 1960s, of British companies building tonnage in British yards and complaining about high costs when lower prices were available overseas, where yards, some rebuilt after the war, benefited from more modern equipment and techniques. An inducement was the availability, from 1957, of a 40 per cent investment allowance for new tonnage. (In its 120-year history Royal Mail ordered and took delivery of only two ships that were not built in Britain; in 1959 two 1,300-ton refrigerated meat lighters for use on the River Plate and its tributaries were built in Germany.)

In May 1956 the chairman advised, in his report for 1955, that the building of *Reina del Mar* was essential 'to maintain and extend the passenger service' and noted that her considerable cost, originally anticipated at £3m, had been much greater due to wage and material cost rises. He added ominously: 'it will be very difficult to secure an adequate return to cover interest and depreciation', and warned that a 'more reasonable basis of taxation' was needed or the lifeblood of the shipping industry would be drained away.[24]

---

23 Rollie E. Poppino, 'Brazil Since 1954', in Bello, *A History of Modern Brazil 1889–1964* (Stanford, 1966), pp. 335–8. Fausto, *A Concise History of Brazil*, pp. 237–48.

24 RML, Report of the Directors, May 1956.

The timing of the decision, in 1956, to build the three new passenger/cargo liners for the Brazil/Argentina service was unfortunate. The general trade situation worsened appreciably, rather than improved, as the directors hoped it would, and meat supplies became progressively uncertain. The Company's situation in the trade was precarious, with the four *Highland* ships, 30 years old by the time new tonnage might be available, becoming increasing unreliable and expensive to operate. Without urgent replacements the Company's important passenger services would cease and its share of homeward refrigerated freight would be severely reduced.

The decision to build the new liners at minimum cost of £15m was a gamble. By 1960 it was very evident that passenger numbers were falling due to the dramatic increase in the number of flights servicing the South American countries. In that year all the major European airlines offered services to South America. Britain's national airline, BOAC, operated two weekly flights to Buenos Aires using Comet aircraft with accommodation for 61 passengers, the numbers of passengers growing as new and larger airliners entered service and frequencies increased. The route was circuitous, with a transatlantic connection between Dakar and Recife, but the benefits, especially to business travellers, were great.

Alcantara was withdrawn from service in 1958, sold to Japanese ship-breakers for £235,000, and *Asturias* and *Empire Ken*, troopships managed for the Ministry of Transport since 1945, were withdrawn and sold for breaking up. The Southampton office and stores, opened in 1841, were, as a result, severely curtailed, although *Andes* continued to use the port on her cruising schedules. In the period 1957–60 four cargo ships were sold for scrap and the four wartime-built Liberty ships were sold for further trading for about £135,000 each.

All three of the new A-ships, *Amazon*, *Aragon* and *Arlanza*, made their maiden voyages from London during 1960. They were handsome, white hulled (a departure from the Company's usual black) and able to carry over 4,000 tons of refrigerated and 1,000 tons of general cargo. They had accommodation for 107 first-class passengers, 82 in cabin class and 275 in third class. The ships were described at the outset as 'well supported', but the high cost of their construction, nearer to £6m each than the hoped-for £5m, resulted in the disposal of the Company's substantial holdings of government securities and the need to arrange a bank overdraft.[25]

Pacific Steam's 1931-built *Reina del Pacifico*, no longer profitable, was withdrawn from service in 1957 and scrapped the following year. As early as 1959–60 it was evident that the liner service from the west coast, beset by increasing costs and airline competition, was no longer profitable and consideration was given to withdrawing *Reina del Mar* from service. Application had been made to government for financial support to maintain the trade, but this was not forthcoming. By 1963 she was converted for cruising and chartered to Travel Savings Ltd, a joint operation with Canadian Pacific and Union-Castle, which operated her unsuccessfully out of Liverpool. Later she was chartered for

[25] *The Times* (London), Chairman's Report, 24 May 1961.

Figure 13.1 *Arlanza* (1960). J & M Clarkson Collection

five years, with an additional five-year option, to the British & Commonwealth Shipping Co. *Reina* was never considered as a running mate or, indeed, as a replacement for *Andes*, whose operational results were, by 1964, in decline despite her expensive refurbishment in 1959.[26] She was sold for breaking up in 1971, ending Royal Mail's long involvement in the cruise industry.

The first of the P-class cargo ships, *Parima*, was sold in 1962, having been laid up with several other vessels largely as a result of the closure of the Brazil service, and, by 1964, her remaining five sisters were disposed of, mainly to Greek companies for further trading, for a total of about £514,000. At the beginning of 1965 Pacific Steam owned 14 cargo ships, all but five of them built since 1950, and two oil tankers for a total of 160,000 tons. Royal Mail owned 20 ocean-going vessels, the oldest, the D-class ships built in 1942–44, of 230,000 tons as well as two River Plate meat lighters (see Table 13.1).

[26] Author's correspondence in August 2001 with Sir Brian Shaw, Royal Mail Lines Company Secretary, 1960–65, later a director and chairman of Furness, Withy.

Table 13.1 Ships owned by Royal Mail and Pacific Steam in 1965

Royal Mail	**Pacific Steam**
Andes	*Pizzaro, Potosi, Cotopaxi, Cuzco*
Amazon, Aragon, Arlanza	*Kenuta, Flamenco*
Loch Avon, Loch Garth	*Salamanca, Salinas, Salaverry*
Loch Loyal, Loch Gowan	*Santander, Sarmiento*
Durango, Drina, Darro, Deseado	*Somers Isle, Eleuthera, Cienfuegos*
Eden, Escalante, Ebro, Essequibo	*William Wheelwright* (tanker)
Tuscany, Picardy, Albany, Thessaly	*George Peacock* (tanker)

Financial Decline

When, in 1957, capital was increased to £8m, Company finances were sound, the share price strong and a dividend of 9 per cent was paid. Reserves and undistributed profits were nearly £15m, with heavy commitment to new tonnage. The annual report noted the 'very severe' effects of the fall in freight rates and the scarcity of return cargoes. The 1958 and 1959 reports cautiously summarised future prospects in terms of the Company being in a position to take advantage of 'any improvements when they come along'. References to continued difficult trading conditions followed with 'no prospect of any material improvement taking place for some time to come'.

Dividends suffered, down from 15 per cent in 1956 to 5 per cent in 1960 and the share price slumped from 38s in 1957 to 20s in 1958, recovering to 31s in 1960 (see Table 13.2). The Stock Market had taken note of the situation. The confidence of shareholders was shaken.

Table 13.2 Profits, reserves, assets and liabilities, 1955–64

	Capital (£m)	Operating profit (£m)	Reserves & undistributed profits (£m)*	Liabilities (£m)	Assets (£m)	Dividend (%)	Share price*
1955	4	2.1	13.7	10.3	28.1	10 + 2	34s 6d
1956	4	3.7	15.9	10.8	30.8	15	33s 4d
1957	8	3.5	14.8	10.8	33.7	9	38s
1958	8	2.7	16.0	8.6	32.6	8	20s
1959	8	2.5	15.7	13.5	37.2	8	23s
1960	8	1.9	13.9	18.6	40.4	5	31s
1961	8	2.0	15.7	16.5	40.2	Nil	21s
1962	8	1.9	19.1	11.5	33.9	3	12s
1963	8	2.1	20.0	9.0	37.5	3	9s
1964	8	79,834	18.7	9.5	36.2	Nil	17s

* Share prices are as at early January unless otherwise indicated.

The financial burden of new-tonnage building was reflected in the 1960 accounts, which showed liabilities increased from £13.5m in 1959 to £18.6m, including a bank overdraft of £7.4m, creditors, various, £6.5m and investments reduced from over £2m to £120,375. Chairman Bowes's report to shareholders in 1961, his first, was unremittingly gloomy. He was obliged to advise them that 'in view of the fall in profits and the urgent need to conserve cash resources the directors found it necessary to reduce the dividend from 8% to 5%'. He added that, due to the very high building costs of new tonnage, most of the Company's government securities had been disposed of and temporary financial facilities had been arranged with the bank.[27] Already referred to was the move in 1962 to bolster the Company's financial situation by transferring dividends from Pacific Steam.[28]

The accounts for 1963 included the advice that full disclosure of the profits and reserves of the Company was now being made. *The Times* welcomed the decision to no longer hide behind the clause in the Companies Act that allowed certain companies, shipping, banking and so on not to fully disclose financial information. The move, investors were assured, would enable them to make a better assessment of the true value of their investments. The 3 per cent dividend paid from reserves was straightforward enough.[29]

In 1964 reserves were still in excess of £18.7m, with liabilities of £9.5m and assets of £36.2m, the majority of that being the fleet value. But profits and return on capital had collapsed and there was, clearly, little or no prospect of short-term recovery. The combination of poor trading conditions and the introduction of national-flag restrictions had progressively damaged Royal Mail's business.

There was always, especially from the late 1950s, in the tone of pronouncements by Company chairmen the implication that passengers and, more importantly, cargo shippers 'supported' the Company and that governments of countries with which Royal Mail/Pacific Steam had traded for many years had an obligation to help preserve that link. In point of fact, shippers supported the Company if the freight rates and delivery arrangements were acceptable, and passengers travelled in Royal Mail ships when the schedules were convenient, the fares competitive and onboard conditions to their satisfaction. Countries with which the Company had traded for many years not surprisingly pursued their own national interests.

Frequently stated by management were pleas that the British government owed a debt of gratitude to the Company for Royal Mail's service to the nation over many years in transporting vital imports and exports, sometimes in difficult conditions. The fact that the Company's objective was profit for shareholders was not dwelt upon. There was some merit in the arguments: a more lenient tax regime with loans for new tonnage, introduced in 1957, would have been helpful at times, as would fewer restrictions that adversely affected trade. More vigorous representation to foreign governments regarding matters such as flag preference

---

27 *The Times* (London), 24 May 1961, Chairman's Report.

28 *The Times* (London), 30 May 1963, Chairman's Report.

29 *The Times* (London), 27 April 1963.

and discrimination was demanded. These viewpoints were common within the shipping industry and they were compounded by the belief that things would get better – a belief that was dangerous and, ultimately, ruinous for some.

A resolution within a document titled 'Shipping and Government action' prepared by the Chamber of Shipping in 1962 drew attention to the 'increasing difficulties facing British shipping in making its full contribution to the national economy in the face of competitive services to meet the needs of the nation and of world trade'. A key argument was against 'the distortion of trade caused by government interference', specifically, flag discrimination and flags of convenience. By the early 1960s both of these were well established and they were not going to go away. Likewise, various forms of subsidy by foreign governments to their national shipowners were seriously disadvantageous to British companies.[30] An additional uncertain element for shipping interests was the effect of the new European Common Market. Fearing that preferences might be applied to the meat and other trades, representations were made to the government on behalf of owners with highly specialised ships operating in the River Plate and other meat trades.

Added to these problems, in the case of Royal Mail and Pacific Steam was the ongoing totally unpredictable situation in South America. The persistent belief that Royal Mail's future in South America was assured was restated in 1962 when Chairman Bowes, acknowledging that many South American countries confronted severe problems – political, economic and financial – stated: 'Our faith in the future of South America is unshaken.'[31] This was on top of the poor results for 1960, with a dividend cut to 5 per cent and bank borrowing to clear costs outstanding on the building of the three new A-ships, and even poorer results in 1961. The share price, generally a reliable indicator, reacted, falling from 21s 7d early in January 1961 to 14s in October and 12s in January 1962.

General Trade Decline

From the mid-1950s it was clear that Royal Mail's trade with South America was in serious decline as cargo volumes reduced and freight rates fell. Despite the Company's constant protestations and those of the British government, the protectionist move towards national shipping fleets was pursued by most South American countries, greatly affecting trade on both the east and west coasts and in the Company's West Indies services.

Royal Mail's most profitable freight over many years, the carriage of frozen and chilled meat from Argentina, had become totally unpredictable. The situation was made still more difficult by the Argentine intention to reduce its long-standing dependence on the British market by shipping more of its exports directly into other European markets. Adding greatly to the difficulties was the reduced share

---

30 *Shipbuilding and Shipping Record*, 1 March 1962.

31 *The Times* (London), 30 May 1962.

of export quotas available to European shipping services as developing Argentine lines were given preferences. This was a relatively slow process from the post-Second World War period, but it was inevitable. The same applied to Brazil, with a merchant fleet almost doubled in the 1939–55 period. Hope comments that the Brazilian preferences 'halved the service given by British ships'.[32]

Royal Mail's South American service was reduced from nine passenger/cargo ships plus a number of cargo vessels in 1939 to only three passenger/cargo ships and four refrigerated cargo vessels operating in very difficult, frequently unprofitable, circumstances in the 1960s. The Company was progressively squeezed out of its important general cargo services to Southern Brazil and the Argentine from the mid-1950s, a further major blow.

The one successful service, at least until the early 1960s, was that to North Pacific ports operated jointly with Holland America Line, although precisely how profitable the service was cannot be gauged from the accounts. (This service sailed from continental ports and London. Furness, Withy operated a similar, less frequent, service out of Manchester and Glasgow.) Outward freights were generally satisfactory and homeward shipments of fresh, dried and tinned fruits and other cargo were maintained. However, from the early 1960s outward and homeward freights declined as costs on the Pacific coast increased dramatically, and competition, including container services, rose. The frequency of sailings was reduced by agreement with Furness, Withy.

World trade increased progressively in the post-1949 period, as did the total of world shipping; although British tonnage lagged behind most European countries, its total tonnage advanced by less than 2 per cent per annum up to 1960. By comparison, even France's growth was nearer to 5 per cent in the same period from a smaller base.[33]

Shipowners worldwide were obliged to become more flexible and more efficient, to seek new trading opportunities and to reduce costs so that freight shippers were offered more efficient and cost-effective means of transportation. The major problem for shipping companies, especially liner operators with fixed arrival and departure schedules, was their inability to reduce costs incurred by the long-established, labour-intensive, break-bulk cargo-handling processes common in ports around the world. The practice was to load and discharge general and refrigerated cargo in slings or nets, the cargo moving to or from dockside transit sheds, usually on a two-wheeled trolley. This involved gangs of stevedores on the quayside and in the ship's holds handling individual sacks, boxes, crates and larger items, as well as unpackaged motor cars, machinery and steelwork, and stowing them in the cargo spaces. The sheds received or shipped out cargo by lighter, road or rail. The procedure was slow and subject to weather and labour delays and, frequently, pilferage and breakages.

---

32 Hope, *A New History*, p. 396.

33 Sturmey, *British Shipping*, table p. 392.

During the 1950s the increased use of pallets and forklift trucks, which could, in some cases, be used to move goods around within the cargo holds as well as on the quayside, improved matters. The essential was to speed up the process and reduce costs. In the 1930s cargo-handling costs were estimated at about 13 per cent of freight earnings: by 1955 costs were nearer to 40 per cent.[34] All general-cargo ships were thus affected, scheduled sailings more so: the Company's A-ships regularly spent two weeks per voyage unloading and loading cargo in London and in Buenos Aires in the 1950s and 1960s, so that 40 to 50 per cent of their voyage time was spent in port. In January 1965 a Cabinet Docks Committee noted that 'the movement of goods in and out of the country represented one of the least efficient parts of our economy'. A commentator added: 'The port acted not so much as a conduit for trade but as a potential bottleneck.'[35]

Shipowners recognised the need for change: at a meeting of the London Chamber of Commerce in early 1961 Sir Nicholas Cayzer, of Clan Line, underlining the urgent need for government support in matters such as credit facilities and discrimination, argued: 'The ship-owners must be ready to face, if necessary, reorganisation and reorientation in the industry to make it more efficient.'[36] The frustrations of owners are understandable: trade discriminations, by now widespread, were applied by foreign governments and required intervention by the British government. And the government did make many representations on behalf of the industry, but with little or no helpful outcome.

During the late 1950s the development of container shipping, the carriage of general cargo in a standardised 'box' (the 20-foot TEU (twenty-foot equivalent units) later became the most common), was in its early stages. British cargo vessels would, on occasion, carry a small number of boxes (it is unlikely that the term 'container' was in use at that time), which were usually stowed securely lashed on deck for ready loading and discharge. In 1955 the Harrison Line built a small number of refrigerated boxes for use in its London to West Indies service. The boxes, with capacity for 450 cubic feet of cargo, connected with the vessel's electricity supply, were equipped with lifting slings and were suited to road transportation.[37]

The rapid extension of long-distance air travel was a factor anticipated in some measure by Royal Mail even before the Second World War. A number of shipping companies, including Royal Mail and Union-Castle, invested in the fledgling British Airways, which began operating in 1937. Royal Mail withdrew when the airline merged with Imperial Airways, becoming British Overseas Airways Corporation (BOAC), although the Company retained its interest in air travel. In 1943 the General Council of British Shipping urged shipowners to

---

34 Hope, *British Shipping*, p. 402.

35 Alan G. Jamieson, *Ebb Tide in the British Maritime Industries. Change and Adaptation, 1918–1990* (Exeter, 2003), pp. 84–5.

36 *Shipbuilding and Shipping Record*, 2 March 1961.

37 *Shipbuilding and Shipping Record*, 3 February 1955.

develop air services and Royal Mail, Blue Star and others with interests in the South American trade became shareholders in what emerged in 1945 as British South American Airways (BSAA). Services began in early 1946 but by 1947/48 the airline was absorbed into BOAC. A 1943 report by the Company's passenger manager anticipated competition from air lines but appeared to conclude that, with increased numbers travelling, shipping companies might hold their own in terms of passenger numbers but they must resort to increased promotional activities.[38]

By the late 1950s, air travel, with larger, faster aircraft and shorter flight times than could possibly have been anticipated 15 years previously, was significantly affecting passenger volumes on the South American routes and making older ships, namely *Alcantara* and *Reina del Pacifico*, with their limited cargo-carrying capacities, no longer profitable to operate. Between 1950 and 1959 the total of arrivals and departures by sea between Britain and non-European nations was, broadly, unchanged. The figures for movements by air more than trebled (see Table 13.3).[39] Royal Mail's introduction in 1960 of the three new A-ships capable of carrying in excess of 400 passengers, nearly 200 of them in first and cabin class, does not suggest that Royal Mail's board members were yet convinced, in the mid- to late 1950s, at a time when they were spending lavishly on new tonnage, that air travel was an imminent threat.

Table 13.3 Passengers entering and leaving the UK to and from non-European countries, 1953–59 (thousands)

		1950	**1953**	**1956**	**1959**
Arrivals	By sea	269	302	325	312
	By air	125	176	250	428
Departures	By sea	333	369	386	334
	By air	130	185	260	414

Source: Annual Abstract of Statistics, no. 97 (1960), p. 39.

Sturmey, a reliable commentator, noted: 'The critical period for British shipping was that between 1920 and about 1958. In this period tremendous changes in trading patterns, in competition, in cargoes, and in the movement of passengers occurred to which the industry was slow in adapting itself.' He added: 'the lack of competition within the conferences, together with the group structure of the industry, appeared to be sufficient to produce a situation completely lacking dynamism'.[40]

[38] Nicol, *Macqueen's Legacy*, Vol. 1, pp. 176–8.

[39] Sturmey, *British Shipping*, p. 164; Furness, Withy & Co. Ltd, Accounts for 1961–2. Into the 1960s the company held substantial investments in British United Airways.

[40] Sturmey, *British Shipping*, p. 398.

This was certainly a difficult period for Royal Mail, as it was for all British shipping companies. The directors were fully alert to the significance of the changes taking place in the Company's long-established services but their public utterances suggested that they were completely unable to contemplate effective responses to the situation. In 1961, the chairman told shareholders that the increase in flag discrimination had reached such a point as to make normal trading impossible. He called for 'a little understanding' on the part of those responsible and for greater enterprise in the business of selling goods to South America.[41]

However, others were not about to resolve Royal Mail's problems. The Company's financial situation was dire, with substantial debt accrued as a result of the building of new tonnage. The cost savings made were entirely inadequate. Management's hands were tied: no evidence exists of consideration being given to moving into alternative trades and businesses, the introduction in 1959–60 of the two tankers operated by Pacific Steam apart. Difficulties would have been experienced in raising the capital required. Alternative uses for the fleet were limited. None of the Company's non-South American routes was appropriate to the refrigerated tonnage. The four D-ships were now above 20 years old, with profitability uncertain. On occasion one or other of them was chartered to Shaw, Savill for the New Zealand meat trade. The prospect for the 1960s-built A-ships was even more limited.

Freight income from 1964 refrigerated produce from South America was over £1m less than the previous year, itself not a good year, with drastic curtailment of shipments continued from 1963. Chairman Bowes, in his review of the year, in early 1965, noted:

> This deterioration is mainly accounted for by the severe reduction in shipments of Argentine chilled beef to the United Kingdom. Although the beef trade can be expected to recover, it is now considered by the authorities best qualified to assess the position that the recovery will take longer than was being predicted up to the middle of last year.

Other cargo trades in which the Company's ships were operated all suffered setbacks. Freight rates in general failed to keep pace with rising operating costs. Finding profitable homeward cargoes from the west coast of South America, the Caribbean and North Pacific ports was a recurring difficulty that was accentuated during 1964. The frequency of cargo-ship sailings was reduced in order to cut costs and a number of vessels were sold; non-Company vessels were chartered for the outward voyage only.

---

[41] *Shipbuilding and Shipping Record*, 23 February 1961.

'What of the Future?'

'What', Chairman Bowes asked, 'of the future?' He spoke of improvements in the current year (1965), with meat shipments increased. There were, he said, signs of vigorous revival in many Latin American republics and the directors retained their faith in their future prosperity. He added that he, personally, had not changed his mind about prospects. Nevertheless, he acknowledged that the Company was poorly placed financially and that no dividend was likely to be paid in 1965. He then announced that the directors had accepted the offer of Furness, Withy & Co. to purchase the 66 per cent of Royal Mail shares it did not already own and commended the offer to shareholders.[42]

At a board meeting a few weeks earlier, on 4 May, Chairman Bowes advised his colleagues that he had received from Sir Errington Keville (note: one of his own directors) an indication of the terms on which Furness, Withy would be prepared to make an offer for the whole of the ordinary stock not already held by them, but only if the Royal Mail board were prepared to recommend the offer to shareholders. Some directors favoured a share swop arrangement but, following discussions with financial advisers and, having informed the Northern Ireland government, a significant shareholder, of the situation the board accepted the offer and on 11 May the following press notice was issued.[43]

> The Directors of Furness, Withy & Co. are of the opinion that although Royal Mail is not at present trading on a profitable basis, there should in due course be considerable scope for improvement from closer cooperation between the two Companies which can only be achieved if Royal Mail is under the complete ownership of Furness, Withy & Co. The directors of Royal Mail share this view.

The offer was 20s cash for each of the 5,283,174 (66 per cent of £8m) ordinary £1 shares not already held or £1 of 4.5 per cent convertible unsecured loan notes. Shareholders, who had as recently as 1957 enjoyed a share price of 38s and a dividend of 9 per cent, as well as a one-for-one share issue, can hardly have been happy, although they were obliged to bear in mind recent price weaknesses. The chairman welcomed the bid and advised shareholders that the Company was poorly placed to finance several years of adverse trading conditions. He added that Royal Mail would benefit from becoming a part of a more widely based organisation.[44]

---

[42] *The Times* (London), 3 June 1965, extract from the Company Chairman' Bowes's Report to Shareholders at the 25 June AGM. Copies were circulated to shareholders in advance of the meeting.

[43] *Annual Return of Shareholders of Royal Mail Lines, Limited*, 9 July 1965. The chairman's contacts with the Northern Ireland government resulted from the fact that their long-time representative on the board, Frank Charlton, had recently resigned that position due to ill-health.

[44] *The Times* (London), 3 June 1965.

One City commentator described the deal as 'the best of a bad job' in light of the 1964 results.

Brian Shaw, Royal Mail's company secretary in the mid-1960s, states that in 1965 'Furness, Withy became unhappy with the performance of Royal Mail and its management'.[45] The comment is surprising in that Royal Mail's board continued to be, as it had been from 1932, effectively controlled by Furness's representatives. Chairman Bowes and his colleagues had little or no option but to defer to the opinions and influence of Furness's three senior representatives on the board, Messrs Charlton, Keville, (the Furness, Withy chairman) and Burnett.[46]

A financial statement produced by Furness, Withy and published within the offer-to-buy document addressed to shareholders in June 1965 illustrates infinitely more clearly than Royal Mail's own accounts the alarming situation of the Company in the period 1960–64 (see Table 13.4). The bottom line is not readily identifiable within the Company's Reports and Accounts and, clearly, took note of information not available to the public.

Table 13.4 Furness, Withy profit and loss figures for Royal Mail, 1960–64 (£)

	1960	**1961**	**1962**	**1963**	**1964**
Profit (loss)	(758,232)	(1,255,061)	(932,780)	(568,159)	(1,741,698)
Less previous profit	217,263	188,420	135,029	179,520	250,384
Investments	104,610	32,338	27,305	33,412	60,898
	(436,140)	(1,034,303)	(720,396)	(337,227)	(1,430,416)
Taxation	787	5,048	4,917	2,781	6,631
	(437,146)	(1,039,351)	(775,313)	(340,000)	(1,437,047)
Income tax recov'y	146,475	233,314	414,672	235.765	321,438
	(290,671)	(806,037)	(360,641)	(104,243)	(1,115,609)
Dividends (%)	5	Nil	3	3	Nil

The announcement of the Furness, Withy offer was not unexpected. Royal Mail's woes were well known in the City of London, and other shipping companies were experiencing similar difficulties. But the real measure of the concerns of shareholders was recorded by the Stock Exchange. The £1 Royal Mail ordinary shares languished at around 8s in 1962, improving marginally to 12s–15s through 1963 and 12s in October 1964. The offer price of £1 per share a few months later, a substantial percentage premium, was, most probably, welcome. When the first indication of

[45] Brian Shaw, *True to Myself* (2005), p. 53.

[46] RML 81/13. Charlton resigned as representative of the government of Northern Ireland on 28 June 1965.

Furness's intention was made public the shares were marked up sharply to 18s 3d. Furness, Withy shares reacted adversely, falling from 36s 6d in December 1964 to 30s 6d at the end of May, recovering to over 34s by August.

Furness, Withy was a major liner company, second only to P&O in tonnage. It held controlling shareholdings in Shaw, Savill & Albion, which operated passenger liners and cargo services to Australia and New Zealand. It also owned 46 per cent of the stock of Manchester Liners, which served the Manchester to Canada and the Great Lakes cargo trades and 49 per cent of the shares in Houlder Brothers, which included the refrigerated tonnage of the Furness–Houlder Argentine Lines. Furness was represented on the boards of all three, usually by one or two senior directors.[47]

Post Mortem

When Leslie Bowes took over as chairman of Royal Mail in 1960 his options were few, a situation of which he must have been entirely aware, having been managing director for two years. The Company was burdened by debt and it was being squeezed out of its principal trades, South America and the West Indies, which it had operated for more than a century, and the North Pacific. The circumstances were entirely out of the control of management. Apart from his cost-cutting exercises there was little he could do. It was already too late: the move to national fleet preferences was here to stay. The chairman's persistent plea when addressing shareholders was for a return to the status quo of 20 years earlier, with foreign governments acquiescent and British shipping still powerful. Although he must have been aware of the move towards containerisation, no record has been found that he referred to it.

Were the interests of shareholders in the 1950s and into the 1960s properly safeguarded by the Company's directors? Was the presence of senior and broadly experienced Furness, Withy directors beneficial? The Furness representation on the board in 1964 was dominant and always had been from the time of Royal Mail's establishment in 1932: Sir Errington Keville was the Furness chairman and R. Peyton Burnett was his deputy. Frank Charlton, a Royal Mail director since 1932, was a former chairman. Royal Mail's company secretary noted in 1965 that when problems arose, Chairman Bowes had no option but to defer to the influence and opinions of the three Furness, Withy representatives.[48]

The Company's problems began in the mid-1950s when Walter Warwick was in the chair. Informed leadership with some anticipation of likely future developments was required, with special reference to the longer-term effects of discriminatory practices: it was not forthcoming. It is arguable that the single factor that led to the collapse of the Company was the 1956 decision to build the

---

[47] In 1970 Furness acquired control of Manchester Liners, its bid being initially contested.

[48] Author's correspondence with Brian Shaw, August 2001.

three A-ships at a cost of over £15m and the resulting serious financial difficulties. It is equally arguable that there was a pressing need for new passenger tonnage on the South American route, which ignores entirely the effects of the dramatic increase in air travel. Perhaps Royal Mail's directors were no wiser than those of other British companies that continued to build liners for transatlantic and Australian services. Whatever the truth, within seven to eight years the Company was in ruins. No one emerged from Royal Mail's desperate situation in 1965 with credit and shareholders must have been less than happy.

For Furness, Withy, which increased its capital from £11.5m to £15m to fund the acquisition of Royal Mail's substantial assets, the outcome was considered satisfactory. Chairman Sir Errington Keville advised an extraordinary meeting of Furness shareholders in July that over 90 per cent of Royal Mail shareholders had already accepted the offer and the remaining shares would be obtained in due course through the Company's Act of 1948. Of the acceptances, more than 60 per cent had opted for cash, so that the up-front cost was approximately £3.3m, less than one year's cash flow for the Group. He added that a benefit of the merger was the great opportunities for development in South America, echoing the persistently stated forlorn hopes of Royal Mail's chairman.[49]

Just a few months later Chairman Keville, speaking at a dinner in November 1965, advised guests that 'The British shipping industry has to rationalise.' He added, 'The industry is facing a period of complete change. It is a change equally as important as the change from sail to steam.' Further references were to too many ships chasing too many cargoes, despite the fact that world trade had doubled in the past ten years.[50] The remarks were made a few months after Furness, Withy was invited by the other three participants to join the OCL (Overseas Container Ltd) container-ship consortium and hint at a late appreciation of a development already well in train.

The Furness Group, which had enjoyed improved trading figures in 1963–64, began, in 1963, a programme to simplify its considerable shareholding structure, which included investments in non-shipping companies. In 1965 Furness Ship Management was established to bring under single management the ships and trades of Furness, Withy, Royal Mail, Shaw Savill, Prince Line and Johnson Warren Ltd and others. Passenger, freight and other large departments were merged and agency arrangements were restructured, effecting, no doubt, substantial cost savings.[51] Staff in Royal Mail's Leadenhall Street head office were transferred to the Furness office in Fenchurch Street, with considerable job insecurity both ashore and afloat.

---

[49] *The Times* (London), 7 July 1965. Chairman Leslie Bowes retired at the end of 1965.

[50] *Fairplay*, 4 November 1965.

[51] D. Burrell, *Furness Withy. The centenary history, 1891–1991* (Kendal, 1992), pp. 146–7.

From the time of the establishment of the Company in 1932 Furness's interest in Royal Mail was that of an owner, despite its minority shareholding and Chairman Warwick's denial of an intention to take over the company. Its approach to other companies in which it had only minority holdings was not dissimilar, although it does seem that its control was less complete. Others diversified: Houlder entered into a joint venture with the British Iron and Steel Corporation Ore Carriers Ltd in 1954 to ship iron ore into the UK, and by 1960 it had built and begun to operate eight bulk carriers. Shaw Savill and Manchester Liners appear have to retained a measure of autonomy. But Royal Mail had no strong 'family' management presence and the introduction of the two tankers placed under Pacific Steam management apart, there is little or no evidence of anticipation of future developments and planning, in terms of tonnage, for those eventualities.

No fewer than eight of the Company's traditionally built 'tween-deck cargo ships, the 1952–56-built E-ships and the 1956–57-built Y-ships, were effectively obsolete, expensive to operate and less than ideally suited to alternative trades where they were obliged to compete with an increasing international fleet of ships maintained by low-cost operators. In 1966 *Drina* and *Durango* were transferred to Shaw, Savill and renamed. The following year, reflecting increasingly difficult trading conditions, *Darro* and *Deseado* and *Loch Garth* and *Loch Avon* were sold, along with Pacific Steam's five S-ships, all by now over 20 years old. Between 1968 and 1970 the four E-ships were sold for further trading, two of them barely 15 years old, and, in 1970, the North Pacific service was terminated in the face of spiralling costs.

The three A-ships continued on the South American service until, in December 1967, meat imports were banned due to an outbreak of foot and mouth disease in Britain. *Amazon* was refitted as an all-tourist-class ship and transferred to Shaw Savill, renamed *Akaroa*, and operated on the New Zealand and round-the-world service. Despite the resumption of meat shipments, in late 1968 it was announced that *Arlanza* and *Aragon* would also move to Shaw Savill the following year. *Aragon* finally ended Royal Mail's South American service early in 1969, making a brief, sentimental, homeward call at Southampton 118 years after *Teviot*'s initial departure from that port and 100 years since *Douro* made the first through sailing to Buenos Aires. *Aragon* continued to Rotterdam and London to discharge passengers and cargo.

A press report in November 1970 commented on a Furness, Withy announcement that 23 ships were to be sold, adding that the announcement was forced out prematurely by persistent stock market rumours that a takeover bid was in the offing.[52] The report and accounts for 1971, published in early 1972, made no reference to the bid, although other approaches were received in the next two to three years. The report did, however, confirm that a total of 30 ships had been sold, nine of them formerly owned by Royal Mail, including *Andes*, now more than 30 years old and no longer profitable, and the three A-ships and four PSNC vessels.

52 *The Times* (London), 14 November 1970.

Others sold were ships of Prince Line, Houlder Bros and Manchester Liners. The report further noted: 'The deterioration in profitability from ship operating which is by far the major activity of the Group is responsible for losses of £1.76mn incurred during the year.' References were made to 'cost explosions, depressed freight rates and port delays to all of which cargo and passenger liner operations were especially vulnerable'. A dock strike in the UK in 1970 cost the Group at least £0.5m. Substantial job cuts were inevitable.

The purchase of Royal Mail by Furness, Withy may well have have appeared to be a sound financial move in light of balance-sheet assets and the prospect of profitable rationalisation of trades, although the huge costs accumulated in the following five or six years cannot have been properly factored in. The Furness plan was to incorporate the Royal Mail fleet and assets within its associated companies so that full advantage might be taken of improving trading conditions, which they were determined were around the corner. They weren't. Conventionally constructed shipping was out of date by the mid-1960s: the three 1960s-built A-ships were retired from service in 1971, two years earlier than intended, because 'they have proved to be so peculiarly vulnerable to recent increases in operating costs and to the deterioration in productivity especially in respect of cargo working'. They were sold for rebuilding as vehicle carriers.

Nevertheless, Furness remained profitable, at £4.17m in 1969 with a dividend of 15 per cent, £1.9m the previous year. Through the 1970s there were persistent rumours of takeover approaches and, in September 1980, Kenwake Ltd, a subsidiary of Orient Overseas (Holdings) Ltd, took control.[53]

The Shape of Things to Come

The movement to sea-borne container transport in Britain developed from 1960 when the British India Company, owned by P&O, commissioned a study of systems for unitising cargo, presumably stimulated by the activities of Malcolm McLean and the Matson Line in the USA.[54] Other companies participated in research, including Furness, Withy's Shaw, Savill Line from 1964, all recognising the need for the dramatic changes demanded in order to speed the movement of increasing volumes of cargo, reduce operational costs and minimise persistent labour problems. In 1965 a new company, OCL (Overseas Containers Ltd), emerged, with P&O, Alfred Holt (Blue Funnel and Glen Lines) and British &

---

[53] Burrell, *Furness, Withy*, p. 171.

[54] Frank Broeze, *The Globalisation of the Oceans. Containerisation from the 1950s to the Present*. Research in Maritime History No. 23 (St Johns, Newfoundland, 2002), pp. 32–4. The early container carriers were converted wartime-built T2 tankers and C2 cargo vessels used in the 1950s. The Matson Line, in 1956, began to research the needs of its California to Hawaii trade. In 1958 it began to ship containers on deck in conventional vessels and, by 1960 it used its own converted vessels for the trade.

Commonwealth jointly involved. Some weeks later Furness, Withy was invited to join.[55] OCL's focus was on the Australian trade.

The requirement for combined action lay in the great capital costs anticipated for the building of new tonnage. OCL was duly incorporated and in January 1967 orders were placed for six vessels, five of them from German yards, each with capacity for 1,572-TEU (twenty-foot equivalent unit) containers. The first of these, *Encounter Bay* (27,000 tons), manned by P&O, sailed from Rotterdam for Australia in March 1969; industrial action had delayed the introduction of the newly built Tilbury facility.[56] Broeze estimates the cost of the six new vessels at US$100m, with a further US$85m spent on three sets of containers, one carried on board with two ashore for distribution purposes.[57]

Progressively the country's traditional dock systems, notably London's vast upriver Royal Docks, fell into disuse. The requirement now was for ready access from the sea to large deep-water quays with vast dockside areas for container storage as well as good connections with road transport to facilitate delivery and collection of the containers. In time, larger and faster vessels, built specifically for the trade and capable of carrying increased numbers of standard-sized containers, operated from specially developed berths, very different from those used by conventional cargo services. By the 1990s ever-larger ships were able to carry 7,000 containers; in 2006, the Danish *Emma Maersk* (170,794 gross tons) entered service with capacity for 15,000 TEU containers. The vessel had a crew of 13.

New port facilities were essential and, in 1968, Tilbury's deep-water river berth was opened, with further terminals building in Felixstowe, Southampton and Liverpool and on the continent, the USA, Australia. The berths were equipped with large cranes, capable of lifting over 40 tons, which moved the containers from the storage areas to and from the ship. This arrangement enabled speedy dock-side turnarounds with greatly reduced numbers of stevedores and lower operational costs. Enclosed docks were a thing of the past. The laying off of thousands of dock workers in the period resulted in disputes and strikes, but the dramatic changes in work practices were inevitable.

The statistics starkly illustrate the effects of the changeover: the first ship to use Tilbury's new berth was the US Line's *American Lancer*. Fifteen dockers took only 13 hours to unload and load containers in the ship before she sailed on the next tide. Using the traditional break-bulk procedure would have taken 176 dockers (96 on the ship and 80 on the quay) four or five days.[58] A comparison

---

[55] Broeze, *The Globalisation of the Oceans*. A second group of major companies, concerned that OCL sought to gain control over the British liner industry, formed Associated Container Transportation (ACT) with Ellerman, Blue Star, Ben Line and Harrison and Port Line as partners; pp. 43–4.

[56] A. Bott (ed.), *British Box Business. A History of OCL* (London, 2009) pp. 23–4, pp. 29–31.

[57] Broeze, *The Globalisation of the Oceans*, p. 29.

[58] Jamieson, *Ebb Tide*, p. 106.

made in 1985 between the time spent in port and at sea by a conventional liner and a container ship of 22,000 and 25,000 tons, respectively, showed that the former spent 216 days at sea per annum compared with 300 for the container ship. Comparisons of time in port per annum were 149 days for the former and 64 days for the container vessel.[59] An additional cost benefit was that the container ships operated with dramatically reduced crew numbers.

Although American shipowners, notably Malcolm McLean, who is credited with the early development of the concept, had operated container services using converted tonnage from the 1950s, it was not until 1966 that McLean's Sea-Land Service opened a transatlantic service. Other British companies and international consortia quickly established North Atlantic and Australian services. Notable was that of Manchester Liners' (a Furness, Withy subsidiary) 1968 service from Manchester to Montreal.[60]

An assist with the costs of new tonnage was, from 1957, a 40 per cent government investment grant available to British shipowners. This was altered, in 1966, to a 20 per cent cash grant provided the vessel was retained in British registry for at least five years. Sadly, few British shipyards were updated sufficiently to reliably produce the large-tonnage vessels required to schedule and agreed cost. A further credit inducement was offered from 1967 to shipowners who built in Britain. Bott notes that in that period Britain offered some of the most generous state aid to shipping in the world. These several initiatives ensured that British liner companies were at the forefront of the development of worldwide container services, second only to the USA, although most individual companies lost their historic identities.[61]

By the 1970s the nature of maritime transportation had changed out of all recognition from the post-Second World War period. The change could not be described as a development, in the manner of the nineteenth-century move from sail to steam; it was, rather, a revolution, one that began in the mid-1950s and gathered momentum through to the 1970s. Large container ships, bulk carriers and very large tankers played an increasingly important role in international shipping, both in numbers and ever-increasing size, and they progressively displaced the long-established liner networks and the traditional vessels. Passenger liner services succumbed to the inroads made by rapidly developing air transport. Cargo liner trades, once dominated by British tonnage, were under pressure from the expanding merchant fleets of newly developing nations that applied cargo preferences and other sanctions to support their national services.

---

[59] Martin Stopford, *Maritime Economics* (London, 1988), pp. 192–4. The figures are from a paper by M. Meek, 'Operating experience of large container ships', to the Institute of Engineers and Shipbuilders of Scotland in 1985.

[60] Jamieson, *Ebb Tide*, pp. 35–7.

[61] Bott, *British Box Business*, pp. 44–5. In 1971 the US companies owned 75 container ships, out of a world total of 231. Britain was in second place with 51 ships; p. 38.

The Rochdale Report of 1970 identified possible reasons why some British shipping companies failed to keep pace with the development of the industry and the changes affecting it. These included the absence of corporate machinery to quantify the effects of external commercial, economic and political influences on its interests and the neglect of economic research of trade trends. Also cited were financial conservatism and the lack of interest outside their own sectors as well as the common failure to appreciate the benefits of university and professional training for staff who would then progress through to senior positions, an oblique reference to the preponderance of elderly 'shipping men' on company boards.[62] Bott commented that in years past ships had attracted an almost reverential status: 'their owners' pride in them verged on the inordinate, with commercial consideration pushed into second place'.[63]

[62] *Report of the Committee of Inquiry into Shipping* (The Rochdale Report), (HMSO, London, 1970).

[63] Bott, *British Box Business*, p. 23.

Appendix: The Fleet List, 1850–1965

Only RMSP and RML ships owned and employed at some time in the passenger/cargo services to South America are listed. All tonnages are gross. Note that cargo-only vessels are not included.

Before the early 1900s, when tonnage was built specifically for the South American service, some vessels, usually older tonnage, were engaged regularly, running to Brazil and The Plate; others were switched from the West Indies or other routes for only an occasional relief voyage. The A and the 1911–12 D-classes of passenger/cargo liners were built for the service to Brazil and Argentina and, apart from wartime years, seldom diverted.

All vessels listed are steamships. The earliest were wooden paddle ships, w/p, followed by iron paddle ships, i/p, and then iron screw ships, i/scr. *Orinoco II*, 1886, was the Company's first steel-hulled vessel, st/scr. Virtually all Company vessels carried passengers, P, and cargo, C. By 1900 some of the cargo space was refrigerated, C/R. From 1900 some larger vessels were twin screw, Tw.Scr, and triple screw. Tri.Scr. Two ships were motor powered, M, and Andes was turbine powered, Tur.

From about 1900, cargo ships, some carrying 12 passengers, might make a number of sailings to South American ports before reverting to an alternative trade, or they might trade on a regular basis to Brazil. These ships are not listed, although their activities are referred to in the text.

Table A.1 The Fleet List

1841	*Thames*	1,889 w/p	PC	Out of service 1865
1841	*Tay*	1,858 w/p	PC	Wrecked 1856
1841	*Medway*	1,895 w/p	PC	Broken up 1861
1842	*Severn*	1,886 w/p	PC	Broken up 1856
1841	*Teviot*	1,744 w/p	PC	Broken up 1864
1842	*Avon*	2,069 w/p	PC	Wrecked Colon 1862
1838/acqd 1847	*Great Western*	1,775 w/p	PC	Broken up 1856
1851	*Magdalena*	2,943 w/p	PC	Broken up 1866
1851	*Parana*	2,943 w/p	PC	Hulked 1868, sold 1876
1851/acqd	*Prince*	398 i/p	P	Out of service 1862
1852/acqd Cunard to replace *Amazon*	*La Plata*	2,404 w/p	PC	Sold 1871 (£7,600)
1851/acqd	*Camilla*	539 w/p	P	Sold 1862
1853	*Solent*	1,804 w/p	PC	Broken up 1869
1854	*Tamar*	1,850 w/p	PC	Out of service 1871
1855/acqd 1858	*Oneida*	2,293 i/scr.	PC	Sold 1874 for further trading
1859	*Shannon*	3,609 i/p	^PC	Wrecked 1875
1859	*Mersey*	1,039 i/p	PC	Sold 1876
1860	*Seine*	3,440 i/p	PC	Broken up 1871
1864	*Douro*	2,824 i/scr.	PC	Sunk, collsn 1882
1865	*Rhone*	2,738 i/scr.	PC	Wrecked 1867
1865	*Danube*	2,000 i/p	PC	Sold 1871 for further trading

1868/bought on stocks, replaced *Rhone*	*Neva*	3,025 i/scr.	PC	Broken up 1890
1869	*Elbe*	3,108 i/scr.	+PC	Sold 1902 (£10,000)
1870/acqd 1873 (*ex De Ruyter*)	*Larne*	1,670 i/scr.	+PC	Sold 1900
1871	*Tagus*	3,298 i/scr.	+PC	Scrapped 1897
1871	*Moselle*	3,298 i/scr.	+PC	Wrecked 1891
1866/acqd 1871 (*ex Kaikoura*)	*Tiber*	1,591 i/scr.	+PC	Wrecked 1882
1866/acqd 1871 (*ex Rakaia*)	*Ebro*	1,509 i/scr.	PC	Sold 1881 for further trading
1865/acqd 1871 (*ex Ruahine*)	*Liffey*	1,589 i/scr.	PC	Wrecked 1874, River Plate
1872/acqd 1874 (*ex Santiago*)	*Mondego*	2,564 i/scr.	+PC	Sold 1887 for further trading (£9,500)
1872/acqd 1874 (*ex Leopold II*)	*Minho*	2,541 i/scr.	+PC	Sold 1887 for further trading (£7,500)
1874/acqd 1875 (*ex State of Florida*)	*Guadiana*	2,504 i/scr	+PC	Wrecked 1885, Brazil coast
1873/acqd 1878 (*ex Vancouver*)	*Tamar II*	2,923 i/scr	+PC	Sold/broken up 1897
1873/acqd 1878 (*ex Vasco da Gama*)	*Trent II*	2,912 i/scr.	+PC	Sold/broken up 1897
1872/acqd 1875 (*ex Corcovado*)	*Don*	4,028 i/scr.	+PC	Tpl. exp. 1879, broken up 1901
1872/acqd 1875 (*ex Puno*)	*Para*	3,805 i/scr.	+PC	Tpl. exp. 1890, broken up 1903
1872/acqd. 1875 (*ex Minnesota*)	*Dee II*	1,864 i/scr.	+PC	Broken up 1901
1877	*Medway*	3,687 i/scr.	+PC	Out of service 1899

1878	*Solent*	1,908 i/scr.	+PC	Broken up 1909
1879	*Derwent II*	2,466 i/scr.	+PC	Out of service 1902
1880	*Avon*	2,162 i/scr.	+PC	Broken up 1903
1879/acqd 1882 (*ex Norfolk*)	*La Plata II*	3,240 i/scr.	+PC	Sold for further trading 1893
1882	*Eden*	2,145 i/scr.	+PC	Wrecked 1909, West Indies
1882	*Esk*	2,145 i/scr.	+PC	Broken up 1910
1883	*Dart*	2,641 i/scr.	+PC	Wrecked 1884, off Santos
1886	*Orinoco II*	4,572 st/scr.	PC#	Broken up1909
1888	*Atrato II*	5,347 st/scr.	PC#	Sold for cruising 1912
1889	*Magdalena II*	5,373 st/scr.	PC#	Broken up 1921
1889	*Thames II*	5,621 st/scr.	PC/R#	Broken up 1914
1890	*Clyde II*	5,618 st/scr.	PC/R#	Broken up 1913
1893	*Nile II*	5,855 st/scr.	PC/R#	Sold for further trading 1911
1893	*Danube II*	5,891 st/scr.	PC/R#	Sold for further trading 1920
1896	*La Plata III*	3,445 st/scr.	PC/R#	Sold for further trading 1900
1896	*Minho II*	3,445 st/scr.	PC#	Sold for further trading 1903
1896	*Ebro II*	3,445 st/scr.	PC#	Sold for further trading 1903
1898	*Severn III*	3,760 st/scr.	PC#	Sold for further trading 1913
1899	*Tagus II*	5,545 st/scr.	PC/R#	Sold for further trading 1920
1899	*Trent III*	5,525 st/scr.	PC/R#	Broken up 1922
1900	*Tyne III*	2,902 st/scr.	C	Torpedoed, sunk 1917
1900	*Eider II*	1,236 st/scr.	C	Sold for further trading 1927

1882/acqd 1901 (*ex Moor*)	*La Plata IV*	4,464 st/scr.	PC#	Sold for cruising 1908
1904	*Parana II*	4,515 st/scr.	PC/R#	Broken up 1933
1904	*Pardo*	4,538 st/scr.	PC/R#	Broken up 1934
1904	*Potaro*	4,378 st/scr.	PC/R#	Captured/sunk 1915
1905	*Aragon*	9,588	Tw.Scr.PC/R##	Sunk 1917
1906	*Amazon*	10,037	Tw.Scr.PC/R##	Sunk 1918
1906	*Araguaya*	11,537	Tw.Scr.PC/R##	Sold for further trading 1930
1907	*Avon III*	11,073	Tw.Scr.PC/R##	Sold/broken up 1930
1889/acqd 1906	*Oruba*	5,737	PC/R#	Sold Admiralty 1914
1892/acqd 1906	*Marima*	2,742	C/R#	Sold for further trading 1911
1892/acqd 1906	*Manau*	2,742	C/R#	Wrecked 1906
1907	*Asturias*	12,105	Tw.Scr.PC/R##	Renamed *Arcadian* 1923, scrapped 1933
1911	*Deseado*	11,475	Tw.Scr.PC/R##	Broken up 1933
1911	*Demerara*	11,484	Tw.Scr.PC/R##	Broken up 1933
1911 Royal Mail Lines	*Arlanza*	14,930	Tri.Scr.PC/R##	Broken up 1938
1912	*Desna*	11,483	Tw.Sc.PC/R##	Broken up 1933
1912/acqd 1916/17	*Darro*	11,493	Tw.Sc.PC/R##	Broken up 1933
1912/acqd 1914/15	*Drina*	11,483	Tw.Sc.PC/R##	Torpedoed, sunk 1917
1913 RML	*Andes*	15,620	Tri.Sc.PC/R##	Renamed *Atlantis* 1929, broken up 1952
1913/chartered	*Alcala*	10,660	Tw.Scr.PC##	Retd Lamport & Holt 1913
1914	*Alcantara*	15,831	Tri.Scr.PC/R##	Sunk 1916
1914	*Essequibo*	8,489	Tw.Scr.PC/R##	Sold to PSNC 1922

1915 RML	*Almanzora*	16,034	Tri.Scr.PC/R##	Broken up 1948
1925 RML	*Asturias*	22,048	Tw.Scr.M.* PC/R	Broken up 1957
1926 RML	*Alcantara*	22,181	Tw.Scr.M.* PC/R	Broken up 1958
1915 RML	*Nela*	7,206	Tw.Scr.C/R	*Ex* Nelson, broken up 1946
1915 RML	*Nasina*	7,206	Tw.Scr.C/R	*Ex* Nelson, sold 1935
1915 RM.	*Nalon*	7,206	Tw.Scr.C/R	*Ex* Nelson, sunk 1940
1928 RML	*Highland Monarch*	14,139	Tw.Scr.PC/R	*Ex* Nelson, broken up 1960
1928 RML	*Highland Chieftain*	14,131	Tw.Scr.PC/R	*Ex* Nelson, sold for further trading 1959
1928 RML	*Highland. Brigade*	14,131	Tw.Scr.PC/R	*Ex* Nelson, sold for further trading 1959
1929 RML	*Highland Princess*	14,128	Tw.Scr.PC/R	*Ex* Nelson, sold for further trading 1959
1932 RML	*Highland. Patriot*	14,157	Tw.Scr.PC/R	*Ex* Nelson, sunk 1940
1920 RML	*Nagoya*	8,442	S.Scr.C/R	*Ex* Nelson, sold for further trading 1936
1939 RML	*Andes*	26,689	Tur. PC/R	Broken up 1971
1942 RML	*Deseado*	9,641	Tw.Scr.C/R	Broken up 1968
1943 RML	*Darro*	9,733	Tw.Scr.C/R	Broken up 1967
1944 RML	*Drina*	9,785	Tw.Scr.C/R	Broken up 1968
1944 RML	*Durango*	9,806	Tw.Scr.C/R	Broken up 1968
1949 RML	*Magdalena*	17,547	Tw.Scr.PC/R	Sank Rio Bay 1949
1959 RML	*Amazon*	20,348	Tw.Scr.PC/R	Sold for further trading 1971
1960 RML	*Aragon*	20,362	Tw.Scr.PC/R	Sold for further trading 1971
1960 RML	*Arlanza*	20,362	Tw.Scr.PC/R	Sold for further trading 1971

Details are from Bushell, *Royal Mail* (until 1939), where possible confirmed and supplemented by directors' reports. Nicol, *MacQueens's Legacy*, gives additional useful information on a small number of ships. Bushell gives only out-of-service dates: where firm alternative details are available, these are quoted.

** *Danube* was the last paddle-steamer built by Royal Mail.

^ *Shannon* was lengthened, re-engined (compound) and converted to screw propulsion in 1874.

+ Compound engined. *Elbe* was the first Royal Mail-built ship with a compound engine. Subsequently most ships were fitted with compound engines, but not all.

Triple-expansion machinery. *Orinoco II* was Royal Mail's first ship fitted with triple-expansion machinery and the first equipped with electric lighting.

Quadruple expansion.

RML indicates ships acquired by the 1932 establishment of Royal Mail Lines Ltd or built subsequently. **Asturias*, 1925, and *Alcantara*, 1926, were built as motor ships. Both were re-engined in 1934 with Parsons geared turbines.

Bibliography

Books

Akers, C.E., *A History of South America*, new edn, with additions, L.E. Elliot (London, 1930).

Behrens, C.B.A., *Merchant Shipping and the Demands of War* (London, 1955).

Boase, F., *Modern English Biography* (London, 1965).

Bonsor, N.R.P., *South Atlantic Seaway* (Jersey, 1983).

Bott, A. (ed.), *British Box Business. A History of OCL* (London, 2009).

Broeze, F., *The Globalisation of the Oceans. Containerisation from the 1950s to the Present*. Research in Maritime History No. 23 (St Johns, Newfoundland, 2002).

Bulmer-Thomas, V., *The Economic History of Latin America Since Independence, 2nd edn* (Cambridge, 2003).

Burns, E.B., *A History of Brazil*, 3rd edn (New York, 1993).

Burrell, D., *Furness Withy. The Centenary History* (World Ship Society, Kendal, 1992).

Bushell, T.A., *Royal Mail. A Centenary History of the Royal Mail Line 1839–1939* (London, 1939).

Bushell, T.A., *Eight Bells, Royal Mail Lines War Story*, (London, 1950).

Cain, P.J. and Hopkins, A.G., *British Imperialism, 1688–2000* (London, 1993).

Calogeras, J.P., *A History of Brazil* (trans. and ed. P.A. Martin) (Chapel Hill, 1930).

Church, R.A., *The Great Victorian Boom 1850–1873* (London, 1975)

Corlett, E., *The Iron Ship: The Story of Brunel's S.S. Great Britain* (London, 1975, rev. edn 1990).

Critchell, J.T. and Raymond, J., *A History of the Frozen Meat Trade* (London, 1969).

Davies, P.N., *The Trade Makers: Elder Dempster in West Africa, 1852–1972, 1973–1989* (London, 1973).

Deakin, B.M. and Seward, T., *Shipping Conferences: A Study of their Origins, Development and Practices* (Cambridge, 1973).

Fausto, B., *A Concise History of Brazil* (Cambridge, 1999).

Ferns, H.S., *Britain and Argentina in the Nineteenth Century* (Oxford, 1960).

Graham-Yooll, A., *The Forgotten Colony: A History of the English-speaking Communities in Argentina* (Buenos Aires, 1999).

Graham, R., *Britain and the Onset of Modernization in Brazil 1850–1914* (Cambridge, 1968).

Green, E. and Moss, M., *A Business of National Importance. The Royal Mail Shipping Group, 1902–1937* (London, 1982).

Griffiths, D., *Brunel's Great Western* (Wellingborough, 1985).

Hanson, S.G., *Argentine Meat and the British Market* (London, 1938).

Haws, D., *Merchant Fleets, Royal Mail Line and Nelson Line* (Crowborough, 1982).
Haws, Duncan, *Triumph of a Great Tradition, 1840–1990. A souvenir history of the Cunard Line* (London, 1990)
Hope, R., *A New History of British Shipping* (London, 1990).
Howat, J.N.T., *South American Packets, 1808–1880* (York, 1984).
Howarth, D. and S., *The Story of P&O* (London, 1986).
Hyde, F.E., *Shipping Enterprise and Management 1830–1939. Harrisons of Liverpool* (Liverpool, 1967).
Hyde, F.E., *Cunard and the North Atlantic 1840–1973* (London, 1975).
Jamieson, A.G., *Ebb Tide in the British Maritime Industries. Change and Adaptation, 1918–1990* (Exeter, 2003).
Jones, E., *Accountancy in the British Economy 1840–1980* (London, 1981).
Knightly, P., *The Rise and Fall of the House of Vestey* (London, 1981).
Leslie, H.W., *The Royal Mail War Book* (London, 1920).
Manchester, A.K., *British Pre-eminence in Brazil. Its Rise and Decline* (New York, 1964).
Mathias, P., *The First Industrial Nation, An Economic History of Britain 1700–1914* 2nd edn (London, 1969).
Miller, R., *Britain and Latin America in the Nineteenth and Twentieth Centuries* (London, 1993).
Nicol, S., *MacQueen's Legacy, A History of the Royal Mail Line*, 2 vols (Stroud, 2001).
Perren, R., *Taste, Trade and Technology, The Development of the International Meat Industry since 1840* (Aldershot, 2006).
Perren, R., *The Meat Trade in Britain 1840–1914* (London, 1978).
Perry, S., *The Vestey Group. History of a Global Family Business* (London, 2008).
Platt, D.C.M., *Business Imperialism 1840–1930. An Inquiry based on British experience in Latin America* (Oxford, 1977).
Platt, D.C.M., *Latin America and British Trade, 1806–1914* (Edinburgh, 1972).
Ridings, E., *Business Interest Groups in Nineteenth Century Brazil* (Cambridge, 1994).
Rock, D., *Argentina, 1516–1987* (London, 1986).
Salter, J.A., *Allied Shipping Control. An Experiment in International Administration* (Oxford, 1921).
Saul, S.B., *The Myth of the Great Depression 1873–1890* (London, 1969).
Scobie, J.R., *Argentina: A City and a Nation* (Oxford, 1971).
Scobie, J.R., *Revolution on the Pampas. A Social History of Argentine Wheat, 1860–1910* (Austin, 1964).
Shaw, B., *True to Myself* (2005).
Stone, I., *The Composition and Distribution of British Investment in Latin America, 1865–1913* (New York, 1987).
Stopford, M., *Maritime Economics* (London, 1988).
Sturmey, S.G., *British Shipping and World Competition* (London, 1962).
Thornton, R.H., *British Shipping*, 2nd edn (Cambridge, 1959).

Vice, A., *Financier at Sea. Lord Kylsant and the Royal Mail* (Braunton, 1985).
Walsh, Robert, *Notices of Brazil in 1828 and 1829*, vol. II (London, 1830).
Wardle, A.C., *Steam Conquers the Pacific* (London, 1940).
Woodman, R., *The History of the Ship* (London, 1997).
Woolward, R., *Nigh on Sixty Years* (London, c. 1894).
Wright, W.R., *British-Owned Railways in Argentina. Their Effect on Economic Nationalism, 1854–1948* (Austin, 1936).

Articles/Papers

Albion, R.G., 'British Shipping and Latin America, 1806–1914', *Journal of Economic History*, Vol. X1, No. 1V (Cambridge, 1951), 361–74.
Arnold, A.J., 'Privacy or Concealment? The Accounting Practices of Liner Shipping Companies, 1914–1924', *International Journal of Maritime History*, VIII (1) (June 1996).
Bulmer-Thomas, V., 'The Latin American economies, 1929–1939', in L. Bethell (ed.), *The Cambridge History of Latin America, Vol. VI, Part I, 1930 to the Present* (Cambridge, 1994).
Bulmer-Thomas, V., 'The Latin American economies, 1929–1939', in L. Bethell (ed.), *The Cambridge History of Latin America, Vol. VI, Part I, 1930 to the Present* (Cambridge, 1994).
Clark, J.F., 'Railway Ports. Southampton', *The Railway Magazine*, March–May 1909.
Cortes Conde, R., 'The growth of the Argentine economy, c.1870–1914', in L. Bethell (ed.), *The Cambridge History of Latin America, Vol. V, c. 1870–1930* (Cambridge, 1986).
Cottrell, P.L., 'Domestic Finance, 1860–1914', in R. Floud and P. Johnson (eds), *The Cambridge Economic History of Modern Britain, Vol. II: Economic Maturity, 1860–1939* (Cambridge, 2004).
Crossley, C. and Greenhill, R., 'The River Plate Beef Trade', in D.C.M. Platt (ed.), *Business Imperialism 1840–1930. An inquiry based on British experience in Latin America* (Oxford, 1977).
Davies, P.N. and Bourn, A.M., 'Lord Kylsant and the Royal Mail', *Business History*, Vol. 14, no. 2, July 1972.
Dean, W., 'The Brazilian Economy, 1870–1930', in L. Bethell (ed.), *The Cambridge History of Latin America, Vol. V, c.1870–1930* (Cambridge, 1986).
Fausto, B., 'Brazil: the social and political structure of the First Republic, 1889–1930', in L. Bethell (ed.), *The Cambridge History of Latin America, Vol. V, c.1870–1930* (Cambridge, 1986).
Glover, J., 'On the Statistics of Tonnage' (decades of the 1850s through the 1880s), *Journals of the Statistical Society*, March 1863 to 1892.
Gravil, R., 'The Anglo-Argentine Connection and the War of 1914–1918', *Journal of Latin American Studies*, Vol. 9, No. 1 (May, 1977).

Greenhill, B., 'Steam before the Screw', in R. Gardiner (ed.), *The Advent of Steam* (London, 1993).

Greenhill, R., 'The Royal Mail Steam Packet Company and the Development of Steamship Links with Latin America, 1875–1900', *The Journal for Maritime Research.*

Greenhill, R., 'Shipping 1850–1914', in D.C.M. Platt (ed.), *British Imperialism 1840–1930. An Inquiry based on British Experience in Latin America* (Oxford, 1977).

Humphreys, R.A., 'Latin America and the Second World War', in Rosemary Thorp, *Latin American Economics*, 1939–1950, p. 124

Lewis, C., 'British Railway Companies and the Argentine Government', in D.C.M. Platt (ed.), Business Imperialism 1840–1930. An Inquiry based on British Experience in Latin America (Oxford, 1977).

Lewis, C., 'Anglo-Argentine Trade, 1945–1965', in David Rock (ed.), *Argentina in the Twentieth Century* (London, 1975).

Love, J.L., 'Economic ideas and ideologies in Latin America since 1930', in L. Bethell (ed.), *The Cambridge History of Latin America, Vol. VI, Part I, 1930 to the Present* (Cambridge, 1994).

Magee, G.B., 'Manufacturing and Technological Change', in R. Floud and P. Johnson (eds), *The Cambridge Economic History of Modern Britain, Vol. II: Economic Maturity, 1860–1939* (Cambridge, 2004).

Palmer, Sarah, 'Experience, Experiment and Economics: Factors in the Construction of Early Merchant Steamers', *Proceedings of the Conference of the Atlantic Canada Shipping Project*, St John's, Newfoundland, March–April 1977.

Rock, D., 'Argentina from the first world war to the revolution of 1930', in L. Bethell (ed.), *The Cambridge History of Latin America, Vol. V, c.1870 to 1930* (Cambridge, 1986).

Stemmer, J.E.O., 'Freight Rates in the Trade between Europe and South America, 1840–1914', in E. Bethell, V. Bulmer-Thomas and L.Whitehead (eds), *Journal of Latin American Studies*, Vol. 21, February 1989.

Torquist, Ernesto & Co., 'The Economic Development of Argentina in the Last Fifty Years' in D. Rock, *Argentina, 1516–1987* (London, 1986), pp.

Official Report

General Council of British Shipping, *Survey of British Shipping* (London, 1960).

Report of the Committee of Inquiry into Shipping (The Rochdale Report), (London, 1970).

Unpublished Theses

Gebhardt, R.C., 'The River Plate Meat Industry since c.1900: Technology, Ownership, International Trade Regimes and Domestic Policy', Ph.D. thesis, London School of Economics, 2000.

Greenhill, R.G., 'British Shipping and Latin America 1840–1930: The Royal Mail Steam Packet Company', Ph.D. thesis, University of Exeter, 1971.

Archive Material

The Royal Mail Steam Packet Company (RMSP) and Royal Mail Lines Ltd (RML) held in the Caird Library of the National Maritime Museum, Greenwich, the Library of University College, London and the Library of the Maritime Museum, Liverpool.

Furness, Withy (FW) material held in the archive section in Southampton Civic Centre.

Stock Exchange Annual Reports, Guildhall Library, London.

S. Nicol, *Scrapbook.* A compilation of material from Royal Mail archives. Available on CD in the libraries of the National Maritime Museum and the Merseyside Maritime Museum.

Newspapers and Periodicals

A Link of Empire or 70 Years of British Shipping, published by The Royal Mail Steam Packet Company in 1909.

Dictionary of Business Biography, IV/2

Fairplay

Lloyd's List

Oxford Dictionary of National Biography, Vol. 44.

Royal Mail News (Newsletter for members of the Royal Mail Association, published 1990–2010)[1]

Shipbuilding and Shipping Record

The Stock Exchange Annual Reports

The Economist

The Financier

Financial Times

The Hampshire Independent

The Shipping World

The Siren and Shipping

[1] Bound copies of all 80 issues of *Royal Mail News*, an eight-page quarterly publication, 1990–2010, for members of the Royal Mail Association are held in the National Maritime Museum and in the Liverpool Maritime Museum.

The Times (London)
Weddell & Co., *Review of the Frozen Meat Trade*
Stock Exchange Daily Official List

Correspondence

Letter dated 21 August 2001, Sir Brian Shaw to author.

Index

Modern Economic and Social History Series

General Editor
Derek H. Aldcroft, University Fellow, Department of Economic and Social History, University of Leicester, UK

Derek H. Aldcroft
Studies in the Interwar European Economy
1 85928 360 8 (1997)

Michael J. Oliver
Whatever Happened to Monetarism?
Economic Policy Making and Social Learning in the United Kingdom Since 1979
1 85928 433 7 (1997)

R. Guerriero Wilson
Disillusionment or New Opportunities?
The Changing Nature of Work in Offices, Glasgow 1880–1914
1 84014 276 6 (1998)

Roger Lloyd-Jones and M.J. Lewis with the assistance of M. Eason
Raleigh and the British Bicycle Industry
An Economic and Business History, 1870–1960
1 85928 457 4 (2000)

Barry Stapleton and James H. Thomas
Gales
A Study in Brewing, Business and Family History
0 7546 0146 3 (2000)

Derek H. Aldcroft and Michael J. Oliver
Trade Unions and the Economy: 1870–2000
1 85928 370 5 (2000)

Ted Wilson
Battles for the Standard
Bimetallism and the Spread of the Gold Standard in the Nineteenth Century
1 85928 436 1 (2000)

Patrick Duffy
The Skilled Compositor, 1850–1914
An Aristocrat Among Working Men
0 7546 0255 9 (2000)

Robert Conlon and John Perkins
Wheels and Deals
The Automotive Industry in Twentieth-Century Australia
0 7546 0405 5 (2001)

Sam Mustafa
Merchants and Migrations
Germans and Americans in Connection, 1776–1835
0 7546 0590 6 (2001)

Bernard Cronin
Technology, Industrial Conflict and the Development of Technical Education in 19th-Century England
0 7546 0313 X (2001)

Andrew Popp
Business Structure, Business Culture and the Industrial District
The Potteries, c. 1850–1914
0 7546 0176 5 (2001)

Scott Kelly
The Myth of Mr Butskell
The Politics of British Economic Policy, 1950–55
0 7546 0604 X (2002)

Michael Ferguson
The Rise of Management Consulting in Britain
0 7546 0561 2 (2002)

Alan Fowler
Lancashire Cotton Operatives and Work, 1900–1950
A Social History of Lancashire Cotton Operatives in the Twentieth Century
0 7546 0116 1 (2003)

John F. Wilson and Andrew Popp (eds)
Industrial Clusters and Regional Business Networks in England, 1750–1970
0 7546 0761 5 (2003)

John Hassan
The Seaside, Health and the Environment in England and Wales since 1800
1 84014 265 0 (2003)

Marshall J. Bastable
Arms and the State
Sir William Armstrong and the Remaking of British Naval Power, 1854–1914
0 7546 3404 3 (2004)

Robin Pearson
Insuring the Industrial Revolution
Fire Insurance in Great Britain, 1700–1850
0 7546 3363 2 (2004)

Andrew Dawson
Lives of the Philadelphia Engineers
Capital, Class and Revolution, 1830–1890
0 7546 3396 9 (2004)

Lawrence Black and Hugh Pemberton (eds)
An Affluent Society?
Britain's Post-War 'Golden Age' Revisited
0 7546 3528 7 (2004)

Joseph Harrison and David Corkill
Spain
A Modern European Economy
0 7546 0145 5 (2004)

Ross E. Catterall and Derek H. Aldcroft (eds)
Exchange Rates and Economic Policy in the 20th Century
1 84014 264 2 (2004)

Armin Grünbacher
Reconstruction and Cold War in Germany
The Kreditanstalt für Wiederaufbau (1948–1961)
0 7546 3806 5 (2004)

Till Geiger
Britain and the Economic Problem of the Cold War
The Political Economy and the Economic Impact of the
British Defence Effort, 1945–1955
0 7546 0287 7 (2004)

Anne Clendinning
Demons of Domesticity
Women and the English Gas Industry, 1889–1939
0 7546 0692 9 (2004)

Timothy Cuff
The Hidden Cost of Economic Development
The Biological Standard of Living in Antebellum Pennsylvania
0 7546 4119 8 (2005)

Julian Greaves
Industrial Reorganization and Government Policy in Interwar Britain
0 7546 0355 5 (2005)

Derek H. Aldcroft
Europe's Third World
The European Periphery in the Interwar Years
0 7546 0599 X (2006)

James P. Huzel
The Popularization of Malthus in Early Nineteenth-Century England
Martineau, Cobbett and the Pauper Press
0 7546 5427 3 (2006)

Richard Perren
Taste, Trade and Technology
The Development of the International Meat Industry since 1840
978 0 7546 3648 9 (2006)

Roger Lloyd-Jones and M.J. Lewis
Alfred Herbert Ltd and the British Machine Tool Industry, 1887–1983
978 0 7546 0523 2 (2006)

Anthony Howe and Simon Morgan (eds)
Rethinking Nineteenth-Century Liberalism
Richard Cobden Bicentenary Essays
978 0 7546 5572 5 (2006)

Espen Moe
Governance, Growth and Global Leadership
The Role of the State in Technological Progress, 1750–2000
978 0 7546 5743 9 (2007)

Peter Scott
Triumph of the South
A Regional Economic History of Early Twentieth Century Britain
978 1 84014 613 4 (2007)

David Turnock
Aspects of Independent Romania's Economic History with Particular Reference to Transition for EU Accession
978 0 7546 5892 4 (2007)

David Oldroyd
Estates, Enterprise and Investment at the Dawn of the Industrial Revolution
Estate Management and Accounting in the North-East of England, c.1700–1780
978 0 7546 3455 3 (2007)

Ralf Roth and Günter Dinhobl (eds)
Across the Borders
Financing the World's Railways in the Nineteenth and Twentieth Centuries
978 0 7546 6029 3 (2008)

Vincent Barnett and Joachim Zweynert (eds)
Economics in Russia
Studies in Intellectual History
978 0 7546 6149 8 (2008)

Raymond E. Dumett (ed.)
Mining Tycoons in the Age of Empire, 1870–1945
Entrepreneurship, High Finance, Politics and Territorial Expansion
978 0 7546 6303 4 (2009)

Peter Dorey
British Conservatism and Trade Unionism, 1945–1964
978 0 7546 6659 2 (2009)

Shigeru Akita and Nicholas J. White (eds)
The International Order of Asia in the 1930s and 1950s
978 0 7546 5341 7 (2010)

Myrddin John Lewis, Roger Lloyd-Jones, Josephine Maltby and Mark David Matthews
Personal Capitalism and Corporate Governance
British Manufacturing in the First Half of the Twentieth Century
978 0 7546 5587 9 (2010)

John Murphy
A Decent Provision
Australian Welfare Policy, 1870 to 1949
978 1 4094 0759 1 (2011)

Robert Lee (ed.)
Commerce and Culture
Nineteenth-Century Business Elites
978 0 7546 6398 0 (2011)

Martin Cohen
The Eclipse of 'Elegant Economy'
The Impact of the Second World War on Attitudes to Personal Finance in Britain
978 1 4094 3972 1 (2012)

Gordon M. Winder
The American Reaper
Harvesting Networks and Technology, 1830–1910
978 1 4094 2461 1 (2012)

Julie Marfany
Land, Proto-Industry and Population in Catalonia, c. 1680–1829
An Alternative Transition to Capitalism?
978 1 4094 4465 7 (2012)

Lucia Coppolaro
The Making of a World Trading Power
The European Economic Community (EEC) in the GATT Kennedy Round Negotiations (1963–67)
978 1 4094 3375 0 (2013)

Ralf Roth and Henry Jacolin (eds)
Eastern European Railways in Transition
Nineteenth to Twenty-first Centuries
978 1 4094 2782 7 (2013)